UNIVERSITY LIBRARY
W.S.U. · STEVENS POINT

D1544295

Inside the Money Market

THE RANDOM HOUSE SERIES IN FINANCE & INVESTMENT

EDITORS: Peter L. Bernstein & Gilbert E. Kaplan

Inside the
Money Market

Wesley Lindow

RANDOM HOUSE : NEW YORK

Copyright © 1972 by Wesley Lindow

All rights reserved under International and Pan-American
Copyright Conventions. Published in the United States by
Random House, Inc., New York, and simultaneously in Canada
by Random House of Canada Limited, Toronto.

Library of Congress Cataloging in Publication Data

Lindow, Wesley, 1910–
Inside the money market.

Bibliography: p.
1. Monetary policy—U.S. I. Title.
HG538.L643   332.4'9'73   70–37059
ISBN 0–394–47885–1

The editorial entitled "Topless Ceiling" which appeared in the February
22, 1967 issue of *The New York Times* is reprinted with permission.
Copyright © 1967 by The New York Times Company.

Manufactured in the United States of America by Kingsport Press,
Kingsport, Tenn.

98765432

HG
538
L643

To Ellie, Kitty, John
and Eric, who helped a lot

215173

291748

ACKNOWLEDGMENTS

This book about the money market is based on personal experience. It is not a textbook in the usual sense, but rather an attempt to provide a practical approach to the subject using my own background. I have worked in the money market on behalf of management for the largest borrower, the U.S. Treasury, and also for a leading New York bank.

Writing this book proved more difficult than I thought. Important changes kept taking place as I was writing, and innumerable technical matters had to be threshed out. Fortunately, my associates at Irving Trust Company and my friends outside the bank gave freely of their time and ideas. In the bank I particularly want to acknowledge the assistance of Dorothy R. Funck, who helped in many ways, from clarifying technical writing to checking details for accuracy. From time to time the following all helped graciously as I called on them: Richard J. Chouinard, James C. Cooper, Eleanor M. Johnson, David M. Jones, George W. McKinney, Robert J. Richardson, Robert W. Stone, Rosemary Truempy, and Edward G. Webb.

Outside the bank I am indebted to Thomas R. Atkinson, Peter M. Bernstein, Gilbert Edward Kaplan, George W. Coleman, George Garvy, Edwin A. Heard, the late Leroy M. Piser, Robert V. Roosa, Duane Saunders, and Kenneth M. Wright.

Obviously, I need to emphasize that certain controversial matters covered in the book are handled in my own way and may not have the concurrence of those who helped me.

Wesley Lindow

CONTENTS

Contents

An Overview

PART I

The Money Market: What It Is and Why It Keeps Changing

CHAPTER 1   Like all Gaul, the financial market domain is divided into three parts: the stock market, the money market and the bond market. Since the three markets are interrelated, there is some difficulty in delineating the separate areas.

To avoid confusion, let us agree at the outset on the following short definitions. The stock market means trading in corporate equities that are already outstanding. The money market generally encompasses activity in short-term high-grade debt instruments that carry a minimum element of risk so that they may be readily turned into cash without material loss. The bond market covers trading in debt issues other than those involved in the money market.

These definitions are perhaps too brief but they would be accepted by most observers in the United States today. We must recognize, however, that the term money market does not mean the same thing in other countries. Thus, the thirteen-volume edition of the Oxford English Dictionary says, "The money market is a sphere of operations of the dealers in loans, stocks, and shares, etc." [1] This definition is so broad that it includes the stock market and the bond market. To add to the confusion, the word stocks means bonds in British terminology, while shares mean stocks or equities.

First Money Market in London

I found it interesting to study the Oxford Dictionary to see when the term "money market" was first used. Since each volume is the size of a large telephone book and much of the text is in fine print, there is a tremendous amount of detail. Searching for "money market," I found that it first appeared in 1861 in a British text on foreign exchange. The reference was to the power which "foreign capitalists, holders of bills of exchange upon England, may exert over our money market." [2] We in the United States seem to have a similar situation today in that the chronic deficit in our international balance of payments is giving foreigners dollars which they may hold or which their central banks up until recently could exchange for gold.

The first modern money market grew up in London. The words "grew up" are very appropriate because this market developed bit by bit as the need for it evolved over the years. The gold standard to a very considerable extent operated through the pound sterling. The importance of Britain in world trade was stimulated by the Industrial Revolution. With the passage of time, it was England which dominated world trade, selling manufactured goods and buying raw materials; it was British shipping which delivered the goods both ways; it was the British Navy which enforced the peace. Funds were flowing into and out of England at all times and new institutions developed along with new financial customs to meet the growing needs of the industrial and trading nation. Naturally, at any one time there were people who had funds to invest for a few days or months before they were needed for some commitment and there were other people who needed money for a short time, perhaps in

4

anticipation of payments which were to be made to them later. Trading in foreign bills (payments due on imports) developed rapidly in this situation. The market that specialized in short-term funds, the nearest thing to money,* clearly was the place to invest or to borrow such funds. London became the financial center of the world.

In 1870 a very perceptive book entitled *Lombard Street* appeared in London. Written by Walter Bagehot, long-time editor of the *London Economist,* the book showed keen insight in describing the way the British financial system developed over the years to meet the needs of the country both in terms of domestic requirements and of the unique position occupied by London with respect to the rest of the world. Considerable attention was paid to the way the Bank of England evolved from a commercial bank to a central bank and the painful mistakes which were made along the way. But the most fascinating aspect of the book, even today, is the manner in which Bagehot weaves together the theory of how things should be expected to be done on a logical basis and how they actually do get done as the various financial institutions play their role. In the introduction he refers to the power of the financial institutions centered about Lombard Street. This follows:

> The briefest and truest way of describing Lombard Street is to say that it is by far the greatest combination of economical power and economical delicacy that the world has ever seen. Of the greatness of the power there will be no doubt. Money is economical power. Every one is aware that England is the greatest moneyed country in the world; every one admits that it has much more immediately disposable and ready cash than any other country. But very few persons are aware *how much* greater the ready balance— the floating loan-fund which can be lent to any one or for any purpose—is in England than it is anywhere else in the world.[3]

* Money may be defined as ready cash on hand or *immediately* available in the bank.

And a little later in the same introduction: "But in exact proportion to the power of this system is its delicacy—I should hardly say too much if I said its danger. Only our familiarity blinds us to the marvelous nature of the system. There never was so much borrowed money collected in the world as is now collected in London." [4]

As we shall see, the money market in the United States also developed in an evolutionary way to fill the emerging needs of the various participants. It is fascinating to see how institutions keep evolving as the needs for them, and the ability to meet these needs, change. Time after time the money market in the United States has demonstrated this.

What Is Traded in U.S. Market

In the United States today, the "money market" covers one specialized type of "money," one type of commercial bank deposit, and several kinds of "near money."

The specialized type of money is the super-money represented by reserves which member banks maintain on deposit at Federal Reserve Banks as the major part of the reserves required against their demand and time deposits.* These reserves are very important in the money market in several ways. For one thing, if the banks as a group find themselves growing short of reserves, the efforts of individual banks to replenish their reserve positions cause monetary tightness to spread throughout the money market and short-term interest rates tend to rise with the pressure at times spilling over into longer-term interest rates; vice versa, if the banks find themselves with a growing amount of excess reserves, the whole money market becomes easier, with interest rates tending to fall. Second, these reserves themselves are traded in the market, as banks with excess reserves lend their Federal

* The remainder may be in the form of currency and coin in the banks' vaults.

Reserve balances to banks with insufficient reserves. This is known as trading in Federal funds. Third, if banks are short of reserves, they may borrow them from the Federal Reserve through what is known as the discount window, at a price known as the discount rate. Accordingly, both the discount rate and the access of banks to the discount window are important aspects of Federal Reserve operations in the money market.

The commercial bank deposit referred to as a money market instrument is the negotiable certificate of deposit (CD). I include it because it is competitive with securities and is, in a sense, near to being a security in terms of the function it serves.

Turning to "near money," we find a number of types of credit instruments that qualify for that description. We shall define these as short-term, high-grade credit instruments that meet the liquidity needs of the various kinds of investors who acquire them. They are highly liquid through marketability or cashable at their near-term maturity.

In money market circles there is a vague, indistinct line somewhere in the twelve- to twenty-four-month maturity area which separates money market transactions from bond market transactions. Obviously, Treasury bills due tomorrow are indeed short-term and qualify as a money market instrument. In contrast, a long-term Government bond due in, say, fifteen years does not qualify. The maturity is so far off that it will be a long time before the bond can be converted into money by redemption at the Treasury. In the interim, interest rates might rise and the market price might go down substantially. Thus, long-term securities do not have the basic characteristic of a money market instrument, *i.e.*, a relatively stable market value at all times.* In discussing Government securities in this book, however, we shall sometimes go beyond the two-year money market area because the entire Government market is so important.

---

* Although the interest rate may fluctuate widely, the price on a short-term instrument changes by only a small amount, as will be explained in Chapter 14.

How Market Is Organized

Now let us pause to consider the term "market." The Oxford English Dictionary gives the following definition: "The meeting or congregating together of people for the purchase and sale of provisions or livestock, publicly exposed at a fixed time and place." This is an interesting definition and we need to make only two changes to describe the money market: first, substitute short-term, high-grade paper (and Federal funds) for provisions or livestock; second, change the first few words to explain that there is no one "place" and that transactions are arranged by telephone. The money market is a highly dispersed affair with operations scattered around the Wall Street area of New York City and with telephone tielines across the country to many other financial centers.

The money market is an impersonal market like the farmers' market. Each participant is acting in the purest sense of Adam Smith's economic man; he is always trying to get himself the best deal. Because credit risks are minimal and the product in each group highly uniform, transactions are usually consummated on an impersonal basis between buyer and seller. They involve little of the personal relationships which frequently color transactions in other markets where established customer relationships (and loyalty) are understood to be a factor.

In the farmers' market, a few more bushels of supply usually mean that prices will decline; a few less bushels and prices will rise. Throughout the time the market is open and goods are changing hands, bargaining is going on. Competition is the keynote of the farmers' market—competition between sellers, competition between buyers, and competition between products.

It is the same, only more sophisticated, in the money market in the United States. There are many buyers and sellers and there are many different products involved. There is great competition among all these products and among all the participants on a highly impersonal basis. In fact, the pressure of great compepetion is a major reason the money market is so volatile, with prices and interest rates ever changing, and so resilient and resourceful in developing institutions, customs, and instruments to meet ever-changing needs.

Purpose of Book

The basic purpose of this book is to get inside the money market. After this brief overview, we shall begin with a description of the types of paper that the money market uses. Next we shall consider the needs and objectives of money market participants. Then we shall study the larger universe in order to understand the dynamic pressures as well as the functional procedures and adjustments that make the market operate. Our primary purpose is to bring out the relationship of the money market to our whole financial structure.

As we go, we shall try to examine the importance of the tangible forces in the money market as well as the psychology that may intensify a force beyond the point that the actual volume of supply and demand would suggest. This psychological factor is the economist's "expectations," namely, the anticipation of things to come. Participants in the money market are a sophisticated group and are frequently influenced as much by expectations as by the actual current tangible facts.

Another purpose will be to explore the pressures from Government on the money market. We shall discuss not only operations of the Federal Reserve as they affect the money market but the importance of the Federal budget, as well as Treasury public debt operations. We shall consider the impact of attitudes of the White House and of actions in Congress. For it is true today that the money market must take into account what Congress is doing to influence financial conditions and economic developments. If some Representative is trying to get a bill adopted that will limit the interest rates payable by banks or that will hamper the flexibility of the Federal Reserve in its operations, the money market will be quick to consider the possible repercussions.

In short, we shall examine some of the myriad financial and political forces that participants in the money market must understand. We shall try to explain how these forces may be anticipated and how trends may be overshot. We shall explore the psychology of men as distinct from statistical quantities and shall study the dynamics that cause the money market to move as it does, continuously ebbing and flowing.

In the last section of the book, we will provide a brief glimpse of some possible future developments in the money market.

The Instruments and How They Function

PART II

Federal Funds: The Esoteric Leader in Daily Volume

CHAPTER 2   Many investors do not know what Federal funds are even though the daily volume of transactions * outstrips that of all other money market instruments, and the interest rate on them is one of the most volatile in the money market. Federal funds are not securities that anyone can buy; they are not loans between individuals or ordinary businesses; and they have nothing to do with the Federal Government in spite of the name.

What are Federal funds? They are simply deposits in Federal Reserve Banks. Remember that every bank which is a member of the Federal Reserve System is required by law to maintain a certain amount of reserves against its deposits in the form of balances with the Federal Reserve Bank of its district (cash in its

---

* Figures on the aggregate volume of Federal funds traded daily are not available but the Federal Reserve compiles weekly averages of daily figures on such operations from forty-six banks throughout the country. Federal Reserve Governor Andrew F. Brimmer stated in a speech on July 9, 1969, that the daily average volume of gross purchases plus gross sales in May 1969 was more than $9 billion, compared with $3 billion five years earlier.

vault also counts). These are known as reserve requirements and vary with the size of the bank and the type of deposit. The requirements are formulated as a set of percentages which are applied to average daily deposits to determine the amount of reserves required for the seven-day computation period which ends on Wednesday of each week.

As of early 1972, the following reserve requirements were effective:

	For Reserve City Banks †	For Country Banks ††
	(Percent of Deposits)	
Net Demand * Deposits:		
Under $5 million	17	12½
In excess of $5 million	17½	13
Time Deposits:		
Savings	3	3
Other time (including Certificates of Deposit)		
Under $5 million	3	3
In excess of $5 million	5	5

* Gross demand deposits minus cash items in process of collection and demand balances due from domestic banks.
† Banks located in the forty-six cities which the Federal Reserve Board has designated as reserve cities.
†† Banks located outside reserve cities.

During each reserve computation period, every member bank must have reserves § on deposit at its Federal Reserve Bank and cash in vault equal to the required percentages of its average net deposits for the period two weeks earlier. Excesses or deficiencies averaging up to 2% of required reserves may be carried forward to the next period. If the total of cash and reserves is running below requirements, a bank will consider various possibilities to raise cash, such as (1) borrowing reserve funds (Federal funds)

§ Reserves consist of average balances at the Federal Reserve Bank during the computation period and average vault cash held two weeks earlier.

from another bank; (2) in the case of some banks, such as major U.S. banks with branches abroad, tapping funds in the Euro-dollar market; (3) building up deposits, particularly CDs, if feasible; (4) selling securities or possibly other assets, such as loan participations; (5) calling loans, particularly money market loans; and (6) borrowing from the Federal Reserve Bank at the discount rate currently in effect.

Let us focus here on number (1) above, namely Federal funds. At certain times some banks have more reserves on deposit than are required, i.e., they have excess reserves, while other banks may have less reserve balances than they need. A bank with excess reserves is a potential lender of these reserves, called Federal funds in the money market, and a bank with a deficiency is a potential borrower. The Federal funds market developed for such lenders and borrowers. In the commonly used terminology, transactions in the market are known as sales and purchases of Federal funds.

Obviously, bank deposits fluctuate from day to day and indeed from hour to hour, so every bank must keep alert to carry at the Federal Reserve Bank only the amount of reserves required to be maintained on average against its deposits over the prescribed settlement period. If a bank has too much when the settlement period is over, it will have sacrificed earnings, since the Federal Reserve pays nothing on these deposits. If a bank has too little, there may be a penalty charged against it at the end of the settlement period. Hence, banks calculate their figures frequently to estimate how much they need to carry at the Federal Reserve Bank in comparison with what they actually have there. This leads to the situation in which banks with excess reserves sell reserves to banks that have shortages. As noted in the example below, such transfers may be made within or across Federal Reserve district boundaries through the Federal Reserve's wire transfer facilities. Since the loan is typically for one day, a transfer in the opposite direction on the following day reverses the transaction and shifts the funds back to the seller. Recently some transactions have been tailored to periods longer than overnight, but not more than a few weeks.

A Typical Transaction

A specific example will help to illustrate how Federal funds are traded. A large commercial bank (Sellers National Bank) might, on a typical morning, find that it has a surplus in its reserve position. It knows that it can make money by selling (lending) this surplus in the Federal funds market for one day. It decides to call a Federal funds broker to inquire about the market. The broker says that several banks, including Buyers State Bank, have called in within the last few minutes looking for Federal funds.

Assume that Buyers Bank needs $1 million, which is the usual minimum amount involved in a transaction between large banks.* The price (rate of interest) for these overnight transactions is negotiated between the buying and selling banks. In conferring with the broker, Sellers Bank asks "What's the market?" *i.e.*, what the prevailing rate on Federal funds is. The broker says that funds opened "tight," meaning that there was more demand than available supply. He reports that there have been some transactions in funds this morning at 5⅛%. Sellers Bank is satisfied with the rate and tells the broker that it is willing to sell (lend) Buyers Bank $1 million in Federal funds for one day at 5⅛%.

Buyers Bank agrees and, as is customary, Sellers Bank immediately notifies its local Federal Reserve Bank to transfer the funds by wire to the Federal Reserve Bank (or branch) of Buyers Bank. The Federal Reserve then charges the reserve account of

---

* Most trading is done in multiples of $1 million but some of the smaller banks around the country are now participating in the Federal funds market with large banks on an accommodation basis, as noted later, with transactions as small as $25,000 or $50,000.

Sellers Bank and credits the reserve account of Buyers Bank. On the following business day the funds will be sent back by Buyers Bank through the same Federal Reserve wire transfer system, thus reversing the entries of the day before. The interest charge of $142.36 ($1 million at 5⅛ % for one day computed on a 360-day basis) is debited and credited to the respective bank account balances of the banks involved if they have a correspondent relationship; otherwise, an interest check will be sent through the mail.

Note that Sellers Bank must approve the individual bank that it will sell to because a sale of Federal funds is really an unsecured loan. Banks do not carelessly lend Federal funds to other banks because the possibility of a credit problem is always present if the other bank should get into some kind of trouble. Hence, banks usually keep a list indicating the maximum amounts that they are willing to lend to approved banks in the form of Federal funds. Small banks, of course, are assigned smaller limits by lenders than are large banks. In some cases, the deposit of collateral is required to comply with State laws for State-chartered banks.

The fascinating thing about Federal funds transactions is the rapid speed at which they are consummated. High-speed teletype and teletape systems are installed in the large commercial banks and the Federal Reserve Banks located in the large banking centers across the country. No physical handling of funds takes place, just a confirmation via teletype or over the telephone, and a debit and credit acknowledgement from the two Federal Reserve Banks that are involved.

Federal Funds Rate

The rate on Federal funds varies with conditions in the money market. Thus in a recession period, when money tends to be plentiful, the Federal funds rate is usually relatively low: most

17

banks have more cash than they need and must press to keep it working. In the boom phase of a recovery, on the other hand, the rate on Federal funds will rise: banks have an active demand for loans, yields on securities are high, and idle reserves tend to be in short supply. The exact situation will depend on how restrictive Federal Reserve policies are.

RELATION TO THE DISCOUNT RATE

How do fluctuations in the rate on Federal funds compare with the discount rate, *i.e.*, the rate set by the Federal Reserve on loans to member banks? For many years the rate on Federal funds never exceeded the discount rate, since member banks typically have the option of borrowing at the discount window rather than borrowing Federal funds. Beginning in late 1964, however, the rate on Federal funds has from time to time exceeded the discount rate. At first, it was considered peculiar that a bank would be willing to buy Federal funds from another bank at a rate above the discount rate when it could go to the Federal Reserve Bank and borrow more economically at the stated discount rate. As money tightened, especially in 1966 and 1969, the rate on Federal funds rose more and more above the discount rate. With the discount rate at 6% in 1969, the Federal funds rate averaged close to 9% and transactions were reported as high as 11%. Why would a bank be willing to pay up to 5% more than the discount rate? Put in perspective, we shall see that it is another example of the flexibility and ingenuity of the money market in meeting new situations.

Look at it this way. Banks borrow at the discount window of the Federal Reserve Banks as a privilege and not as a right. Federal Reserve officials are likely to check into lending and investing policies of a bank if it persistently uses the discount window. Accordingly, a bank that has borrowed recently from the Federal Reserve faces the prospect of Federal Reserve questioning, or "surveillance," of its policies. The bank thus finds it desirable to pay a premium in order to avoid going to the discount window. Many banks apparently share this feeling, some because of past substantial borrowing at the Federal Reserve and some simply as a matter of prudence to "save" their discount window "privilege" for even more difficult times. So a real scramble often develops to obtain needed reserves through the Federal funds market.

RELATION TO OTHER MARKET RATES

Banks have come to think that buying large amounts of Federal funds every day may be preferable to selling securities (often at a loss) or to borrowing in other forms, such as trying to sell additional certificates of deposit (CDs)—a special form of time deposit to be discussed later. At times, such as 1966, 1968, and 1969, banks were forced to buy more Federal funds because CDs could not be sold when Federal Reserve ceilings made them noncompetitive with other money market instruments. Thus the Federal funds rate is related to yields on securities and rates on CDs, as well as the discount rate.

SIGNIFICANCE OF FEDERAL FUNDS RATE

Over the years the Federal funds rate has been the most volatile rate in the money market, because of its sensitivity to the varying degree of tightness of bank reserve positions and the fact that it is a one-day rate and thus reflects conditions at the moment. A careful student in the money market could watch the Federal funds rate and tell quite accurately what was happening to the pulse, or the degree of tightness, of commercial bank reserve positions. In fact, Federal Reserve technicians are known to regard the Federal funds rate as a key indicator of money market conditions. Quite often the rate on Federal funds has moved up or down ahead of other short-term money market rates. It would perhaps be stretching the point to say that the Federal funds rate predicts the movement of other interest rates but on occasion it has helped in appraising future trends. The careful technician watching changes in the Federal funds rate could frequently detect events leading to a broad tightening or easing of conditions in the short-term money market before this was generally apparent. Some market specialists look to this rate for clues on changes in Federal Reserve policy.

It follows that the thorough student of the money market should watch the rate on Federal funds carefully in the daily newspapers. He may keep a chart on Federal funds rates and compare trends with other money market rates to see whether there is a persistent degree of pressure showing in Federal funds. Or, he might try to keep up to date on a less formal basis, simply by watching the newspapers from time to time so that in periods of impending change he is alert to what is going on. Quotations on Federal funds rates are published in *The New York Times, The Wall Street Journal, American Banker,* and several other newspapers and financial magazines.

Market Structure for Trading

How are buyers and sellers of Federal funds brought together? Does the Federal Reserve play a part in making the arrangements? The answers to these questions will illustrate the resourcefulness of the money market in developing instruments and operating methods in accordance with need. The Federal Reserve has nothing whatsoever to do with *arranging* the transactions even though a shift of ownership of balances on the books of Federal Reserve banks takes place.

In the early years of the development of the Federal funds market, arrangements between banks were largely made by one or two stock exchange firms. One of these in particular kept a "book" on buyers and sellers. A buyer might call this broker and ask that his name be entered in the book to be matched against a seller. There was no charge for this service but the hope was that the eventual receipt of stock exchange commissions would provide a *quid pro quo.*

Today there are at least four brokers arranging Federal funds transactions. Two of these are stock exchange houses, one is a money broker, and one is a commercial bank: the Garvin Bantel Corp.; Mabon, Nugent & Co.; George Palumbo & Co., Inc.; and Irving Trust Company.

Meanwhile, another important type of arrangement has been developed through what is called "accommodation for customers." Under this system a large bank will buy and sell Federal funds in transactions with correspondent banks simply to help out these customers. This means that the transactions are made by the bank acting as a principal for its own account rather than as a broker or agent for another bank. Some of the larger banks have set up accommodation systems for smaller bank correspondents that virtually assure the smaller banks that their Federal funds needs, either as buyers or sellers, will be taken care of automatically. Some of the smaller banks may also use Federal funds brokers.

While only commercial banks deal in Federal funds, settlements of certain financial transactions are made in the form of Federal funds. For example, transactions in U.S. Treasury obligations are usually settled in Federal funds. Hence, when a corporation buys a Treasury bill from a dealer in Government securities, the buyer must have Federal funds—"good" or collected funds—in order to make payment. It is customary for the dealer to deliver the bills to the corporation's bank in New York which makes payment on behalf of the corporation in Federal funds, usually via Federal payment wire, and debits the corporation's account for the amount of the purchase. In the event that the corporation's account has insufficient "good" funds, the bank may request the corporation for compensation in the form of one day's interest at the Federal funds rate. Payments for municipal securities are generally made in Clearing House funds, *i.e.,* by check drawn on a commercial bank.

To understand the distinction between Federal funds and

Clearing House funds, it is necessary to note that the only immediately available "good" money is money that is already collected and in the bank's account at the Federal Reserve. Such money is available to cover reserve requirements or may be sold in the Federal funds market. In contrast, a check received by a commercial bank which is drawn on another local bank is not "good" funds until the next day when it has been cleared through the Clearing House. At that point the Federal Reserve will transfer funds from the account of the bank on which the check was drawn to the account of the bank receiving the funds.

Over the years, more and more transactions have come to be settled in Federal funds. In effect, such transactions result in shifts of funds between customers' respective banks in the Federal Reserve system. Recently, banking committees have been working on plans to simplify the clearing of financial transactions by requiring all settlements in the form of Federal funds.

Government Securities: United States, Agency, and Municipal Issues

CHAPTER 3   In the money market, three groups of issues come under the heading of government securities: obligations of the United States Government, securities issued by Federally sponsored agencies, and obligations of states, municipalities, and other political subdivisions. The money market is vitally interested in these obligations because there is a large volume of securities maturing within one or two years, which means they are attractive holdings for purposes of liquidity. Moreover, in the case of U.S. and Federal agency issues, dealers maintain a ready market, that is, they stand ready to purchase or sell securities in reasonable amounts over the telephone with no delay. The market for obligations of states and municipalities is much more limited.

Obligations of the U.S. Government

The obligations of the U.S. Government which are of principal interest to the money market are Treasury bills and Treasury notes and bonds maturing within two years.

TREASURY BILLS

Treasury bills are the "backbone" of the money market. As of July 7, 1971, when the distribution of available bills was quite typical, some $89 billion of Treasury bills were outstanding and they represented about 35% of the Federal public debt outstanding in the form of marketable issues. Treasury bills are important to the money market because they are available in very large supply and are scattered over a wide range of maturities with the maximum running to one year. The distribution of outstanding Treasury bills as of July 7, 1971, in terms of the number of days to maturity is shown below:

Amount Outstanding (In Billions of Dollars)	Days to Maturity	Amount Outstanding (In Billions of Dollars)	Days to Maturity
3.8	6	1.7	114
3.8	13	1.4	118
3.8	20	1.7	125
1.7	22	1.4	132
3.8	27	1.4	140
3.8	34	1.7	144
3.6	41	1.4	146
3.7	48	1.4	153
1.7	53	1.4	160
3.7	55	1.6	167
3.7	62	1.6	174
3.7	69	1.7	175
1.8 TAB *	74	1.6	181
3.8	76	1.7	206
5.5	83	1.7	235
3.9	90	1.7	266
1.6	97	1.2	296
1.4	104	1.2	327
1.4	111	1.2	357

* TAB: Tax Anticipation Bills, see page 27.

With such a distribution, a short-term investor is almost certain to find an issue close to the maturity he wishes at any time.

The U.S. Treasury sells new issues of bills at auction each week. Bids for three- and six-month bills are usually received on

Monday for payment and delivery the following Thursday. Bills normally mature on Thursday and are always paid off in cash. However, proceeds may be used in payment for new bills which an investor has successfully bid for in the auction and which are issued on the same date as the maturing bills. The larger part of each weekly issue usually consists of ninety-one-day bills, along with a somewhat smaller offering of 182-day bills. In addition, the Treasury offers during the third week of each month issues of nine-month and twelve-month bills dated as of the end of each month. All bills are issued only in bearer form: they are not registered in an individual name, but, like money, belong to the person who has possession.

The marketing of Treasury bills through auctions is unique. Consider the issues in a typical offering on July 6, 1971. The Treasury stated that a total of $3.9 billion of Treasury bills would be offered on Monday, July 12: $2.3 billion with a ninety-one-day maturity (October 14, 1971) and $1.6 billion maturing in 182 days (January 13, 1972). Both bill issues were dated July 15 and payment was due on that date. On the morning of July 12, prospective bidders all over the country sharpened their pencils and, probably after a certain amount of agonizing indecision, filled out the forms in order to get them to their local Federal Reserve Bank by the one-thirty P.M. (New York time) deadline. Some of the bidders, we can surmise, were bidding to obtain the bills for holding in their own accounts, while others were hoping for a quick speculative profit. Later on the same day (between five-thirty and six P.M.), the Treasury announced the results of the bill sale as follows:

			Range of Accepted Bids					
	Amount Applied	**Amount**	**High**		**Low**		**Average**	
Maturity	**for**	**Accepted**	**Price**	**Yield**	**Price**	**Yield**	**Price**	**Yield**
	(Millions of Dollars)							
91 days	$4,094	$2,301	98.650	5.341%	98.637	5.392%	98.641	5.376%
182 days	3,225	1,600	97.242	5.455	97.226	5.487	97.228	5.483

Treasury bills are discount issues: interest is not paid in the form of a coupon but is represented by the difference between the price the bidder pays and the par amount which he receives at maturity. In the case of the ninety-one-day bill, the average price accepted was 98.641 per $100. The discount of 1.359 per $100 represented income to be received at maturity. For income tax purposes this difference between price paid and price received is always treated as current income and never as a capital gain.

It is apparent that some buyers were successful in bidding for ninety-one-day bills at lower prices and higher yields than others —a difference of 0.051% between the 5.341% high (price) bid and 5.392% low (price) bid. At this auction 50% of the volume bid for at the low price (high yield) was accepted.

Smaller investors do not have to name a price but can simply subscribe on a noncompetitive basis for amounts from $10,000 to $200,000 of bills, which are awarded at the average rate accepted by the Treasury for the entire issue. On this particular date, $481,260,000 of noncompetitive tenders were made, or about 12% of the total offering.

The following computation shows how the average yield of 5.376% (the average shown above) is derived from the price of 98.641.

1. Derive Discount

$100,000 Par value (receivable at maturity)
−98,641 Issue price (bid)
$ 1,359 Discount

2. Calculate Interest

$$\frac{\text{Discount}}{\text{Par Value}} \quad \frac{1,359}{100,000} = 1.359\% \text{ Interest for 91 days.}$$

3. Calculate Yield (Y)

$$\frac{\text{Interest}}{\text{Days}} \quad \frac{1.359\%}{91} = \frac{Y}{360 \text{ days (not 365)}}$$

$$Y = 5.376\% \text{ yield (annual basis)}$$

A further computation is necessary in order to make a direct comparison of bill yields with bond yields. This is called the bond equivalent yield and recomputes the figures to value the interest in relation to the amount of cash actually put up (instead of par) and puts the computation on a 365-day basis, the same as used for Treasury bonds.

1. Calculate Discount
   (As above)

2. Calculate Interest
   $$\frac{\text{Discount}}{\text{Issue price}} \quad \frac{1,359}{98,641} = 1.38\% \text{ Interest for 91 days}$$

3. Calculate Bond Equivalent Yield (Y)
   $$\frac{\text{Interest}}{\text{Days}} \quad \frac{1.38\%}{91} = \frac{Y}{365}$$
   $$Y = 5.54\% \text{ bond equivalent yield (annual basis)}$$

Thus a ninety-one-day bill yielding 5.38% (rounded) would be equivalent to a ninety-one-day coupon bond yielding 5.54%.

From time to time the Treasury offers issues of Treasury bills called Tax Anticipation Bills (TABs).* These are sold with maturities about a week after tax payment dates for corporations and can be used at par in payment of taxes on tax dates. For example, the TABs which matured on September 21, 1971, could be turned in by taxpayers at face value when they paid their taxes due September 15, 1971. This means that a slight amount of "gravy" was available to taxpayers in getting paid for the six extra days between September 15 and September 21.

The Treasury also sometimes offers a "strip" of bills for sale. On some occasions it has offered a strip of weekly bills representing a small addition to each of a group of seven consecutive weekly issues already outstanding. A buyer of the strip would

---

* Tax Anticipation Bills (and other Treasury issues) are often sold with the provisions that banks may pay for them by crediting the Treasury Tax and Loan Account. The procedure is discussed in Chapter 8. This privilege is valuable to the banks and they generally will bid higher than other investors for bills carrying this privilege.

obtain seven different maturities in this case. On other occasions the Treasury has offered a strip of additional *monthly* bill maturities. Thus, an offering could consist in part of a maturity in three months, another in four months, another in five months, and so on.

After issuance, Treasury bills are traded in large amounts daily and all trades are made on a yield basis. Such a market for trading outstanding securities is called a secondary market and constitutes the largest volume item of the Government securities dealers. Typically dealers do not charge a commission for round-lot transactions (par value of $100,000 or more) but make some profit on the spread between their bid and asked quotations. For example, shortly after it was issued the bill maturing October 14, 1971, was quoted on a bid basis of 5.50% and an asked basis of 5.40%. The price for these yields on a million-dollar amount would be as follows:

| Bid | $986,860 | (5.50% for 86 days) |
| Asked | $987,100 | (5.40% for 86 days) |

The difference would be $240 representing the spread to the dealer if he bought at the one price and sold at the other indicated. Spreads are shaved further on large transactions so a dealer must have an active turnover if this source of income is to be significant. In recent years the high interest rates available in the bill market have brought in considerably more investors and trading has increased substantially. Dealers treat transactions under $100,000 as odd-lot trades; they are usually arranged at yields a few basis points wider than the quoted bid and asked figures and are usually subject to a fee.

OTHER TREASURY SECURITIES

The money market is also interested in other short-term Treasury issues outstanding because their broad and active markets give them a high degree of liquidity. On September 30, 1971, approximately $29 billion of Treasury issues other than bills were due within one year. These were represented by $21 billion of Treasury notes and $8 billion of Treasury bonds.

The characteristics of different Treasury securities may be summarized as follows: Treasury bills, as already noted, are discount issues which have original maturities of one year and under. Treasury notes and Treasury bonds have original maturities of over one year. They are generally issued in bearer form, *i.e.*, possession indicates ownership, and pay interest on presentation of semiannual coupons attached to the security, cashable one by one at designated dates. However, the owner may choose to have the security registered in his name and receive a check covering the interest directly from the Treasury. Notes were by law limited to maturities of not more than five years but in 1967 Congress extended the range of Treasury notes to seven years. Treasury bonds can be any maturity but have been customarily issued with maturities in excess of five years; now presumably seven years will be the minimum maturity in view of the 1967 change in notes.

Certificates of indebtedness have a maturity not exceeding one year and usually have semiannual interest coupons attached, similar to bonds and notes. Dating from as far back as the 1920s to recent years, such issues had been outstanding in substantial amounts. In the past few years, however, certificates have been replaced by Treasury bills with maturities up to as long as one year and no marketable certificates have been issued since 1966. Since bills are sold on an auction basis but certificates are not, the Treasury apparently finds it easier to let the market set the rate of interest on a new issue of bills than to sell a new certificate on which the Treasury would have to fix the coupon rate. The bill issues also offer a broader range of maturities than certificates for the investment of liquid funds. The emergence of bills and the fading of certificates is evidence of the flexibility of the money market and of the Treasury's response to its needs.

It is not unusual for a Treasury bond to change hands several times during its life, particularly as it gets closer to maturity. By the time it becomes a short-term issue, the original long-term holder probably has moved out of it into some other issue with a longer span to maturity. Short-term investors become interested in such an issue since only the remaining life to maturity is relevant. Such an outstanding short-term instrument is just as good for use in the money market as if it were a new short-term issue. Unlike Treasury bills which are traded on a yield basis, notes and bonds are traded on a price basis in terms of 32nds. For example, a bid quotation of 98-5 and an asked quotation of 98-9 mean buyers are willing to pay $98\frac{5}{32}$ per $100, but sellers are only willing to sell at $98\frac{9}{32}$. Frequently the trade is consummated somewhere between the bid and asked prices.

Income on Treasury certificates, notes, and bonds is subject to all Federal and state income taxes.

The minimum amount of U.S. Government obligations usually traded is $100,000 although smaller amounts are feasible with the charge of a transaction fee by banks and dealers. U.S. Government obligations are usually sold for delivery the next business day when amounts of $100,000 or more are involved. On some occasions delivery may be on the same day and on rare occasions on some later day, termed "delayed delivery" basis. In the case of amounts under $100,000, delivery must be made the second day (skip day) following sale. Settlement is normally made in Federal funds.

OWNERSHIP OF SHORT-TERM GOVERNMENT SECURITIES

As this is written, the latest Treasury survey of ownership of Government securities was April 30, 1971. On that date there was $113 billion of marketable Treasury debt outstanding which was due within one year, including $88 billion of Treasury bills. The total was about 46% of the total marketable debt. According to the Treasury survey, the Federal Reserve Banks, with close to $33 billion, held about 29% of the $113 billion total due within one year, of which approximately $26 billion was in bills. U.S. Government agencies and trust funds held $2.6 billion. This left almost $78 billion of up to one-year issues outstanding in the hands of the public. Of this total, commercial banks reporting in the Treasury survey held $14.7 billion; State and local governments $5.6 billion; corporations $1.7 billion; other financial institutions approximately $1.8 billion; and all other types of investors about $54 billion. The latter figure includes holdings of smaller banks, and institutional and other investors not reporting in the Treasury survey.

Securities of Federal Agencies

Securities issued by Federal agencies are also outstanding in substantial volume. Agency securities are either guaranteed directly by the United States Government or are fully backed by the individual agencies which are, in turn, supervised and/or owned by the Government.

As of April 30, 1971, there were about $50.4 billion of agency obligations outstanding. Maturities range from short-term to long-term, just as in the case of direct Government issues.

Fanny May, as the Federal National Mortgage Association is

	Obligatons Outstanding (par value) April 30, 1971	
Federal Agencies	**Total**	**Maturing within One Year**
	(Millions of Dollars)	
Federal National Mortgage Association	$15,078	$5,733
Federal Home Loan Banks	8,448	3,800
Federal Land Banks	6,857	2,047
Government National Mortgage Association	6,075	150
Federal Intermediate Credit Banks	5,395	4,768
Export-Import Bank of the U.S.	3,125	550
Banks for Cooperatives	1,915	1,815
Tennessee Valley Authority	1,285	610
Subtotal	48,178	$19,473
Other	2,210	*
	$50,388	

* Not available

popularly known, was the largest issuer, with its securities representing about 30% of the total, the Federal Home Loan Banks accounted for about 17%, and Ginny May—the Government National Mortgage Association—for about 12%. Issues of the three agencies dealing largely with the housing market thus comprised almost 60% of the outstanding agency issues. The remainder was issued largely by agencies dealing in agricultural credit: the Federal Land Banks, the Federal Intermediate Credit Banks, and the Banks for Cooperatives.

The table shows that agency debt is quite liquid, with about 40% maturing within one year. Some agencies customarily limit their securities to short-term. The Federal Intermediate Credit Banks, for example, while authorized to issue debt with a maturity of up to five years, ordinarily offer issues with maturities ranging from three months to one year.* Similarly, the Banks for Cooperatives customarily issue only short-term obligations. The Federal Land Banks, on the other hand, often offer bonds with maturities up to ten years. Fanny May has issued short-term discount notes and also debentures with maturities up to twenty years.

About $7.3 billion of the total consisted of participation certificates originally issued by the Export-Import Bank of the United States and the Federal National Mortgage Association. Those issued by Fanny May were later assumed by Ginny May when Fanny May became a Government-sponsored, privately owned corporation in September 1968 (more fully explained later in this chapter).

According to the U.S. Treasury survey of ownership, Federal agency issues were distributed among the same investor groups as U.S. issues. Out of total agency issues of $50.4 billion, holdings of reporting commercial banks, as of April 30, 1971, amounted to $9.4 billion. Other financial institutions owned $6.3 billion and corporations held $820 million. U.S. Government

* In February 1970, the FICBs announced that they planned to issue twice a year debentures with maturities from two to five years, reflecting the greater volume of term loans being made to farming institutions.

investment accounts and Federal Reserve Banks owned $2.2 billion and holdings of state and local governments were $4.4 billion. All other investors, including smaller banks and institutional investors not reporting in the survey, held the remaining $27.1 billion of agency issues outstanding.

The income from agency issues is subject to Federal income taxes and is exempt, with two notable exceptions (Fanny May and Ginny May), from state, municipal, and local taxes.

Federal agency securities are usually sold initially by fiscal agents who work with securities dealers. They are sold initially on both a discount and coupon basis. At issuance, as well as in the trading market, agency issues usually sell at higher yields than comparable Treasury obligations. This apparently reflects the fact that many investors are not familiar with the issues and a somewhat more limited market exists than in the case of direct obligations. A market for Government agency issues is maintained by practically all dealers in direct Government obligations and they are traded on the same basis. Quotations may be found on the same dealer offering sheets as direct Government securities. Since the volume of agency issues outstanding is about one-fifth of the volume of marketable U.S. Government obligations, the market for agency issues is usually less active and quotations tend to show a wider spread than in the case of direct Government securities. This is particularly true for the long-term issues; in some instances spreads between bid and asked quotations are one whole point, contrasted with only one-quarter point or less for Governments. In the very short-term area, on the other hand, the spread of a few thirty-seconds in agency issues is similar to that in Governments. Dealers maintain some inventory of agency issues and on occasion the Federal Reserve has purchased such obligations under repurchase agreements with dealers.

Another agency, not included in the above, which issues obligations guaranteed in a different way by the Government is the Department of Housing and Urban Development (HUD), which is responsible for administering the program of Federal financial assistance to public housing agencies and urban renewal agencies

33

of local communities. Notes of these local housing authorities are referred to as Project Notes. With maturities up to one year, the Notes are sold in monthly auctions. Technically, local authorities issue these obligations, which are backed up by an agreement between the local authority and the U.S. Government acting through HUD. Under this agreement the Government unconditionally agrees to make a loan to the local authority in an amount sufficient to pay the principal of and interest on the notes to maturity. Unlike other agency securities, these housing obligations are exempt from Federal income taxes because they are considered to be municipal issues. The amount of such issues outstanding is now more than $3 billion. When construction of the housing is completed, the Project Notes are refunded usually into forty-year serial PHA bonds which are also tax exempt and are secured by the Government's pledge to pay annual contributions in sufficient amount to meet principal and interest payments.

Under the Housing and Urban Development Act of 1968, Fanny May was divided into two parts. Fanny May continued as one part but became a Government-sponsored privately owned corporation responsible for market operations involving the purchase and sale of Government insured mortgages. The second part remained a Government-owned corporation with a new title, namely, the Government National Mortgage Association (Ginny May). It took over from Fanny May the special assistance functions involving the extension of subsidies in the form of mortgage purchases to certain Federal Housing programs and also assumed the trustee function for pooling participation certificates (PCs).

Repurchase Agreements (RPs)

RPs are contracts in money market instruments, usually in U.S. Government securities, although Federal agency issues as well as other obligations are frequently used. An RP involves a borrower who needs funds for a few days and enters into a contract to sell an investor a security from his inventory. This will usually be an issue due in eighteen months or less. The borrower agrees to purchase it back, say, three days later, at a given price. Often the price is stated simply as that which is necessary to provide a certain yield basis to the purchaser of the security for the three days. Interest is calculated on an actual day basis for a 360-day year on the dollar amount invested.

The development of RPs is an example of the inventiveness of the money market in creating instruments that are needed at a given time. Although the first RPs appeared in the 1920s, more refined versions began to show up in the mid-fifties. Money was getting tighter and the Government bond dealers were beating the bushes to try to find funds to finance their inventories.

Today Federal Reserve Banks, commercial banks, and Government security dealers use RPs (also known as Repos) as normal money market transactions. Reverse RPs (also called reverse Repos or matched sale-purchase transactions or buy-backs) refer to transactions involving temporary purchases of securities rather than temporary sales.* These RPs arise from time to time from different sources.

Dealer RPs are arranged with corporations, state and local governments, and others, including agencies of foreign banks in the American market. These deals may take the form of an RP for overnight or two or three days, or for longer periods, sometimes for several months. The maturity is tailored to the exact day corporations or other lenders will need the funds repaid.

When initiated by a bank, the RP serves the same purpose as Federal funds, except that it is usually arranged with a nonbank investor and is a secured loan made to the bank. Furthermore, whereas Federal funds transactions are usually for overnight or

---

* Note that the language used describes the position of the instigator of the transaction rather than the other party. It is well to remember this to avoid confusion about all of these RP transactions.

over a weekend, a bank RP is usually for three or four days or more.

Participation Certificates (PCs)

PCs were first authorized and subsequently issued in negotiable form under the Housing Act of 1964. This provided for the issuance of certificates backed by a pool of assets, such as Veterans Administration mortgages and loans by the Small Business Administration. Fanny May acted as trustee of the pooling arrangement in selling PCs. The Export-Import Bank has also issued guaranteed PCs in portfolio funds which hold pooled notes of borrowers. The volume outstanding from both agencies on April 30, 1971, was $7.3 billion, of which $6.1 billion represented PCs originally issued by Fanny May.

Two seemingly extraneous factors encouraged the issuance of PCs, namely, the problems of the budget deficit and the public debt limit set by Congress. Up to 1968, when the unified budget * was adopted, the Government was on a rather elementary cash system of bookkeeping, combining all expenditures, whether for current expenses or for capital outlays and whether made directly or through certain Federally sponsored agencies.† Under this procedure repayments of loans or sales of assets showed up as negative expenditures. Accordingly, the sale of participations in the assets of certain Federal lending institutions effectively reduced the amount shown as outlays by these agencies and so reduced the Federal deficit. In the 1950s, the Eisenhower Administration sold certain loans of Government agencies for this purpose. In 1966, the Johnson Administration carried this a step further and sold participations in a pool of assets of an agency rather than the assets themselves. The Johnson approach

* Discussed in Chapter 8.
† This was not true of Government trust accounts, which operated independently of other accounts.

was more convenient for investors than the Eisenhower approach. Fanny May and the Export-Import Bank issued PCs through mid-1968.

Chapter 8 on the Treasury will show that the public debt limit has sometimes made it necessary or politically convenient for the Government to use artificial devices to reduce the portion of the Federal deficit financed by the issuance of securities subject to the debt limit. In 1966, for example, the public debt limit was so tight that efforts were made to issue a larger than usual amount of PCs. Unfortunately, the PCs had disruptive effects in tightening the money and bond markets and thus helped to raise interest rates beyond what had been visualized. In the latter half of the year, when the money market became congested in the great money squeeze, the sales of PCs were dropped altogether by the Government.

In 1967, the sale of PCs was resumed, again under pressure of the public debt limit. This time there were no serious adverse market effects. However, Congress then enacted legislation that made new PCs issued in 1968 subject to the public debt limit. This meant that issuance of new PCs no longer alleviated the problem of the public debt limit. As a result, only a small volume have been issued since 1968. In addition, the Federal agencies which had earlier issued PCs are no longer part of the unified Federal budget and therefore the issuance of their securities is not subject to the debt limit. The earlier use of PCs illustrates, however, a basic characteristic of the money market: the development of new and sometimes unorthodox techniques to serve a particular need of a borrower or lender.

Obligations of States, Municipalities, and Other Political Subdivisions

There is a continuous flow of new security offerings in the municipal bond market by states, municipalities, and other political subdivisions. These are usually called "tax exempts" because the interest is exempt under existing regulations from Federal income tax and from income taxes of the state in which they are issued. In recent years, the volume of offerings has been very substantial, reflecting the need for funds to finance rising state and local public expenditures. The securities have ranged from short-term tax, bond, and revenue anticipation notes to long-term obligations. A large volume of outstanding municipal obligations that were originally offered as long-term maturities now, with the passage of time, have a life of one or two years or less. These maturities, both the new offerings and outstanding obligations, offer important vehicles for the investment of funds earmarked for liquidity purposes.

New issues of municipal obligations are generally sold to investors by investment firms who have been awarded the offerings in competitive bidding. Direct offerings to investors, which are usually limited to short-term maturities such as tax anticipation obligations, may be negotiated between the comptroller or treasurer of a municipality and banks and other investors in the immediate area. Other issues, often in the form of serial maturities, are usually advertised publicly and awarded to the highest bidder. In most cases, several firms specializing in municipal securities form a syndicate and bid for the issue. The successful syndicate reoffers the issue to investors.

Most of these firms are also active in the secondary market, *i.e.*, buying and selling outstanding issues. They maintain a market in the same manner as for U.S. Government securities. In fact, many dealers are active in both markets. They accumulate an inventory of municipal issues and often post the bonds and notes available for sale in the "Blue List," a trade publication listing the inventory of the various issues being offered by different investment syndicates and individual municipal dealers.

Public housing authorities (local agencies whose securities in effect are guaranteed by the Federal Government as noted above) are large borrowers in the State and local field. Yields on these issues reflect their tax exemption, their Government "guarantee," and the size and therefore marketability of the issue.

Recent data on volume are not available, but the Department of Commerce reported that as of December 31, 1970, there was a net total of $143 billion of State and local debt outstanding. All but a small portion represented long-term debt of States, counties, municipalities, townships, school districts, public housing authorities, and other agencies.

Settlement for municipal obligations is usually made in Clearing House funds and delivery is customarily made on the fifth business day following the transaction. Trading in municipals is generally in multiples of $5,000 because most major issues since 1960 have limited their minimum denominations to that amount. Municipals sold before 1960 and most small issues have $1,000 denominations.

The Old Stand-bys—Bankers' Acceptances, Commercial Paper, Brokers' and Dealers' Loans

CHAPTER 4   While the money market paper discussed in this chapter has been around for a long time, what is new is that there has been a renaissance in the use of such paper by business as interest rates have risen. In particular, there has been a dramatic growth in the volume of bankers' acceptances and commercial paper outstanding.

Bankers' Acceptances

This is the oldest type of paper in the money market. According to the Federal Reserve Bank of Chicago,[1] "A bill of exchange . . . and . . . the bankers' acceptance are virtually as old as international trade itself. The earliest known bills of exchange date from 1156 but it is believed that their initial use dates back to the Roman or Byzantine Empires. The development of bankers' acceptances as a form of commercial credit and a means of money transfer by banking houses of Florence, Genoa, and Venice in the thirteenth century initiated an era that commonly is referred to by historians as the 'commercial revolution.' " Provision for growth of the acceptance market in the United States was one of the main features of the original Federal Reserve Act of 1913.

A banker's acceptance usually results from a short-term contractual obligation of a business firm to pay on a specific date for merchandise shipped by a seller. This obligation can be fulfilled by the buyer's bank accepting a time draft drawn on it by the seller. The "accepted" draft has the credit of the bank behind it (and is negotiable in the money market), thus giving the seller the opportunity to raise cash and eliminating the ordinary waiting time of the buyer's promise to pay at maturity. The instrument is of the highest quality, for no losses have ever been suffered by holders of bankers' acceptances in the United States. Certain acceptances, depending on maturity and purpose, are eligible at the Federal Reserve Banks for discount or purchase.

For example, let us say a New York importer buys a shipment of toys from a German manufacturer. The importer goes to his local bank and opens a ninety-day letter of credit authorizing the German manufacturer to draw a time draft, *i.e.*, an obligation of the importer's bank to pay the German manufacturer at a specified date in the future. If the manufacturer wishes immediate payment, he may present the draft to his German bank to obtain the face value of the draft minus the discount representing the interest rate prevailing in the market. The German bank then forwards the draft along with the shipping documents to the New York bank which will stamp it "Accepted." The accepting bank usually charges a fee (minimum annual rate of 1½%) for its obligations. This acceptance can then be sold in the market. Normally, the German bank would ask this to be done on behalf of its customer. The American Bank might buy it and hold it as an investment, or it might sell it to a customer who is searching for a short-term, high-grade liquid investment or to a dealer in acceptances. The disposition will be determined by money market conditions. The bank will tend to hold the acceptance during periods in which money is easy but not when money is tight.

In addition to financing imports into and exports from the United States, acceptances are used to finance trade between foreign countries and to create dollar exchange. They may also be used to finance the storage and shipment of goods within the United States.

At the end of May 1971 the volume of bankers' acceptances outstanding was approximately $7.5 billion. This is about six times the amount outstanding in early 1960.

Dealers play a key role in the bankers' acceptance market. By providing an active secondary market, they give a high degree of liquidity to acceptances. They raise or lower their bid and offered yields to reflect both money conditions generally and the relative supply and demand situation in acceptances.

The rate structure on acceptances is indicated by posted bid and asked quotations by dealers at any given time.* Thus, for example, the dealer rate may be 5⅞% bid and 5¾% asked for a ninety-day acceptance. The quotations are in terms of a discount rate, representing interest, rather than in terms of price, but it will be recognized that the effect of a higher rate would naturally mean a lower price. The borrower would in effect pay the bid yield plus at least the minimum fee of 1½% (for prime names) to the bank for lending its credit by accepting the draft. In this case, the total charge to the borrower would be 7⅜% (5⅞% + 1½%). As money gets tighter, banks encourage the use of acceptance financing to save their lending capacity; this enables their customers to raise money without any disbursement of bank funds.

Of some $8 billion of acceptances outstanding in late 1971, commercial banks held about $3 billion with the remaining $5

---

* In December 1969, two dealers, Merrill Lynch, Pierce, Fenner & Smith, Inc., and Salomon Brothers announced they would not continue to post fixed rates at which they will buy and sell acceptances but would allow rates to fluctuate in response to supply and demand as in the case of Treasury bills.

billion held largely by corporations and foreign investors. The latter consist largely of foreign central banks, since dollar acceptances are typically permitted as legal investments under foreign banking laws. Federal Reserve Banks held a token amount, about $50 million.

Commercial Paper

Commercial paper is a very convenient device by which corporations borrow from other corporations for short-term periods without any SEC formalities. Unsecured promissory notes are issued with maturities ranging up to 270 days. Recently, banks began to issue commercial paper—not directly, but through their holding companies and subsidiaries.

There are two types of commercial paper: that issued by direct placement and that issued through dealers. All commercial paper is issued in bearer form, at a discount calculated on the basis of a 360-day year and payments are made in Federal funds. Ordinarily, rates are from $\frac{3}{8}\%$ to $\frac{1}{2}\%$ over the yields on Treasury bills of corresponding maturities.

DIRECT PLACEMENT

The major finance companies sell their paper directly to investors. They have found that it is an ideal market in which to raise funds to supplement their normal bank lines. Maturities are worked out, ranging from a few days up to 270 days, to meet the precise needs of investors. Such finance paper is issued in bearer form, with denominations generally running from $50,000 to $1,000,000 and more. The issuing company will usually repurchase outstanding paper before maturity at the request of the holder but such repurchasing is understood to be an accommodation rather than an obligation. As a result, there is no secondary market in this paper. In late 1971, the volume

44

of outstanding directly placed paper of finance companies was slightly under $18 billion.

ISSUED THROUGH DEALERS

Dealers in commercial paper underwrite the commercial paper of several hundred industrial, utility, and other corporations, including smaller finance companies. Most dealer-marketed paper is written for three-month multiples, *i.e.*, usually ninety days or six months. However, paper can sometimes be written to order, as in the case of direct placements by finance companies. In the formal sense, there was no active secondary market until fairly recently in dealer-type commercial paper, although dealers stood ready to assist if a buyer of the paper wished to sell it prior to maturity. More recently, however, a true secondary market appears to be emerging, as dealers offer to make a market in paper they have underwritten. In late 1971, about $12 billion of commercial paper was outstanding which had been underwritten by dealers specializing in this market or offering such facilities in addition to activities in U.S. Government agency, corporate, or municipal securities.

SALES BY BANKS

In 1969, bank-related companies (bank subsidiaries, and one-bank and multi-bank holding companies) began to issue commercial paper both through direct placement and through dealers. Banks are not permitted to issue such paper themselves. The volume of bank paper outstanding rose rapidly to nearly $8 billion at its peak in the summer of 1970. The typical arrangement was that a bank sold existing loans for cash to a related company which simultaneously sold commercial paper on the basis of the loans received. Generally the maturities of the loans closely matched the maturities of the commercial paper issued.

The growth of bank paper was of course stimulated by the

tight money situation. Banks were forced to search out new sources of funds as well as to restrict their lending activities. Corporations in turn were motivated to seek other means of financing. When they could not meet all borrowing needs, many banks encouraged customers to turn to the commercial paper market.

Bank sales of commercial paper turned sharply downward as money conditions eased in the recession of 1970–71. Also, the attractiveness of commercial paper to banks was reduced after October 1, 1970, when the Federal Reserve imposed a 5% reserve requirement on funds reaching banks from the commercial paper market via their related companies. By late 1971, bank-related paper was down to $1.6 billion.

EFFECTS OF THE PENN CENTRAL BANKRUPTCY

The commercial paper market is limited to borrowers with a high credit rating and most issues are supported by bank lines of credit as a standby. As a result, the credit record of commercial paper was excellent—until the Penn Central bankruptcy in 1970. A study made in the early sixties showed that in the twenty-five-year period 1937 through 1961, only seven defaults occurred and there were no losses.

The Penn Central bankruptcy shook the commercial paper market severely. Just before this event, commercial paper outstanding, excluding bank-related paper, amounted to slightly more than $32 billion. Penn Central's failure, with $82 million of commercial paper outstanding, made it clear that buyers had better check on the credit of issuers more carefully. The volume of commercial paper fell off $3 billion in the subsequent six weeks. Then volume began to move up again and for dealer paper reached a new high in March 1971. Subsequently, the widespread efforts of corporations to refund their short-term debt reduced the volume of nonbank-related paper to about $29.4 billion by late 1971.

OWNERSHIP

The largest portion of commercial paper outstanding is held by corporations: as of September 30, 1971, $19.3 billion out of the $29.5 billion total outstanding. Commercial banks owned $5.5 billion of commercial paper near the end of 1971 and the remaining $4.7 billion was held by life insurance companies and mutual funds.

Brokers' and Dealers' Loans

Loans to brokers and dealers have long been used by commercial banks as liquid investments. Since they are callable or are of very short maturity—frequently overnight—they are included among bank assets available to meet liquidity needs. At the end of June 1971 large commercial banks reported about $5.6 billion of loans outstanding to brokers and dealers. Loans are also made to dealers by corporations and other investors interested in money market instruments. Loans to brokers and dealers are negotiated directly between banks, and other lenders, and the borrowers.

The demand for brokers' loans stems from the purchase of stocks on margin by brokers' customers (or for the account of brokers themselves). A bank's loan to a broker is secured by stocks left with him by customers. The loan is represented by a demand note which usually states that the loan will be repaid at the option of the borrower or lender, *i.e.*, "on call." However, loans may also be made to brokers for a period of up to six months, evidenced by time notes. The interest rate charged on new demand loans is the "call" rate and is subject to day-to-day adjustment. Similarly, the renewal rate may be changed from day to day and may differ from the rate on new loans. For example, if a bank's money position is relatively tight, it will not be eager to take on new loans but may be willing, perhaps reluctantly, to maintain its current loans with its broker customers. It will discourage and shut off new loans by quoting a higher call loan rate. In 1969, some banks began charging a rate at a varying spread above the prime rate, depending on the broker's deposit balances and the size of the loans.

Loans made to dealers in securities are most often secured by U.S. Government obligations but may also be secured by municipal or corporate obligations. These loans are usually for the purpose of financing inventories that arise from normal trading activity, as dealers make a market in Government and other issues, or that represent unsold portions of new security issues. Interest rates on dealers' loans have usually been more sensitive than brokers' loans to changes in money market conditions. Also, loans secured by U.S. Governments usually bear a lower rate of interest than loans secured by Stock Exchange collateral or other obligations, but in 1969 this relationship was reversed for a time as money market rates of interest rose above the bank prime rate.

The volume of dealers' loans varies widely from time to time, depending largely on the volume of new security offerings, both Government and private, and dealers' inclinations with respect to accumulating inventories. Loans to dealers in U.S. Government securities represent the largest volume of dealers' loans.

New Money Market Instruments of Commercial Banks: CDs and Other Approaches

CHAPTER 5   In the last decade commercial banks found their positions so tight that they endeavored to tap the money market through newly created instruments. The first of these was the negotiable certificate of deposit, commonly known as the CD, which was developed in 1961. The volume of CDs outstanding rose rapidly for several years but sales were severely impeded at times because the Federal Reserve Board refused to raise the maximum interest rates permitted to levels necessary to allow CDs to compete with other money market instruments. As CD volume then fell off, commercial banks began to tap the Euro-dollar * market. In a sense what they did by this was to sell CDs abroad through foreign branches. Since Federal Reserve in-

---

* Euro-dollars are simply dollars deposited in banks outside the United States. The ownership of these deposits may change frequently from one holder to another. A buyer of good credit standing in Europe can usually obtain such deposits if he is willing to pay the going price, which tends to fluctuate considerably. The home office of an American bank in New York may instruct its London branch office to obtain Euro-dollar deposits for home use, so the London branch would offer to pay whatever rates were necessary. The exact procedure is spelled out in Chapter 7 in a section on Euro-dollar operations.

terest rate ceilings do not apply abroad, the amount of Euro-dollar deposits borrowed rose rapidly as the volume of domestic CDs was curtailed. Unfortunately, interest rates in the Euro-dollar market also rose sharply, reaching levels as high as 12% and 13%, and causing some banks to search for other substitutes in the domestic market. This led to the use of commercial paper by bank-related companies, the issuance of paper known as documented discount notes (DDNs), and the use of ineligible bankers' acceptances.

The reader may wonder why CDs are treated here as a money market instrument. And if this deposit is to be counted, why should not demand deposits be considered, since they also may represent liquidity to corporations? The answer is that CDs were designed to attract short-term investment funds of corporations and not the daily working funds represented by demand deposits. Functionally, the CD comes very close to being a security even though it is technically a deposit. In fact, it can be purchased and sold through dealers in the secondary market in the same way as Treasury bills. Competitively, it is an alternative to short-term securities.*

The development of these new bank money market instruments illustrates clearly how resilient the money market is in responding to the emergence of new needs.

Negotiable Certificates of Deposit

BIRTH AND GROWTH

Let us go back to 1961, when the negotiable CD was first offered. What were the conditions that led to its creation?

One key factor was that interest rates had been rising more or less regularly for about fifteen years. The corporate treasurer was reacting as economists would expect; he was squeezing

---

* The negotiable CD, which is issued in large denominations to corporations, is not to be confused with the nonnegotiable savings certificate, issued in small denominations to individuals.

down his demand deposits, which earn no interest, and putting short-term investment funds to work in money market securities in order to take advantage of increasingly attractive interest rates. In fact, he was becoming a kind of "do-it-yourself" banker, as he lent money by buying short-term money market instruments of various kinds.

Meanwhile, many commercial banks were finding that the slow growth of demand deposits was retarding their ability to meet increasing loan demand. They had been through the experience of 1959 when tight money had held the growth in deposits to near zero and a very large increase in loan demand had been financed only by selling off securities in a sinking market. Clearly the need was to try to find new ways to tap some of the corporate funds available in the money market. The obvious question was: Why not try to develop a kind of interest-bearing money market security that corporate treasurers would be willing to buy competitively with other money market instruments? The reasoning was spelled out quite clearly in a provocative speech in January 1961 by Howard D. Crosse, then Vice President of the Federal Reserve Bank of New York. A few weeks later New York City banks began to issue CDs.

With the CD, individual banks are able to control their own destiny to a much greater extent. They can try to sell CDs more aggressively if they need the funds for loan demands or they can let up on sales if they wish. The key is the ability to increase or lower the interest rate offered in accordance with supply and demand for short-term funds and restrictions imposed by the Federal Reserve. The restrictions, of course, refer to reserve requirements and interest rate ceilings imposed under Regulation Q.

The CD is an ideal instrument for short-term investment by corporations because maturity dates can be tailored to the exact day the corporate treasurers need to have funds on hand to pay taxes, dividends or other claims. Moreover, since it is negotiable, a CD can be resold in the market any time the corporation holding it wishes to raise cash before the stated maturity date.

PRACTICES

Negotiable CDs are normally sold in amounts of $1 million (regulatory minimum is $100,000), in conformity with the concept that they are an attractive instrument for the larger corporations and other large short-term investors. CDs are quoted on a yield basis both on original issuance and in the secondary market, and interest is calculated on an actual day basis for a 360-day year.

Certain government bond dealers make a market in CDs like other money market paper. Yields fluctuate freely; experience has shown that yields are affected by the supply and demand of corporate funds generally and the reserve position of the banking system, as is true of other money market rates.

CURTAILMENT BY FEDERAL RESERVE

The corporate CD was an instant success and the volume outstanding grew rapidly, but serious setbacks occurred in 1966, 1968, and 1969 because the Federal Reserve failed to increase permissible interest rate ceilings to meet competitive rates in the money market. Then a liberalization in Regulation Q ceilings and a less restrictive monetary policy, which produced declining rates in the open market, stimulated a resurgence in CDs and the volume soared to a new high of $34 billion in late 1971. We will discuss this matter in Chapter 6 in connection with Federal Reserve policy matters. Then in Chapter 16 we will consider some major questions about CDs that intrigue bankers.

Other New Instruments

With the sharp decline in CDs outstanding, commercial banks turned to other instruments, some of them quite new and ingenious. Bank commercial paper was described in the preceding chapter. The use of Euro-dollars will be discussed in some detail in Chapter 7. There remains the use of documented discount notes (DDNs) and ineligible bankers' acceptances.

DDNs represent commercial paper, to which are attached irrevocable bank letters of credit. The paper may be issued by customers of the bank, particularly by smaller companies, by firms which are not so well known and by companies whose credit rating may be somewhat less than prime. The attachment of the bank's irrevocable letter of credit places the bank's credit behind the paper and enhances its marketability.

Ineligible acceptances are known variously as working capital bills, marketable time drafts (MTDs), and finance bills. Until the tight money period of the late 1960s, banks generally refrained from issuing acceptances which were not eligible for discounting at the Federal Reserve. As tight money policies ground on, however, bankers' acceptances emerged which were not eligible for discounting but could nevertheless be sold in the market. Such acceptances are usually created to finance an unsecured bank loan. They are accepted by a bank and become a negotiable instrument based on the credit standing of the accepting bank. They reached a peak volume of $550 million in September 1970.

Ralph F. Leach, Chairman of the Executive Committee of Morgan Guaranty Trust Company, described the origin of the MTD as follows:

> We introduced early in 1969 a market instrument which we called the marketable draft. To do this, we used a loan agreement form by which our customer gave us the option of treating his borrowing as an ordinary loan or of creating from it a marketable piece of paper by accepting a draft drawn by him at the time of the borrowing.[1]

The Cast of Participants and What Motivates Them

PART III

The Federal Reserve System:
Keeper of the Money Thermostat

CHAPTER 6   The Federal Reserve plays a vital role in the money market. I like to think of the Fed as controlling the thermostat that regulates the money supply of the country. But the influence of the Fed goes beyond this; major matters like the supply of credit and the level of interest rates are involved; and these in turn lead to questions of economic well-being. This chapter will describe the tools used by the Federal Reserve. In Part IV we will review how these tools are used when major forces affect the economy and the money market.

Paradoxically, as we shall see, the Fed creates the very reserves that member banks are required by law to maintain at their Federal Reserve Banks against their deposits. It is easy for the Federal Reserve to adjust the thermostat to create more or less of these reserves and to start a chain reaction that begins in the money market but affects the whole economic structure. Robert V. Roosa has written that the money market is "a natural meeting ground for the central bank to come into contact with the financial sectors of the economy as a whole" and "that is why the money market is the principal zone for the exercise both of the Federal Reserve System's *defensive* and its *dynamic* responsibilities." [1]

> Defensive responsibilities refer to the task of offsetting seasonal, regional, and random causes of undesired financial stringency or ease. The dynamic responsibilities refer to actions taken "to vary the quantity of reserves . . . by such amounts, and through such methods, as to make the banking system, and the money market as well, an active force in the economy—promoting growth, resisting depression, and limiting inflation."[2]

For money market analysis I find it useful to divide Federal Reserve functions into *direct* money market actions and *indirect* money market actions.*

Direct Money Market Actions

The direct actions are undertaken through operations of the discount function and through purchases and sales of U.S. securities, known as open market operations.

THE DISCOUNT WINDOW

In the discount function, Federal Reserve Banks advance funds to member banks either through discounting customer paper (*i.e.*, in effect taking over the position of lender, the approach used prior to the Great Depression of the 1930s) or through advances on secured notes (the approach used almost exclusively over the last forty years). These advances are secured by U.S. Government securities or other assets. Government securities have been used almost exclusively until recently, when customer paper has been relied upon to an expanding degree as member

---

* The terms "direct" and "indirect" as used here should not be confused with the concepts of "direct" controls (such as wage and price controls) and "general" credit controls, meaning the administration of the discount window, open market operations, etc.

banks' security holdings were reduced. Use of the discount window is one way by which member banks, at their own initiative, can add to their total reserves.

The interest rate at which the Federal Reserve makes advances to member banks is known as the discount rate. When the Fed raises the discount rate, the money market recognizes that the Federal Reserve is trying to accomplish something by way of a tighter credit policy and that this will tend to result in higher interest rates. (Sometimes the discount rate will be boosted to catch up with earlier increases in other rates but even then the Federal Reserve's open market operations may have been a factor making for prior increases in other rates.) Contrariwise, when the Fed reduces the discount rate, the tendency will be to pull down interest rates, because a reduction in the rate usually indicates an easing of monetary policy. The level of the discount rate and changes in the rate thus have a rippling effect on all interest rates and ultimately affect the whole economy. A lower interest rate at any particular time should be more effective in inducing businessmen and individuals to borrow than a higher rate, and vice versa.

The relationship between the discount rate and other rates ought logically to be close, but there are times when, for special reasons, substantial spreads develop. In 1969, for example, the Treasury bill rate reached about 8% while the discount rate remained at 6%. This unusually wide spread would not have been tolerated by the Federal Reserve at most times in the past, for it could be a definite inducement for banks to borrow at the discount window to finance holdings of higher-yielding securities, thereby enabling the banks to "scalp" a substantial profit. Yet in 1969, the Federal Reserve Board chose to keep the discount rate at 6% in spite of such spreads. It presumably did not want to add to the pressures of an unusually tight money market and perhaps it also feared Congressional criticism because of political dislike of the record interest rates prevalent at the time.

The founding fathers of the Federal Reserve System visualized the possibility that there would be different discount rates in effect at the twelve Federal Reserve Banks in accordance with varying regional conditions. In practice, however, different discount rates have proven unworkable, since the money market is really nationwide in scope and disparities between regions lead to unwanted rate (and volume) distortions in the market. There have been only brief periods of a few days and rarely periods involving a few weeks when the discount rates have varied among districts, primarily because some banks were catching up to a new level.

The Board of Directors of each Federal Reserve Bank must take the initial action to change the discount rate and then the change does not go into effect until it has been approved by the Board of Governors in Washington. The law says that a change in rates proposed by the Board of Directors of any of the twelve Banks is subject to "review and determination" by the Board of Governors. The Board sometimes refuses to approve changes adopted by the Banks. For example, in July, August, and September, 1966, seven Federal Reserve Banks asked the Board on several occasions for permission to raise their discount rates. On each occasion the request was refused.

In November 1967, following the devaluation of the pound sterling and an increase in the British discount rate * from 6½% to 8%, the directors of the Federal Reserve Bank of New York "concluded that decisive action was needed to safeguard the position of the dollar and that in the circumstances it would be appropriate to increase the discount rate . . . from 4 to 5%." However, the Board of Governors declined to approve the increase. After reviewing the situation, the directors unanimously reaffirmed their decision but were turned down again. The record shows that ". . . in the light of the Board's action, the directors reluctantly voted to establish the discount rate at 4½%." [3] The other eleven banks made similar discount increases.

---

* Technically called the bank rate.

60

A few months later, in March 1968, following the suspension of trading in the London gold pool,* nine of the Federal Reserve Banks raised their discount rates to 5% effective Friday, March 15. Two other banks followed early the next week but the New York Bank held out to March 22, or a week later, before taking the same action. It had favored a larger increase because "the directors felt that a decisive move was necessary as a demonstration of resolute determination to protect the dollar." Accordingly, it had voted to increase the rate to 6% or, if the Board declined to approve, to 5½%. The Board did not approve either of these increases. The directors of the Bank then "reluctantly voted to establish a 5% rate in the interest of harmony within the System." [4]

Once a change in the discount rate has been inaugurated by one Federal Reserve Bank and approved by the Board of Governors, it is virtually certain that the other Banks will fall in line. However, on more than one occasion the Federal Reserve Bank of New York has held out against changes approved by the Board for other Banks. Thus in August 1968, when the Board approved a reduction from 5½% to 5¼% in the discount rate of the Federal Reserve Bank of Minneapolis, the directors of the New York Bank reviewed the desirability of a discount rate reduction. "They were impressed by the evidence of continued substantial inflationary pressures in the economy and were unanimous in their conclusion that it would be most undesirable to reduce the discount rate. At their next regular meeting on August 29 . . . their assessment . . . was essentially unchanged. Nevertheless . . . this Bank's directors voted to reduce the discount rate to 5¼%." [5]

Borrowing from the Fed is still considered a "privilege," an interpretation consistent with the 1935 change in the Federal Reserve Act which provides that the Federal Reserve Banks *may* (formerly *will*) extend credit to member banks. If a bank begins

---

* The gold pool was a group of central banks operating in the London gold market.

to rely heavily upon the Fed as a source of funds and its business loans and other assets begin expanding more rapidly than the Fed considers desirable, questions will be asked, there may be "surveillance" of the bank's loans and investments and threats of closing the discount window to that bank may be made. The borrowing bank might then find itself in the awkward position of having to sell securities to obtain funds and this might entail substantial capital losses.

Administration of the discount window has raised many questions over the years. Commercial banks have often felt that there was lack of uniformity in the treatment granted by the discount administration of the twelve Federal Reserve Banks. The feeling has been that one Federal Reserve Bank may be more liberal than another in its treatment of member banks in its district. This is a very difficult matter to appraise. Obviously, there can be no variation in the precise legal technicalities of how loans are made at the discount window. The difficulty comes in what may be termed the degree of generosity or toughness in extending and renewing loans to individual banks. Assuming that two member banks in identical circumstances borrow from different Federal Reserve Banks, there is always the possibility that one Federal Reserve Bank will press for repayment more rapidly and thus cause more pressure to be felt on one commercial bank than on the other.*

* A study of the Banking and Financial Research Committee of the American Bankers Association, "The Discount Function," published in 1968, included the results of a survey of bankers' attitudes toward borrowing from the Fed. It reported that of the 415 banks which answered a question dealing with uniformity in the administration of the discount window ". . . one-third felt that there was a difference in the administration of the discount window from district to district. Three-fourths of the banks with deposits of over $500 million felt that there was a difference, and 45 per cent of the banks with deposits of $100 to $500 million believed that the administration of the discount window was different from district to district. . . . In the St. Louis and San Francisco districts more than half the banks felt that the administration was not uniform. In Boston and Philadelphia only about one-fifth of the banks felt that the administration was not uniform. In the remaining districts, 30 to 45 per cent of the banks detected—or believed they detected—some difference from district to district" (p. 50).

62

Over the past few years, the Federal Reserve System has been conducting a series of studies about the administration of the discount window. A Steering Committee headed by Federal Reserve Governor George W. Mitchell has recommended basic overhaul of the discount mechanism. For the first time each member bank would have "a basic borrowing privilege" which would give it the ability to borrow a certain amount from its Federal Reserve Bank with no questions asked. This amount could be borrowed in half the weeks of a given period, say, thirteen out of twenty-six weeks. There would also be a "supplemental adjustment credit" under which the Federal Reserve Banks would continue to make credit available over and above the basic borrowing privilege on essentially the same discount window arrangements in use before the new plan, except that greater uniformity would be achieved among the twelve Federal Reserve Banks. A new "seasonal adjustment credit" would help banks with serious seasonal problems. Finally, the discount rate itself would be changed much more frequently in an effort to keep it closer to rates in the money market. These proposals will be discussed in the last chapter.

OPEN MARKET OPERATIONS

When the Federal Reserve Banks buy or sell U.S. Government securities, they are engaging in open market operations. The primary purpose of open market operations is to affect the volume of reserve balances on deposit at Federal Reserve Banks.* Operations may be undertaken to attain a basic objective of expanding or contracting bank reserves necessary to support an orderly growth of the economy or to meet temporary seasonal factors, such as a rise in currency in circulation (which reduces bank reserves). Purchases of Government securities by the Fed result in the creation of reserves, and sales extinguish reserves. The purchase of a security by the Federal Reserve re-

* See Glossary for explanation of the mechanics.

sults in the issuance of a Federal Reserve check drawn on itself, which ultimately must come into the hands of a commercial bank for collection since only banks have accounts at Federal Reserve Banks. When the check is presented by the commercial bank, the amount is added to its reserve balance on deposit at the Federal Reserve Bank. The transaction is not canceled out (for the system as a whole) until such time as the Federal Reserve makes a sale of a Government security which must result in a check being written to pay the Federal Reserve. Ultimately such a check must be charged against some bank's reserve account at the Federal Reserve.

For perspective, it is important to understand the very close interconnection between the workings of open market operations and the discount window. In general, open market operations and advances at the discount window tend to move in opposite directions in the short run. For example, if the Federal Reserve sells $100 million of Treasury bills under an open market program, banks will find themselves short of reserves and will tend to increase their borrowings at the discount window correspondingly. Conversely, a purchase of $100 million Treasury bills in the market by the Federal Reserve will tend to increase reserves and permit banks to reduce their borrowings by a corresponding amount.

Over the years, by far the largest part of Federal Reserve open market operations has been in short-term Government securities. Major reliance has been on purchases and sales of Treasury bills. Generally speaking, the Federal Reserve tends to prefer to deal in bills; back in the years 1953 to 1960 it followed a "bills only" doctrine. Of course, purchases or sales in any maturities affect bank reserves in the same way, but proponents of this doctrine argued along these lines:

> Transactions in bills interfere least with market forces determining the pattern of interest rates across the whole range of maturities, whereas transactions in longer securities tend to have too much of a direct effect on bond prices and yields of particular

issues or maturity groups. Moreover, transactions in bills can be easily carried out because the pool of bills is so large that it gives the Federal Reserve room to move and with some anonymity. In contrast, transactions in longer securities are more obvious and may both dominate and penalize the market. Fluidity between maturity groups should be expected to transmit the effects of bill purchases to prices and yields in the longer segments of the market.

If this sounds convincing, let me point out that the Federal Reserve no longer follows the "bills only" doctrine. The change came when the international balance of payments deficit began to present a problem and it was felt that short-term interest rates should be pushed upward for international reasons. Federal Reserve Governor Brimmer has explained that "It was in 1960 that U.S. monetary policy began to take explicit account of balance of payments considerations." [6] A new plan was formulated in 1961 by the Federal Reserve which was nicknamed "Operation Twist" by market technicians. The idea was to try to push up Treasury bill rates while keeping longer-term interest rates from rising. The theory was that this could be accomplished by the Federal Reserve selling, or not buying as many, Treasury bills (which would tend to push the rate up) and meanwhile buying Treasury notes and bonds (which would tend to keep longer rates from going up). However, substantial buying of notes and bonds by the Fed proved unnecessary because long-term market yields tended downward into 1963.

Policy concerning open market operations is formulated by the Federal Open Market Committee (FOMC), which consists of the seven members of the Board of Governors of the Federal Reserve System plus five of the presidents of the twelve Federal Reserve Banks. Of these five, the President of the Federal Reserve Bank of New York is a permanent member while the other four serve on a rotating basis from among the other eleven Federal Reserve Banks. Even though only five presidents of the twelve are voting members of the Committee at any one time, the remaining seven presidents are usually present at Committee meetings. The FOMC usually meets every three or four weeks in Washington to review policies then in effect and to formulate changes considered desirable. A number of economists from the staffs of the Board of Governors and the Federal Reserve Banks are always present.

The policy decisions of the FOMC are transmitted to the Manager of the Federal Reserve's Open Market Account at the Federal Reserve Bank of New York for execution. The Manager of the Open Market Account, who is the senior official in charge of the Securities Department or "trading desk," is empowered to undertake open market operations within the framework of the policy decisions of the FOMC. Of course, if sudden economic or financial changes occur, the Account Manager is always able to communicate instantly with senior officials of the FOMC for guidance.

The record of policy decisions made at each meeting of the FOMC is now being released after an interval of approximately ninety days. The release of this information has reduced somewhat public uncertainties regarding Federal Reserve policy and provided significant clues to the trend of the Committee's thinking. The full record is transferred after a period of years to the National Archives, where it is available for inspection by interested persons. For example, the minutes of the meetings during the years 1962 through 1965 were transferred in 1970, those for the year 1961 were transferred in 1967, and those for the years 1936 through 1960 were transferred in 1964.

By late 1971, open market operations of the Federal Reserve had built up the portfolio of Government securities to a total of $68 billion, the highest amount in the history of the System. This volume, along with the nation's gold stock and currency provided by the Treasury, has enabled the public to accumulate more than $60 billion of currency to meet their cash needs,*

---

* Outflows of currency cause a reduction of reserves. See Chapter 16 for a sources-and-uses analysis of reserves.

leaving member banks with reserves of more than $31 billion. The portfolio of $68 billion consisted of $29 billion of Treasury bills, $36 billion of notes, and $3 billion of bonds. About $35 billion of the $68 billion total was represented by obligations with a maturity of less than one year.

In 1966, Congress gave new authority to engage in open market operations for the purchase and sale of securities of certain Government agencies. The Federal Reserve had not requested this authority and indeed indicated that it had absolutely no interest in receiving it. This came about because Congress was restless about the shortage of funds for housing in the very tight money period in 1966 and wished to enlarge the ability of Government housing agencies to put funds into the housing market. One means of accomplishing this was to give the Federal Reserve authority to buy securities of these agencies, replenishing in this way the funds used by the agencies to acquire mortgage loans. It was hoped that the mortgage market would thereby be stimulated. It must be realized, however, that the effect of creating new reserves is the same whether the Federal Reserve does this through purchases of securities of Federal housing agencies or through public debt securities.

The Federal Reserve's lack of enthusiasm about buying issues of Federal agencies was very similar to the arguments made when it decided on the "bills only" doctrine. It wished to provide reserves with minimal effects on particular issues and maturities in the market. In other words, it wished to be "anonymous" in a large market pool rather than aiding or hurting certain issues or areas of the market. The purchase of Federal agency issues to help the housing market was therefore far afield from the basic idea of providing reserves in appropriate amounts for the banking system and the general credit structure.

Nevertheless, the Federal Reserve has purchased Federal agency issues to a limited degree since receiving its new authority. During late 1966 and early 1967 it held as much as $31 million of agency obligations under repurchase agreements with dealers. In the years from 1968 to mid-1971 the amounts ranged up to slightly more than $100 million. In late 1971, an announcement was made that these issues would be purchased for permanent holding under certain guidelines.

The Federal Reserve also holds small amounts of bankers' acceptances. The amounts bought outright or under RP have ranged in the late 1960s from about $50 million to $200 million.

TRANSACTIONS WITH DEALERS

One new technique developed in the field of open market operations in the postwar period involves RPs with dealers in Government securities. The Federal Reserve may buy securities from a dealer with an agreement that the dealer will repurchase the security at a stated price and stated time. Usually the period involved is short, namely a day or a few days. The transaction is usually priced to provide an interest rate equivalent to the discount rate, although the manager of the open market account my specify a higher rate or a lower one (but not lower than the average issuing rate on the Treasury's latest offering of ninety-one-day bills). The purpose of the transaction is for the Federal Reserve to smooth out money market fluctuations or bolster bank reserve positions by putting funds into the market. Use of RPs with dealers can ease a tight situation and particularly help in operations of the dealers themselves if they are pinched for funds. This method has the same effect on reserves as the outright purchase of Government securities. It is quickly reversed with less market impact than the sale of Governments because dealers understand that the Fed obviously wishes to act only on a temporary basis. The RP is used by the Fed mainly to ease temporary market tightness.

The buy-back * is an exactly opposite transaction. This occurs

* RPs are made only with nonbank dealers while buy-backs (sometimes called reverse RPs), or matched sale-purchase transactions, are made also with bank dealers.

when the Federal Reserve sells securities to dealers on a temporary basis and agrees to buy them back in a short period. In this case, the Federal Reserve does not establish an exact price for the buy-back but rather indicates to the dealer involved that it will buy the security back at such a price as will compensate the dealer for the cost of handling and the interest cost of money during the period. The dealer sets a price and the Federal Reserve either accepts or rejects it. For example, suppose that on a Monday, the New York Federal Reserve agrees to sell to a securities dealer $1 million of Treasury bills maturing in eighty days, at a price providing a discount rate of 5.50%, for delivery that day against payment in Federal funds. At the same time, the dealer agrees to sell the Federal Reserve Bank of New York $1 million of the same issue of Treasury bills at a price equivalent to 5.50% for delivery and payment in Federal funds on Tuesday. It should be noted that the rate at which the buy-back is arranged need not be the same as the going market rate (say 5.98%) on that particular issue of eighty-day bills. In fact, it usually would not be the same rate, since one rate applies to the one-day buy-back, and the other rate applies to the much longer maturity date (in this case eighty days). Both the sale and buy-back contracts, incidentally, are stated in terms of specific prices; no direct reference is made to the effective interest rate on the transaction.

As an additional service to dealers, the Federal Reserve in November 1969 began to lend securities (for up to three days) to U.S. Government securities dealers who are unable to deliver securities against contracted sales. However, these exclude short sales. The lending, according to the Federal Reserve, will be made only if the dealer cannot borrow the securities elsewhere. The procedure is designed to assist the dealers in reducing their failures to deliver and to improve the overall performance of the Government securities market. As of mid-1971, approximately $50 million of securities were loaned to dealers by the Federal Reserve Banks.

Indirect Money Market Actions

The indirect operations of the Federal Reserve that affect the money market include changes in reserve requirements, moral suasion, and interest rate ceilings.

CHANGES IN RESERVE REQUIREMENTS

Authority to change reserve requirements was first granted in the emergency banking legislation of 1933 and was made permanent under the Banking Act of 1935.

As already noted, each bank which is a member of the Federal Reserve System is required to keep reserves equal to certain percentages of its net demand and time deposits. From June 1917 to December 1959, all reserve requirements had to be met by maintaining deposits at the Federal Reserve Banks. From December 1959 to November 1960, member banks were allowed to count part of the currency and coin in their vaults as reserves and effective November 24, 1960, they were allowed to count all vault cash as reserves.

Historically, reserve requirements were imposed to protect depositors. It was argued that when a bank maintained a cash fund in other banks it could always meet normal depositor withdrawals. However, such reserves were not adequate to meet withdrawals in times of major stress as indicated by the many banks which failed. To prevent panics and maintain confidence Congress set up the Federal Reserve System and later the Federal Deposit Insurance Corporation.

The role of reserve requirements has changed over the years: today they function largely as a mechanism through which the monetary authorities may influence the money market, the flow of credit, and interest rates. Under present law, the Board of Governors is authorized to set, within the limits specified by the law, the percentage of reserves required against deposits for two classes of member banks: reserve city banks and country banks. A third class, central reserve city banks, was abolished on July 28, 1962.* Changes in requirements may be made in one or both classes of banks at the same time and they must be uniform for all banks in the same class.

The Federal Reserve has made many changes in reserve requirements over the years. Most of the changes were made to meet special situations. For example, the initial increase in 1936 was made to immobilize the large volume of excess reserves that had resulted from the huge inflow of gold. Following World War II, increases were made to tie up excess reserves that had resulted from Federal Reserve open market operations in support of Government securities prices. During the 1950s, requirements were reduced in recession periods as part of the Federal Reserve's efforts to increase excess reserves, thereby making bank credit cheaper and easier to obtain so that the economy would be stimulated.

Changes in reserve requirements were used less frequently in the 1960s. A change in 1960 was to adjust for the effects of making vault cash eligible for meeting reserve requirements. From the end of 1960 through 1965 there was only one change —a reduction in reserve requirements against time deposits. This was partly reversed in 1966 when an increase was instituted against time deposits over $5 million under new legislative authority granted by Congress "designed to exert a tempering influence on bank issuance of CDs and to apply some additional

---

* In testifying on behalf of this legislation before the House Committee on Banking and Currency in Washington, D.C., on July 18, 1962, I said:

Now we think that reserve requirements everywhere are going to have to come down in the years ahead to help finance economic growth. We think requirements in New York and Chicago should come down to the level of reserve cities now or in the very near future. The present discrimination against New York and Chicago is not logical, it is not fair, it serves no desirable monetary purposes, and it could be a deterrent to economic growth if continued indefinitely.

restraint upon the expansion of bank credit to businesses and other borrowers." [7] In 1967 requirements were reduced on savings deposits and time deposits of smaller banks in order to stimulate the mortgage market and housing. Late that year, when monetary policy was shifted to a less expansive stance, the Federal Reserve announced a change in reserve requirements on net demand deposits to become effective in January 1968. Split requirements were imposed for the first time: on amounts up to $5 million the requirement was unchanged; on amounts over $5 million the requirement was raised by ½%. Although another ½% increase in requirements was considered at a meeting of the Board on December 17, 1968, in conjunction with an increase of ¼% in the discount rate, such action was deferred until April 1969, when reserve requirements on net demand deposits were raised ½% across the board, *i.e.*, on deposits both under and over $5 million and for both reserve city and country banks. The increase covered all member banks, in contrast to the previous action in January 1968 which affected only the large banks.

In July 1969, the Federal Reserve Board amended its regulations to classify certain RPs as deposits subject to reserve requirements and interest rate ceilings. Effective August 28, 1969, all RPs entered into on or after July 25, 1969, with a person other than a bank, involving any assets other than direct obligations of the United States or its agencies, or obligations guaranteed by the United States or its agencies, were classified as deposit liabilities subject to reserve requirements and interest rate ceilings. The amended regulation had the effect of eliminating borrowings by banks through the sale of their loans under RPs to corporate and other nonbank investors. This device had been used by several banks as a source of funds earlier in the year when the Fed's policy became increasingly restrictive.

In August 1969, the Federal Reserve Board imposed for the first time a complex system of reserve requirements on Eurodollar borrowings and on the sale of assets to foreign branches. The new requirements were based on borrowings of banks from their foreign branches and on assets acquired by foreign

branches from member banks' head offices in the U.S. A requirement of 10% was imposed on these categories in excess of a base
for each bank defined as the average volume outstanding in the
four weeks ending May 28, 1969.* The requirement became
effective with the four-week reserve computation period beginning October 16, 1969. The Board, in announcing the requirement, stated that the purpose of the action was to moderate the
flow of foreign funds between U.S. banks and their foreign
branches by removing a special advantage to member banks that
had used Euro-dollars not subject to reserve requirements to adjust to domestic credit restraint.

Effective with the four-week reserve computation period ending
December 23, 1970, the reserve requirement on Euro-dollars
above the base was raised to 20%. Furthermore, effective with the
reserve computation period ending January 20, 1971, the reserve-
free base was lowered to the current outstanding volume of Euro-
dollars rather than the May 1969 level.

Reserve requirements were extended to funds received from
commercial paper on October 1, 1970. A 5% reserve requirement
was introduced on such funds at the same time that the reserve
requirement on time deposits in excess of $5 million was reduced
from 6% to 5%.

Returning now to reserve requirements generally, the reason
that they have not been changed very often is that they are considered to be a blunt tool. Changes affect banks as a group at the
same time regardless of the individual bank's position. Even a
change of one half of one percent involves a substantial volume
of reserves and has a material impact on the money market.
When requirements are increased, banks usually have larger
reserve deficits, so they must sell securities or other liquid assets,
buy Federal funds, or borrow from the Federal Reserve banks.
To accommodate an increase in reserve requirements, therefore,
the Federal Reserve will often step up its open market purchases

---

* A minimum base was also provided equal to 3% of deposits subject to
reserve requirements for any bank with a foreign branch regardless of
its previous use of Euro-dollars.

temporarily. Contrariwise, a reduction in reserve requirements will create more excess reserves for member banks and the Federal Reserve may soften the impact by sales of securities. In either event, changes in reserve requirements affect the cost of funds for banks and have usually been interpreted as an important signal of the direction of monetary policy. They tend to have significant effects on the money market as reserve positions of banks become tighter or easier.

MORAL SUASION

Moral suasion, sometimes called "open-mouth operations," may be important to the money market, as the following example will show. On September 1, 1966, during the credit squeeze, the Federal Reserve Board issued a letter cautioning member banks against greater than seasonal expansion of business loans, urging them not to liquidate securities because it would add to pressures on financial markets, and strongly implying that extensions of credit to member banks through the discount window would be curtailed for banks that did not fully cooperate. Although it is not possible to state the specific effects of the letter, the money market almost immediately became tighter as many banks tried to avoid borrowing from the Federal Reserve. In retrospect, it appears that the rate of expansion in business loans was already starting to slacken even before the letter was sent and that economic activity was showing some signs of slowing. In any event, there was much criticism of the letter as an effort to impose a kind of selective lending control designed to curtail particular kinds of loans rather than permitting market forces to work freely through decisions of bank managements. In late December the letter was rescinded.

The effectiveness of other attempts at moral suasion is equally hard to measure. One of the earliest was in 1923 when the Annual Report of the Federal Reserve Board distinguished between "productive" and "unproductive" credit and attempted to guide credit extensions toward the former. In the late 1920s the Federal Reserve Banks insisted that member banks cut back on any extensive stock market loans as a prerequisite for borrowing at the discount window. With the advent of the Second World War and again in the Korean conflict, banks were urged to cooperate in restraint of lending and investing activities.

Another interesting example was in 1955 when the Federal Reserve became concerned about expansion of real estate credit. At that time, large insurance companies were obtaining supplementary funds by "warehousing" mortgage loans with commercial banks. The mortgages were used as collateral to secure short-term borrowing from the banks. The Federal Reserve Bank of New York suggested to individual banks that it was not pleased with this practice of indirectly financing long-term credits and these loans were reduced.

In 1969, Governor J. L. Robertson of the Federal Reserve Board warned bankers against using "various ingenious devices" to evade restrictive credit policies. He deplored such "corner-cutting devices" as sale of commercial paper by one-bank holding companies, solicitation of funds from a nonbank institution with a promise to lend them to another bank through the Federal funds market, and solicitation of deposits of public funds at rates exceeding interest rate ceilings.[8]

INTEREST RATE CEILINGS

The power to set interest rate ceilings on time and savings deposits also has very important money market implications. This power is exercised under Regulation Q of the Reserve Board. "Q" has become a by-word in the money market. "Some bankers quip that Q stands for queer, quixotic, and quicksand. Others quiver and they say Q is for quality of credit and quick assets leading to quiet of mind. Still others contend that Q means quibble and quarrel." *

---

* From remarks by the author introducing a panel discussion in 1964 at the spring meeting of the American Bankers Association in White Sulphur Springs, West Virginia.

The background of the authority to set interest rate ceilings is interesting. In the Banking Act of 1933, Congress ruled that no interest should be paid on demand deposits and that the Federal Reserve should set interest rate ceilings on time and savings deposits. It is usually assumed that these decisions by Congress stemmed from the unhappy banking developments of the twenties with the resulting large-scale failures of banks. There were no hearings on these important matters but controls were the order of the day, as shown by the codes adopted under the National Recovery Administration, which set prices industry by industry in a remarkably detailed way. So it is possible that this philosophy spread also to the group in Congress working on banking legislation. What would be more natural than to give the Federal Reserve powers to hold down bank costs, especially since they were about to rise as a result of FDIC insurance premiums? Anyway, overly aggressive efforts to compete for business might cause unsound pressures.

For approximately two decades, the ceilings were no problem to banks because they were always above market rates. But in 1959 the ceilings on time deposits suddenly bit hard, as market rates moved above them. The problem proved to be temporary and was solved when market rates dropped below the ceilings in the last half of 1960.

The dramatic course of CDs in recent years testifies to the power of the Federal Reserve to let this instrument thrive or virtually die when banks cannot pay competitive rates. By late 1965 CDs outstanding had risen to $15 billion. In December 1965, the ceiling rate on negotiable CDs was raised from 4–4½% to 5½%, as the discount rate was raised from 4% to 4½%. This meant that the CD ceiling was increased to 1% over the discount rate, with the apparent purpose of giving sufficient latitude to banks in setting CD rates so that they could fully meet competitive rates from market instruments.

The upward trend in short-term interest rates continued in 1966, however, and the 5½% ceiling soon did not look so generous. By mid-summer it obviously became repressive, with the result that CDs were frequently not renewed by corporations because it was possible to get a better return from other money market securities. At the peak point of pressure, the rate on 182-day Treasury bills was 6.04% and the bond equivalent * yield on these bills was 6.32%, compared with the 5½% ceiling on CDs. Thus the ceilings were considerably out of line with money market rates. The volume of CDs declined from $18 billion in August to almost $15 billion by year end.

Money conditions soon eased and CDs resumed their growth, reaching a new peak of $24 billion in late 1968. In April of that year, Regulation Q ceilings had been raised for all maturities except thirty to fifty-nine days. For example, the ceiling was raised from 5½% to 6¼% for six months CDs. Again open market rates quickly shot up to the ceilings and even exceeded them temporarily by a few basis points † in May. However, market rates then declined, causing a reversal in the minor downward trend in outstanding CDs which had developed during the second quarter of the year.

On December 18, 1968, the discount rate was raised from 5¼% to 5½% but no change was made in Regulation Q ceilings. Almost immediately open market rates rose to levels about ¼% and more above the ceilings and once more precipitated a sharp attrition in outstanding CDs. The decline became more pronounced as the differentials in favor of open market paper widened to more than 1½% during the last half of 1969. By the end of 1969 the volume of CDs had declined to $11.9 billion.

The reason the Federal Reserve did not increase the ceilings on CDs was that it was uneasy over the growth of bank loans to business, in the inflationary situation then prevailing, and concluded that CDs financed some of these loans. Accordingly, if

---

* See Chapter 3 for explanation of bond equivalent rate.
† Basis point is one hundreth of 1%, *i.e.*, if open market rates were 6.35% vs. the ceiling of 6.25%, the difference of .10% would be termed ten basis points.

CD volume could be reduced, bank loans to business would necessarily be curtailed and this would help to dampen inflationary pressures. In later chapters we will review the 1969 experience in some detail. Here it will be sufficient to say that the use of Regulation Q to squeeze bank credit is controversial, even in Federal Reserve circles. In January 1970 interest rate ceilings on CDs (and other time and savings deposits) were sharply increased. The purpose was not to ease credit but to bring ceiling rates somewhat more in line with market rates and deter the outflow of deposits from commercial banks, savings banks, and savings and loan associations whose customers had been finding it more attractive to buy securities. However, ceilings were not raised sufficiently to make them immediately competitive with market rates. On June 24, 1970, ceilings on CD maturities of thirty to eighty-nine days were "suspended until further notice," in connection with the liquidity crisis precipitated by the Penn Central bankruptcy. CD growth resumed on a rapid basis in late 1970 and 1971, reaching a new high of $34 billion by late 1971.

Service Facilities to the Money Market

In addition to its monetary policy actions, the Federal Reserve System provides service facilities that help the money market to function effectively and rapidly across the country.

FEDERAL FUNDS

The Federal Reserve Banks provide a vital part of the mechanism for trading in Federal funds. Although trading is arranged through a very active network of facilities completely independent of the Federal Reserve Banks, the Federal Reserve System cooperates by providing the instant mechanism for shifting reserves from banks in one Federal Reserve District to banks in other Federal Reserve Districts. Thus, a bank in New York with excess reserves may sell them to a bank in California that is short of reserves. The New York bank simply instructs the Federal Reserve Bank of New York to arrange the shift to the Federal Reserve Bank of San Francisco. Instantly, the reserve account of the New York commercial bank is reduced and the reserve account of the bank in California is increased. This is clearly a vital function to an active market for trading in Federal funds.

TREASURY SECURITIES

In its role as agent to the United States Treasury, the Federal Reserve provides a number of services to the money market. In each Treasury financing the Federal Reserve System is the focal point for subscriptions. For example, each week for the bill bidding, the Federal Reserve Banks across the country have windows open until one-thirty P.M. New York time each Monday to receive bids. A messenger for any institution bidding in the auction can thus leave shortly before one-thirty and run over to the Federal Reserve with the bid or can be at a nearby telephone and receive the figures to fill in the application at the last minute.

The Federal Reserve operates a special wire system across the country for the U.S. Commissioner of the Public Debt. This system makes it possible to transfer Government securities from one city to another by wire. For example, when a security is sold in San Francisco and purchased by a buyer in Boston, the security is delivered to the San Francisco Fed with the proper instructions and it is reissued immediately in Boston. The Fed in San Francisco cancels the old security as the Boston Fed issues the proper new one.

In 1965, the Federal Reserve Bank of New York and two commercial banks in New York City began a pilot test of a new clearing system for the local transfer of U.S. Government securities by teletype. The purpose of the clearing plan was to expedite transfers of Government obligations between banks. It provided for the netting of local trades and greatly reduced the volume of securities deliveries. The test worked so well that it was expanded by the Federal Reserve Bank of New York to include ten commercial banks which are major depositories for securities dealers.

Under this system, the Federal Reserve maintained a clearing account for each of 100-odd issues of Government securities that may be transferred over the teletype network of the participating New York City banks. Instead of receiving or delivering securities for each transaction, as in the past, entries were made to the clearing accounts at the Reserve as the teletype messages were processed during the day. Settlement of the net differences among the banks on each issue were made at the Fed at the close of the day's business.

As this is written, New York banks have moved into a new phase by placing all their Government securities in the hands of the Federal Reserve Bank for safekeeping. This reduces problems of lost and stolen bonds and makes transfers of securities between banks even easier because they are accomplished on a book entry basis at the Fed.

The Federal Reserve also assists foreign central banks in investing in the American money market—primarily in Treasury bills.

Taking the Pulse of the Money Market

The Federal Reserve System has unique facilities for keeping on top of developments in the money market. To begin with, the Fed is a tremendous collector and generator of information on the economic and financial pulse of the nation. The Board of Governors of the System and the twelve Federal Reserve banks all contribute. Moreover, the Fed is in close touch with developments affecting member banks of the system, as well as with the whole field of banking. A large group of member banks submits weekly reports covering all important sectors of their balance sheets.

Beyond all this, the trading desk of the New York Federal Reserve Bank is in almost continuous touch daily with the money position desks of the larger commercial banks and with Government security dealers, as well as with a number of other important elements in the money market. It is something like the weather bureau with its intricate system of tracking weather developments in order to better predict what will happen.

Changing Federal Reserve Objectives

Much has been written about the purposes of the Federal Reserve System and the methods used to achieve the stated objectives. I do not wish to repeat the obvious but changing conditions need to be highlighted for a proper understanding of the Federal Reserve's role in the money market. Most important, the real-life problems of the Federal Reserve and the understanding of them by a student of the money market differ considerably from the textbooks. The trouble is that in real life the problems keep changing and the Federal Reserve is constantly struggling to find solutions to situations that have developed in intensity well beyond the textbook suppositions.

It will be an oversimplification but I would like to illustrate this point by listing a chronology of major monetary and banking developments and the response of the monetary authorities, with the hope of emphasizing not only the evolving needs and tools of the Federal Reserve System but the impact of their operations on the money market over the years.

1918	A large expansion in bank reserves is provided by the Federal Reserve to support Treasury financing but interest rates rise and each War Loan is financed at a higher level of interest rates.
1920–21	A substantial outflow of gold and price inflation motivate the Federal Reserve to push the dis-

count rate up to 7%, the highest rate posted in the life of the System.

1928–29   A large increase in brokers' call loans poses a major problem as margin buying stimulates the speculative binge in the stock market. The Federal Reserve reacts by raising the discount rate.

1931   The onset of the Depression causes a shift in Federal Reserve emphasis to easier monetary policy.

1933–35   The two Banking Acts of the early New Deal serve to correct some of the weaknesses that precipitated the wave of bank failures and the bank holiday in 1933, such as limiting borrowings from the Federal Reserve by banks engaged in certain stock market financing, expanding the lending authority of the Federal Reserve Banks, elimination of interest on demand deposits, etc.

1936–38   The Federal Reserve doubles reserve requirements in three steps during 1936 and 1937 in order to counteract the potential inflationary hazards of the tremendous inflow of gold. Reserve requirements are reduced slightly in 1938 to counter recession.

1941–45   The Federal Reserve pegs interest rates on Government securities in order to finance World War II on a low rate basis and avoid the escalation of rates that occurred in 1917–18. Large amounts of reserves are created as war financing is supported and the setting is laid for a postwar fight between the Treasury and the Federal Reserve.

1951–52   The Federal Reserve wishes to increase its ability to deal with inflationary conditions and reaches an accord with the Treasury to stop supporting Government bond prices. It also adopts the "bills only" doctrine to remove its influence as much as possible from particular maturity groups of securities.

1958　　An intense amount of speculative buying in a Treasury refunding precipitates a sharp decline in bond prices. The Federal Reserve endeavors to intervene to prevent disorderly markets but not to protect the speculators who ultimately lose substantial amounts as bond prices continue to drop. The conflict between the Fed's endeavor to prevent disorderly markets and not to create reserves inordinately is sharply joined.

1959　　The Federal Reserve embarks on a policy designed to reduce inflationary pressures and limits the expansion in bank credit during a year of strong economic expansion.

1960　　The international balance of payments deficit becomes a problem and the Federal Reserve begins to weigh international considerations more heavily.

1962　　The Federal Reserve and the Treasury both try to push short-term interest rates up while holding long-term interest rates down, the purpose being to aid the international balance of payments while not obstructing economic expansion.

1966　　The inflationary expansion in the economy motivates the Fed to adopt an increasingly restrictive policy. Emphasis is directed toward restraining business loans by maintaining restrictive Regulation Q ceilings and through moral suasion in the special letter of September 1.

1967–68　A sharp reversal to an easy money policy to counter recessionary tendencies is succeeded by tightening as economic expansion resumes; a temporary suspension of tighter policy occurs following a tax increase.

1969　　A restrictive policy of "gradualism" is embarked upon, followed later by tough policies designed to restrain continuing inflationary pressures. Again restraint is directed toward limiting expansion in business loans. Highly restrictive Regulation Q ceilings are maintained, reserve requirements are raised, and new restrictive regulations are imposed with respect to Euro-dollar borrowings and proposed for other types of borrowings.

1970–71 A mixed economy consisting of economic sluggishness with continuing inflation poses new problems for the Federal Reserve. Meanwhile, it is giving more attention to the growth in money and bank credit and less attention to interest rates.

Commercial Banks: Nerve Center of the Money Market

CHAPTER 7   Commercial banks are the operating heart of the money market. They act as important principals—investors and lenders on one side and borrowers on the other. Banks by tradition have been lenders and investors in money market instruments for use as liquid reserves. As investors, they are large holders of short-term U.S. Government securities and municipal obligations, as well as other issues. As lenders, they are active in the Federal funds market and perform an important role in financing brokers and dealers in securities.

But developments in the last two decades have created a new mechanism called "liability management" in which banks have become large issuers of money market paper. Thus commercial banks are active borrowers in the Federal funds market and through RPs. They also issue negotiable CDs when the Federal Reserve's Regulation Q ceilings permit. Some banks borrowed substantial amounts of Euro-dollar deposits abroad beginning in 1969. In addition, some bank holding companies and bank subsidiaries began borrowing through commercial paper in 1969. So in a credit squeeze banks have not only the option of selling portfolio securities or reducing loans—they can also balance their accounts on the liability side through issuing CDs, commercial paper, etc.

The prime rate of banks is a key rate in the money market. This rate applies to short-term loans to substantial depositors with the highest credit rating.

Finally, commercial banks provide the facilities and mechanism to effect the large volume of payments and the handling of transactions required by the money market.

Role As Investors and Lenders in the Money Market

Why are commercial banks interested in holding short-term obligations although interest rates are often higher on longer-term investments and loans? The answer of course is that banks need liquidity to take care of both the predictable and the unpredictable outflow of funds from their institutions. While it is true that the Federal Reserve System offers loans to member banks at the discount window to meet unexpected liquidity needs, this has been a somewhat delicate proposition since borrowing is a privilege and not a right. (The proposed new basic borrowing privilege would constitute only a relatively small exception.) In short, the banks fear that if they make frequent use of the discount window, the Fed will interfere in their lending and investing policies. In any event, commercial banks long ago developed the fine art of trying to have just the right amount of liquidity at all times. The exact amount held, of course, varies tremendously from recession to boom periods.

For individual banks, liquidity needs also vary seasonally during the course of the year, as well as from week to week and sometimes even from day to day. Commercial banks have different systems for determining liquidity needs but, regardless of the variety of approaches to the problem, they must be in a position to take care of outflows of funds resulting from net withdrawals of deposits and net loan expansion.

If interest rates are very low, as they were in the Great Depression of the 1930s, commercial banks may not be very forceful in trying to put new funds to work to earn a return. But that was an exceptional period. Normally, interest rates are an important motivating factor in keeping bankers from overlooking business opportunities and in persuading them to economize on holdings of liquid assets. Funds estimated to be required for liquidity will be invested in some form that will provide a return and yet will take care of cash requirements as needed. The typical money market bank in New York employs a variety of liquid instruments: Treasury bills and other short-term U.S. Government obligations and issues of Federal agencies; loans to securities dealers and brokers; bankers' acceptances; State and municipal issues due in a relatively short time; commercial paper; and sales of Federal funds. The banker wants to maximize his return on these short-term money market holdings, but he wants to do so without impairing the real liquidity he needs. He is careful not to put funds required for such purposes in long-term bonds, since this may possibly involve dangerous market risk; bond prices might go down, which would mean that he could only convert the bonds into cash by taking a substantial loss in a depressed market. Spreads between bid and asked prices are also wider in the case of longer maturities than Treasury bills, thus reinforcing the preference for short-term commitments, even if the banker were willing to assume that market prices would remain stable. So he sticks to relatively short maturities; some banks limit maturities of securities held for liquidity purposes to one year while others use maturities up to eighteen months or two years.

The people at the "money desk" at major commercial banks who handle short-term investments must be fleet of foot: they must be flexible and ready to move quickly from one investment to another in order to maximize earnings, always remembering, however, the basic rule that liquid funds must be kept in instruments which provide true liquidity.

Each week, when the Treasury Department conducts its auctions of Treasury bills, commercial banks are important bidders, seeking to buy bills both for their own account and for the accounts of their customers. Sometimes the banks expect to hold the bills acquired for a period of time or to maturity and sometimes they hope to sell them at a profit. One incidental benefit to the Treasury is very important: the banks (and Government securities dealers) in effect assume the function of underwriting Treasury bill issues—so the Treasury can be sure the entire issue will be sold. This also applies to other new Treasury obligations —both short- and longer-term.

The banks are also involved in the Government securities market indirectly through their loans to dealers. Each day, major money market banks in New York post an interest rate for loans to Government securities dealers. The rate generally has two figures, such as 5⅝–6%. The first figure refers to extensions of loans which are already on the bank's books. The second figure refers to new loans as distinguished from renewals. The posting of these rates tells dealers the attitude of the bank. An increase in the rates signifies something about the position of the bank and the money market situation. If such rates are rising in all banks, it is clear that banks are becoming tighter and less willing to take on loans from dealers. If the rates rise only in one bank, it is an indication that the particular bank is tighter than banks generally and wishes to discourage such loans.

Similarly, loans are made to dealers in bankers' acceptances, CDs, Federal agency, municipal, and corporate bonds (often a dealer is involved in all these markets plus U.S. Governments, but collateral for the loan varies among the different types of obligations). Loans to brokers in stocks also vary with the bank's ability to extend money market loans.

Banks also assist dealers from time to time, when the size and distribution of their portfolios permit, by lending them securities. The purpose of such loans is to provide dealers with securities they have sold but do not own (note that dealers endeavor to make markets in all issues of Government securities whether they own them or not), or have not yet received due to delays in deliveries, or to facilitate a short sale by a customer.* Not all banks lend securities to dealers but the practice represents another money market function of commercial banks.

Federal funds are a key item in bank liquidity management. Sales may be made when the cash position is relatively easy, and purchases when the position is tight. Later in this chapter we will examine more carefully just how Federal funds fit into the daily routine of a bank.

Role as Borrowers in the Money Market

Now let us consider banks as borrowers in the money market. Before the Federal Reserve System was organized in 1913, banks borrowed from each other in the form of ordinary bank loans (not to be confused with transactions in Federal funds). Typically, such borrowing took place by smaller banks from their correspondent banks (larger banks, in larger cities, with which they maintained deposits to support services required). Larger banks seldom borrowed because there was no agency to borrow from. With the establishment of the Federal Reserve System, member banks obtained a new source of borrowing by using the discount window. This was important in the 1920s but, as described elsewhere, use of the discount window has faded except during periods of tight Federal Reserve policy. Since the latter 1950s, borrowing through the purchase of Federal funds or through similar forms, such as RPs, has grown tremendously.

---

* A short sale is a sale of securities not yet owned made deliberately with the expectation of lower prices. The seller must borrow securities to turn over to the buyer; eventually, of course, he must buy them from someone to cover what he has borrowed.

Then, beginning in 1961, CDs became a major borrowing device for commercial banks. More recently banks developed arrangements for borrowing Euro-dollar deposits. This instrument did not become very important to American banks until 1969 when tight money caused major money market banks with branches in London to actively seek Euro-dollars.

Federal funds, CDs and RPs have been described in earlier chapters. A later chapter will discuss new perspective on CDs. Now let us stop for a digression on the background and mechanism of Euro-dollars.

EURO-DOLLARS

First, what is a Euro-dollar? A Euro-dollar is simply a dollar-denominated deposit in a bank outside the United States.

In 1966 and 1969, as it became more difficult to acquire Federal funds and to sell CDs, some banks decided that it would be wise to have their foreign branches acquire Euro-dollar deposits. The rate ceilings under Regulation Q do not apply to such deposits, so that they could be acquired when CDs became difficult, if not impossible, to obtain. Euro-dollars could be acquired on a day-to-day basis, like Federal funds or for longer periods like domestic CDs. A bank could have its London branch solicit Euro-dollar deposits for a day, three days, or several months, and then have the New York office collect the funds for its use. What actually happened was that the New York office became the owner of deposits in another American bank—the bank in which the Euro-dollars had been originally based—and, of course, the New York bank involved immediately collected the funds from the other American bank, on which some foreign owner had a claim. The point is that in this process the home office received reserves at the Federal Reserve just as though it were buying Federal funds. On the liability side, instead of owing another bank, the home office owed its branch which in turn had a deposit outstanding to the person in Europe who had made the Euro-dollar deposit. In short, banks in the United States were taking over some of the demand for Euro-dollars which earlier had been exercised by foreigners. We were reacquiring dollars held abroad and substituting a future promise to pay in dollars.

The mechanics of acquiring Euro-dollar deposits may seem complex but it helps to follow through the steps involved. For example, the London branch of an American bank bids in the market for time deposits denominated in dollars just as the head office does domestically for CDs. To accomplish this transaction, the branch of Bank A in London must locate a potential depositor with dollar funds on the books in another bank (Bank B) in the United States. The depositor must instruct the head office of Bank B by wire to deliver its check to Bank A in the States for the amount involved. If Bank B has a London branch, it will arrange this and will issue a confirmation to the depositor for delivery to the London office of Bank A.

The head office of Bank A will collect the funds from the other bank through the Clearing House the day after the check is issued. The funds will be shown in a "Due to London" account. The bookkeeping entries for Bank A will be:

At London Branch	At Home Office
	1. As Bank B's check is received:
Debit "Due from Head Office"	Debit "Due from Banks"
Credit "Time Deposits"	Credit "Due to London"
	2. The next day:
	Debit "Loans" (or perhaps
	"Other Securities," etc.)
	Credit "Due from Banks"

On a consolidated statement, the "Due to London" item washes with "Due from Head Office." The amount shown in foreign deposits is reflected in the various assets accounts when the money is put to work the next day.

Rates offered in London for U.S. dollar time deposits tend to be higher than those offered for time deposits by the head office in New York. Yet the cost may not be unfavorable as compared with the cost of domestic CDs, since reserve requirements are zero on amounts in the so-called "base" (originally the daily average amounts outstanding in the four weeks ending May 28, 1969, but subsequently any lower amount outstanding) for each bank, and no FDIC premiums are applicable to such deposits. Roughly a 6% rate on Euro-dollar time deposits in a bank's stated base is the same as a 5½% rate on domestic CDs.

The increasing use of Euro-dollars during the 1969 period of credit shortage and high interest rates in the U.S. was evidenced by the position of all large American banks at the end of November 1969 when gross liabilities to their foreign branches were $15.0 billion. Of this total, $9.9 billion were reported by the large New York City banks. The latter total, which represented mostly borrowings of Euro-dollars, compared with borrowings of Federal funds and borrowings from other sources of slightly less than $5 billion.

New Federal Reserve regulations on Euro-dollars adopted in 1969 tended to make them less attractive as a source of funds. The first regulation, effective July 31, 1969, required that the drafts or checks used in settling Euro-dollar transactions be included in the bank's deposit totals, subject to reserve requirements, thus making the net cost of Euro-dollars more expensive.

The second regulation established a 10% reserve requirement on Euro-dollar borrowings in excess of the base (average volume outstanding in four weeks ending May 28, 1969). This new requirement became effective with the four-week reserve computation period starting October 16, 1969. A minimum base equal to 3% of deposits subject to reserve requirements was also provided for a bank with a foreign branch regardless of its previous use of Euro-dollars. The reserve requirement was subsequently raised to 20% with the four-week reserve computation period ending December 23, 1970. Furthermore, the reserve-free base was later lowered to the current outstanding volume. To the degree banks purchase Euro-dollars in excess of their minimum base, the borrowings are subject to a 20% reserve requirement and therefore become more expensive.

Another regulatory change which had considerable impact on U.S. bank participation in the Euro-dollar market was the suspension of the Regulation Q ceiling on interest rates payable on short-term CDs in June of 1970. As domestic sources of credit were expanded, U.S. banks began to repay their liabilities to their foreign branches on a massive scale. The outflow of funds from the U.S. to Europe was aggravated by interest rate differentials, which developed as interest rates rose in Europe in response to restrictive monetary policies and fell in the U.S. in a climate of relative monetary ease. U.S. bank liabilities to their own foreign branches fell from $15 billion in November 1969 to $1.5 billion at the end of June 1971. In the same period, bank CDs rose from $11 billion to $28.5 billion.

Also in 1969, some bank holding companies and bank subsidiaries began borrowing through commercial paper in order to raise funds for their constituent banks. In addition, until new restrictive regulations were imposed by the Federal Reserve, some banks sold participations in their loan portfolios and some developed other new instruments.

But why do banks borrow? Today they borrow primarily as a means to supplement asset liquidity. Obviously, borrowing would not supplant completely the need to carry short-term assets for liquidity but borrowing gives a bank more options in managing its total position.

In day-to-day management decisions, banks use the different kinds of borrowing and asset management in a continually changing pattern, depending on the pressures of the moment and interest costs, as well as the composition of their assets and liabilities. To understand this, we need to consider the interchange of policy actions on the liability side and on the asset side of the balance sheet in day-to-day actions to navigate a bank's position.

Opportunity Cost in Managing a Bank's Position

There is never an idle moment in managing the reserve position of a large money market bank, because the position keeps changing continuously. What seems appropriate at ten o'clock in the morning may not be satisfactory at one forty-five in the afternoon. Something may have to be done to correct an imbalance in the inflow or outflow of funds as against previous expectations. The money desk may be actively borrowing or lending in the money market to correct the position, but a half hour later a reverse course may have to be taken because a new development has upset the position.

The economists' term "opportunity cost" is very useful in thinking about the judgments made by banks each day in their money market transactions. Opportunity cost means the cost of not taking an alternative course of action. Thus, we might think of the cost of not using margarine at home (using butter) or we might think of the cost of not modernizing an outmoded kitchen (taking a vacation at Caneel Bay instead). Similarly, a bank may borrow Federal funds rather than sell short-term Treasury securities on hand, if its calculations of opportunity cost show that it is more economical to pay interest on Federal funds than to lose interest (and possibly suffer a capital loss) by selling securities in the portfolio.

Let us assume that a bank needs to raise $10 million to meet an outflow of deposits. What would be the cost if it liquidated short-term securities held in portfolio as against the cost of borrowing Federal funds? How does this compare with the cost of issuing additional CDs? There may be other options but let us consider these by themselves in some calculations I made in 1971. Assume that the Federal funds rate is 4.75% and that the bank is earning 4.94% on its holdings of Treasury bills which could be sold in the market at a rate of say, 5.11%. The 5.11%

94

would reflect the effective cost, including the capital loss, resulting from sale of the bills below "book" or carrying value. The cost of putting on a new CD is 5½% but this is equivalent to 5.96%, when allowance is made for the cost adjustments involved in meeting reserve requirements and paying FDIC assessments.* Examining these three figures, the least expensive route would be to borrow in the form of Federal funds, because 4.75% is below the other rates mentioned.

But there are other factors to consider as well. Is the loss of the $10 million deposit considered permanent or can another deposit be found? If it is permanent, the use of Federal funds may not be an appropriate way of meeting the situation because as a rule a Federal funds transaction is only for overnight. True, it can be repeated, presumably with another transaction tomorrow and the day following but there may be some doubts as to whether the funds will be available day after day and also considerable uncertainty as to what the rates will be. The officers may argue that even though the need for funds is likely to continue for quite a while, they will still bet that the use of Federal funds will be the best approach. This may be decided more or less on a day-to-day basis, *i.e.*, today's decision holds only for today and a new decision will be made tomorrow based on the facts tomorrow. On the other hand, the officers may conclude that the Treasury bills should be sold, even though the effective cost is 5.11%. Alternatively, the officers may consider trying to obtain additional CDs with the hope of making what is considered a more or less permanent replacement for the deposits which are being lost. Of course, there is no such thing as "permanent" in the competitive world in which we live, but the officers may feel that the pool of CDs that the bank has outstanding is from pretty steady customers who are likely to keep a good hard core of these funds, at least for the time being. There is also the possibility that RPs, commercial paper, or Euro-dollars could be used.

* This is explained in Chapter 16.

While I have been referring in this chapter to the decisions made by the officers collectively in a bank, I should note that in practice the decisions are likely to be made by various people, depending on the organization. In some banks they may be made by a committee. Top management, of course, will participate actively in the formation of policy.

Daily "Diary" of a Money Desk

It is fascinating to watch the endless process that takes place as the money desk of a large bank keeps adjusting its reserve position. Let us consider a more or less typical situation for a Reserve city bank early in 1969 when Fed policy was becoming increasingly restrictive. At that time, when the computation period closed on Wednesday night, *i.e.*, the seven days ending Wednesday, a reserve city bank must have had on average, sufficient cash in vault plus balances at the Federal Reserve Bank to equal 17% of its average net demand deposits over $5 million * for the computation period two weeks earlier, plus 6% of its time deposits over $5 million and 3% of its savings deposits and other time deposits under $5 million for the same period. Any excess or deficiency in reserves may be carried over from one computation period to the next to the extent that such excess or deficiency does not exceed 2% of required reserves.

There are technical definitions involved in determining the requirements; for example, the figure on demand deposits is figured on a net basis so as to exclude checks drawn on other banks which are received from depositors but not yet collected from those other banks. The purpose of this is to avoid double counting by all banks taken together: if a check is put in one bank drawn on another bank but it has not yet cleared the other bank, it would be double counting if reserves were required of both banks for the amount involved.

To read about these reserve requirements is hardly to under-

---

* 16½% on the first $5 million of net demand deposits.

stand the process of constant adjustment in meeting them. Accordingly, I prepared a "diary" illustrating the actions taken in a large bank for Thursday and Friday, the first two days of the computation period, and Wednesday, the last day of the period. Two figures will be given frequently, representing the position for the day and the position cumulatively for the period. The Thursday entries will begin with final figures for the week just ended and these will show a deficit for the preceding day but an overage for the weekly period. This will simply mean that in the six preceding days (Saturday's and Sunday's count) the bank built up a position which was larger than was needed on average for those specific days. These could be carried over to Wednesday so that a deficit for the day would still leave the bank ahead for the seven days as a whole. Furthermore, any overage could be carried over, under certain conditions, into the next computation period.

Below then are the entries for certain major items in the "diary" for early 1969:

Thursday—first day of period

9:00 A.M.   Final reserve figures (deficiency [−], surplus [+] in relation to required reserves) for Wednesday night, end of the preceding computation period:

$−10,500,000 for the day

+15,300,000 for the period

Overage of $15,300,000 for the period represented an overage of $+2,185,000 per day vs. daily required reserves of $235,000,000. Overage therefore amounted to less than 1% per day. This overage can be carried over into the new period, in accordance with Fed regulations. Preliminary Wednesday figures had been:

$−17,500,000 for the day

+ 8,300,000 for the period

	but $7,000,000 in late transfers came in over the Federal Reserve wire.
9:15–9:30	Authorized payment of $90,000,000 in Federal funds bought Wednesday. Checked collateral held at Federal Reserve for Tax and Loan Account and possible borrowing.
10:00	Brokers Loans Department said $45,000,000 loans were being paid off in Federal funds by dealers.
10:15	Sold $10,000,000 acceptances to a dealer.
10:30	First estimates of reserve position for new period after adjusting for pay down of loans (may be partly replaced) and sale of acceptances:

Thurs. $-25,000,000 (day)
         -25,000,000 (period)
Fri.   -40,000,000 (day)
          -65,000,000 (period)

10:45	Considered bidding aggressively on new Treasury Tax Anticipation Bills. (Payment will be through Tax and Loan Account.) Broker quoted Federal funds market at 6¼–6½%. Bought $20 million at 6¼% and will try to place funds in loans to Government bond dealers at 6½–6¾%.
11:15	Treasury made special call of $11,000,000 on Tax and Loan Account. Considered sale of $5,000,000 in short Treasury bills to raise funds but decided to hold off as market might improve.
11:30	Made $20,000,000 in new dealer loans at 6¾%. Position now about $-56,000,000 for the day.
11:45	Arranged RP of $10,000,000 with ABC Corporation for fifteen days at 6⅜%.

12:00   Bought $40,000,000 in Federal funds at 6¼%. Half came through brokers and half directly from out-of-town banks.

12:30   NYSE member firm called to borrow $14,000,000 on unsold syndicate underwriting; loans to be made by official check (so no effect on reserves today but will lose funds tomorrow, increasing our shortage then). Rate 6%.

1:00   Federal funds now quoted at 6½%.

1:30   Loaned $25,000,000 more to two dealers in Federal funds at 6¾%.

1:45   Picked up $20,000,000 in Federal funds at 6½%.

2:00   New estimates of position adjusted by recent moves:

> Thurs. $−32,000,000 (day)
>   −32,000,000 (period)
> Fri.   −47,000,000 (day)
>   −79,000,000 (period)

2:15 $3,000,000 in Federal funds just received from issuance of new CDs.

2:30   Review of future known factors affecting reserves showed:

> Friday: $15,000,000 finance company loan being made by National Division; $34,000,000 CDs maturing—some new ones may go on. Plan to ask London office to purchase $25,000,000 two- or three-month Eurodollar funds on Monday. We would receive Federal funds on Tuesday.
> Monday: We may pick up $100,000,000 in new Treasury Tax Anticipation bills paid for by credit to Tax and Loan

Account—raising reserve requirements by $17,000,000—but we expect to sell around $30,000,000 of new bills for delivery on day proceeds are credited. $20,000,000 more in CDs mature.

Tuesday: $31,000,000 will be received to pay dividends of XYZ Corp. Should keep one-third for ten days or more as some checks are cashed gradually and come against us over the period. Real Estate Division has $12,000,000 payoff scheduled in Clearing House funds. We get Federal funds Wednesday.

3:00 Funds market very tight—offered at 6¾% and little around. Hear story Fed may offer dealers RPs on Friday at 5½%. Could help things over weekend. Decided not to buy funds at this level.

3:15 Arranged RP with international agency for $5,000,000 for six days at 6¼%.

3:30 New figures:
Thurs. final
$−39,000,000 (day)
−39,000,000 (period)
Fri. estimated
$−54,000,000 (day)
−93,000,000 (period)
Thursday results thrown off by revisions, mainly in international accounts.

3:45 Checks are in on weekend Euro-dollar funds bought Tuesday by London office. $15,000,000 (cost 7⅜%) will clear tomorrow and be credited to Fed balance. Money will, of course, go

100

out Monday in repayment. Transactions had been allowed for in estimates since commitment was made two days ago.

Friday—second day of period

10:00   Opening estimates

       Fri. $− 45,000,000 (day)
               − 84,000,000 (period)
       Sat.   − 57,000,000 (day)
            −141,000,000 (period)
       Sun.   − 57,000,000 (day)
            −198,000,000 (period)
       Mon.   − 42,000,000 (day)
            −240,000,000 (period)

Weekend makes the cumulative shortage look bad.

11:30   Funds look easier. Federal Reserve buying bills for cash. Bought $35,000,000 Federal funds at 6¼%, cutting our Monday period shortage by $105,000,000 (3 × $35,000,000).

1:00 $10,000,000 in new CDs sold to two corporations. Monday period figure now $−75,000,000.

2:00   Picked up $20,000,000 more Federal funds at 6%. Estimates now:

       Fri. $+20,000,000 (day)
            −19,000,000 (period)
       Sat.   + 8,000,000 (day)
            −11,000,000 (period)
       Sun.   + 8,000,000 (day)
            − 3,000,000 (period)
       Mon. −35,000,000 (day)
            −38,000,000 (period)

2:30   Learned that loan to finance company of $15,000,000 will go on Monday instead of today, resulting in a + position through Monday.

New figures are:

Fri.	$+36,000,000	(day)
	− 3,000,000	(period)
Sat.	+24,000,000	(day)
	+21,000,000	(period)
Sun.	+24,000,000	(day)
	+45,000,000	(period)
Mon.	−35,000,000	(day)
	+10,000,000	(period)

Wednesday—last day of period

10:00   Opening estimates

$− 6,000,000 (day)
+10,000,000 (period)

Repaid $25,000,000 RP with international agency and $10,000,000 Euro-dollar funds, both maturing today.

2:00   Estimates are:

$−45,000,000 (day)
−29,000,000 (period)

2:15 $4,000,000 in new CDs arranged for tomorrow.

2:30   Managed to buy $10,000,000 funds at 6⅜%. Dealers Clearance reports that delivery of $9,000,000 in Governments may be turned down as too late by another Wall Street bank. May increase shortage after funds purchase back up to:

$−44,000,000 day
−28,000,000 period

Treasury bill market up so sold $5,000,000 bills for delivery today.

2:50 $5,000,000 transferred in from West Coast bank to cover purchase of securities not yet received. Funds being held.

3:15   Bought $8,000,000 Federal funds at 6¼%.

102

Other late transfers coming in. Dealers Clearance says late delivery was accepted. Position now:

$$\$-18,000,000 \ (\text{day})$$
$$-\ 2,000,000 \ (\text{period})$$

3:25 $5,000,000 West Coast payment ordered transferred to other New York bank—presumably for overnight RP as delivery of securities was not made. Payments & Transfers Section reports a last-minute transfer to another Street bank of $4,000,000; earlier instructions from corporate treasurer apparently delayed.

3:40   Bought $3,000,000 in Federal funds at 6⅜%. Figures now

$$\$-20,000,000 \ (\text{day})$$
$$-\ 4,000,000 \ (\text{period})$$

4:00   Considering borrowing at Federal Reserve discount window to meet shortage. Hold up on borrowing, counting on late transfers in from out of town to cover. Still $3,000,000 short for period.

Thursday—first day of new period

9:00   Final Wednesday report:

$$\$-15,000,000 \ \text{day}$$
$$+\ 1,000,000 \ \text{period}$$

Good results—but a little close for comfort.

The "diary" indicates how the money desk is kept posted on developments from time to time during each day and shows how a balance is struck to meet requirements for the day and for the seven-day period. On this basis, the money desk keeps correcting its position to try to meet the exact requirements at the Federal Reserve. It is important not to have a shortage because this may call for a penalty charge against the bank. Technically, there is no penalty if a shortage not exceeding 2% of reserve requirements occurs in one week and is offset by a surplus the following week. But no money desk officer likes a shortage to occur because of the pressure it puts on him the following week. Something unexpected could come up to force him into a deficit again.

It is important also to avoid overages because the Federal Reserve does not pay any return on deposits it holds—the opportunity cost of overages is high. Hence, if the amount shown as an overage in the case above had been in excess of 2%, it would have represented a lost opportunity to make money for the bank. Overages do not occur in large amounts very often in well-managed banks, but they are inevitable from time to time because unexpected developments throw off the figures.

The Prime Rate

The prime rate came into being in the Great Depression of the 1930s. It started out at 1½%, which was the "break-even cost" of handling the paperwork on a large loan with little or no credit risk. Over the intervening years, the prime rate has moved about considerably, reaching a high of 8½% in 1969.

The prime rate is sometimes criticized as a rate that is, in effect, managed by large banks. But I view it as a market rate which cannot hold if it is very far out of line with competitive rates, such as other rates in the money market and rates charged by other types of institutions that are also lending funds to customers of banks. Important competitive rates are to be found in the bond market, the commercial paper market, and the bankers' acceptance market. In short, corporations have the option of borrowing from banks, selling new bonds, selling commercial paper, or perhaps using bankers' acceptances. It is true, of course, that there are other costs and considerations involved in these alternatives, but any material variation in rates between the different sources of funds will lead to a change in borrowing practices by corporations. As an example, in the spring of 1967,

104

corporations appeared to be actively issuing new bonds, putting out commercial paper, and using bankers' acceptances partly because rates were more favorable than bank rates. Bank rates had declined only slightly because bank loan–deposit ratios were high and bank liquidity was relatively low. Hence there was a diversion of some loans to other lenders, but banks welcomed this, at least in part, as they wished to retard their own loan expansion.

In 1969, somewhat the same conditions existed and corporations placed more emphasis on borrowing through commercial paper and bankers' acceptances. A parallel factor which stimulated the expansion in the volume of commercial paper and bankers' acceptances outstanding was the demand from short-term investors, particularly corporations, which found the rates on such paper more attractive than the restricted rate on CDs.

During the early part of 1969 rates on open market paper were below the prime rate, but early in June the new supply of commercial paper became so great that rates advanced to a level above the prime rate. With reserve positions already severely strained and the prospects for even tighter conditions, the banks became fearful that they would be faced with additional demands for funds, as borrowers shifted from the commercial paper market because of the more favorable prime rate. They reacted by raising the prime rate on June 9. The 1% increase—from 7½% to 8½%—was deemed necessary to alert borrowers to the existing extraordinary tight money conditions and to the need to defer borrowings (and the projects which required financing) until there was a dampening of inflationary pressures in the economy. Moreover, even the 8½% was well below rates being paid by banks to raise funds in the Federal funds market and the Euro-dollar market abroad.

In 1971 something new occurred when some banks introduced a floating prime rate set each week on the basis of changes in commercial paper rates.

A word about compensating balances is in order. Such balances are usually required by banks to be retained on deposit in some amount, such as 10% of credit lines extended or 20% of actual loans outstanding. The origin of this idea is that a business which borrows from a bank should carry its account with that bank. It strengthens the ability of the bank to lend and therefore such balances are regarded as compensation to the bank for its readiness to extend a loan when funds are needed. Banks vary in what they demand in compensating balances, and requirements tend to ease or tighten as money conditions change. Some corporations have the power also to force more advantageous terms on banks than the general rules in use. In any event, compensating balances may or may not result in interest rate charges being higher than they appear. Thus a 20% compensating balance might seem to result in a 7½% actual rate when the prime rate being charged a company is 6%. However, in most cases banks provide services to corporations which are paid for by carrying deposits. It is thus very difficult to determine whether compensating balances constitute in effect higher interest rates on loans or represent compensation for services rendered.

Vital Service Role Played by Banks

Virtually all private transactions in the money market are paid for by checks drawn on commercial banks. Even in a utopian "checkless society," the vast majority of payments would be effected via entries in bank accounts. The only exceptions today involve payments to or from the Federal Reserve Banks and transactions in Federal funds.

But it is not only checks drawn on commercial banks that make the money market possible; it is also the facilities of commercial banks in handling the many pieces of paper that change ownership in the money market. Commercial banks operate as agents for their customers, transferring the great bulk of short-term investments between buyers and sellers.

Certain commercial banks act as clearing agents for Government securities dealers. During the trading day securities come in as a dealer makes purchases and they go out from his account as he makes sales. All day long the dealer keeps instructing the bank to accept securities and to pay them out on his behalf. If the total inventory of securities rises, the bank acting as a clearing agent will finance the dealer by in effect carrying his position during the day without charge except for the delivery fees. If overnight loans are needed, the bank will try to accommodate the dealer if he has been unable to finance his position through RPs or other cheaper forms of borrowing. Loans by New York City banks are usually available, but at slightly higher rates if reserve positions are tight; these banks are often considered to be lenders of last resort.

The Treasury Department:
Big Stake in the Money Market

CHAPTER 8   The United States Treasury has a
big stake in the money market. In its role as manager of the
public debt, the Treasury relies heavily on the market. In fact, it
is the largest issuer of short-term securities. But its interest does
not stop there. Unlike other borrowers, the Treasury must consider the national well-being. It is vitally interested in managing
its affairs so as to aid economic growth with price stability for
the country; in recent years it has also been concerned with improving the international balance of payments.

In terms of domestic economic policy, the Treasury will ordinarily have the same objectives as the Federal Reserve.* If
there is economic weakness, the tendency will be to strive for
expansion, and this may cause the Treasury to make decisions
that will help reduce certain interest rates. In times of inflationary pressures, the objective will usually be some restraint of

---

* There is one difference which may be important at times. The Treasury
usually wants to minimize interest costs, whereas this is of little concern
to the Federal Reserve. However, minimizing interest costs is only one of
several Treasury objectives, as noted later in this chapter.

economic activity and rising interest rates will be appropriate.*

The money market watches carefully what the Treasury is doing and tries at all times to understand the rationale and the motivations of the Treasury in its financing.

The Treasury's Role As a Borrower

The Treasury is a frequent borrower in the money and securities markets and has to consider many factors in planning offerings. Among the most important are the current budget situation and the state of the nation's economy. How much financing must be undertaken to provide for budget deficits and refunding operations? What is the condition of the money and bond markets? What economic problems must be given consideration? What international financial aspects must be considered? Such questions must be carefully explored before decisions are made in connection with Treasury borrowing.

EMPHASIS ON SHORT-TERM SECURITIES

Well over $100 billion of United States debt presently falls due within one year. This large sum exceeds the total of all other types of issues which by definition count as money market securities.

The money market, as we have noted, needs a large volume of short-term securities because many of the participants in this market maintain a portfolio to serve their liquidity needs. They either have temporary surplus funds that they wish to invest for a short time or they carry a substantial amount of short-term securities as part of a conscious liquidity program. As we have

---

* These and other objectives were previously discussed by the author in *The Bankers' Handbook* (Homewood, Illinois: Dow-Jones-Irwin, Inc., 1966), "The Influence of Fiscal Policy and Debt Management," pp. 1102–3.

110

seen, the Federal Reserve also holds substantial amounts of short-term U.S. securities.

The Treasury was not always a large borrower. Before World War I the public debt of the United States was only about $1 billion and most of it consisted of bonds held by banks as collateral for the currency that they were then permitted to issue. Thus practically no money market function was served by Treasury securities at that time. When World War I built up the public debt to an unprecedented amount, short-term Treasury securities were issued for the first time in large volume. These were largely confined to certificates of indebtedness (maturities up to one year) which then became an important part of the money market during the twenties. The Treasury bill was not devised in this country until 1929.

Some people will be surprised to hear that the public debt was reduced very substantially (about one-third) during the decade of the 1920s. Since then the public debt has become of growing importance in the money market. It was really during the Great Depression that the Treasury began to develop the role of providing short-term securities to the money market on a massive basis. There was, of course, a tremendous volume of liquid funds in the hands of market participants since the banks had huge excess reserves and interest rates were low. Excess reserves of the banking system grew to almost $7 billion in 1940 compared with less than $100 million in 1930. The interest rate on commercial paper dropped from about $3\frac{1}{2}\%$ in 1930 to about $\frac{1}{2}\%$ by 1940. By 1939, three-month Treasury bills were well established and replaced the certificates of the twenties as the most important money market instrument. However, the rate on bills was down to near zero.

More recently, the volume of outstanding bills has increased for a variety of reasons: bills, of course, are a convenient and often an economical way for the Treasury to finance a budget deficit; there has been an expanding need for such liquidity instruments in the market; the volume of bills outstanding has been increased at times to help keep short-term rates firm in order to strengthen our international balance of payments position; and, finally, the 4¼% interest ceiling on new Treasury bonds has forced the Treasury to rely disproportionately on short-term issues.

In 1951, the Treasury first offered Tax Anticipation Bills to provide corporations with an instrument for the investment of funds being accrued for the payment of income taxes. These issues usually range in maturity up to nine months with maturities scheduled about a week after tax payment dates. They may be used to pay taxes on the tax date at full value or may be redeemed for cash at maturity. After December 1958 six-month bills were also offered every week. In April 1959 the Treasury began to issue bills of up to one-year maturity on quarterly dates and these were replaced in 1963 by a series of nine- and twelve-month bills issued at the end of each month. In June 1961, strip bills were offered for the first time, representing an addition to some or all of outstanding maturities. All these innovations reflected the Treasury's ability to change and to probe the market to meet investors' and its own needs. Recently, the Treasury has tapped the market abroad through issues denominated in Euro-dollars.

OBJECTIVES OF DEBT MANAGEMENT

Debt management represents all measures and decisions which affect the composition and ownership of the public debt of the United States. It includes such matters as the choice and terms of securities to be issued, the selection of the pattern of debt maturities, the efforts to influence ownership by different classes of investors, the decisions to repay or refund maturing obligations, adaptation of new issues to the needs of prospective holders, and other related factors.

In studying the objectives of debt management as enunciated by Treasury spokesmen over a considerable period, nine points

112

stand out (leaving aside the obvious point that needed cash must somehow be raised):

> to maintain confidence in the credit of the U.S. Government;
>
> to use debt management to further current national economic policies, including programs to improve the international balance of payments;
>
> to harmonize debt management with policies of the Federal Reserve System;
>
> to keep the market for United States securities viable (it should have breadth, depth, and resiliency);
>
> to avoid disruptive effects on the money, bond, and mortgage markets and on thrift institutions;
>
> to minimize interest cost for budgetary reasons;
>
> to maintain an orderly scheduling of maturities;
>
> to minimize difficulties caused by Congressional limitations, such as the public debt limit and the 4¼% interest ceiling on marketable Treasury bonds; *
>
> to encourage small savers through the savings bond program, which protects holders from market fluctuations.

Clearly there are many conflicts in these objectives, the resolution of which is bound to vary at different times. People are bound to assign different priorities to these factors as, for example, the objective of minimizing interest cost may be assigned greater significance by one Administration than another.

Some of the objectives obviously point to active use of short-term securities in the money market at certain times. Thus, it is often cheaper in terms of interest cost to use short-term securities.† In the early sixties, however, the persistent deficit in the international balance of payments added a new factor. The Treasury then found it desirable to issue more short-term securi-

---

* I call these "symbolic restraints" imposed by Congress because of frustrations in dealing with the budgetary management and the massive annual Budget document itself.

† See Chapter 14 for a discussion of the yield curve.

ties, not because it was cheaper to put them out than other issues, but because it would help firm up short-term interest rates and thus tend to keep funds from moving abroad to seek higher interest rates in other money markets.

There is also the 4¼% interest limitation on Treasury bonds. Under this legal limitation, which was inaugurated more than five decades ago, the Treasury has frequently been forced to utilize short-term securities because market yields on bonds were above the ceiling. This has had a major impact on the maturity distribution of the debt in recent years and has also limited freedom of action at times by the Federal Reserve. In 1971, Congress authorized the Treasury to issue $10 billion of bonds without regard to the 4¼% limit. There is also an exception for U.S. Savings bonds, which now pay 5½%.

Sometimes there has been still another point, namely, the desire to avoid upsetting longer-term markets when they were under pressure. The short-term market can usually take extra amounts of offerings fairly easily, and this is a comforting situation for the Treasury if the bond market tends to be in a debilitated state. Even if the short-term market is congested, resulting in high interest rates as in 1966, 1968, and 1969, frequent opportunities to refund mean that no funds are committed at very high rates for a long time. At other times, the Treasury has felt that it was desirable not to issue bonds but to concentrate on short-term issues because of a desire to keep down interest rates for mortgages and corporate bond issues—the basic idea being to encourage capital spending for economic growth.

There is always a considerable demand for Treasury bills, reflecting basic needs of the economy for liquid assets, so it simply makes sense for the Treasury to put out such securities to meet a very large part of its borrowing needs. This is true over the entire economic cycle. On the other hand, there may be serious problems if the debt gets too short. For example, the supply of liquidity in the economy may become excessive in relation to current national economic policy. Also the Treasury may, sooner or later, run into problems, if constant refunding of the short debt is required at a time when the money market is choked up by excessive demand for funds. (Note also that this could create difficulties for the Federal Reserve, which might feel it necessary to assist the Treasury by buying securities when, in fact, the appropriate policy might be to sell securities to dampen inflationary pressures.)

TREASURY POWERS

The Treasury has very little control over the total amount of cash it must raise within any given period by borrowing, since the need for borrowing stems from the net effect of Government taxing programs and Government spending and lending programs. The Treasury must simply take care of whatever has to be paid that is not covered by taxes. Since it has very little leeway to spread the amount of borrowing over any given period, it must show considerable skill in endeavoring to get the proper impact by timing the borrowing suitably and by choosing the appropriate instruments and maturity structure.

In debt management, the Treasury's greatest power is probably its ability to feed and starve different maturity sectors in the market. It will always have a given amount of borrowing to do; it can decide to concentrate all this borrowing in very short bills or it can spread it out to somewhat longer bills or into the intermediate and long-term bond market if the interest rate ceiling is not a limiting factor.

In considering economic aspects of debt management, the maturity structure and ownership pattern are very important. Short-term debt provides liquidity to its owners, while long-term debt is not only illiquid but is also subject to the hazards of market loss if interest rates rise. Hence, issuance of more short-term securities will have quite different economic significance than issuance of more long-term issues. Moreover, sales of securities

115

to commercial banks have different significance than sales to nonbank investors. Sales to banks tend to increase bank earning assets and thus lead to the creation of bank deposits, and by definition, therefore, the money supply. Sales to nonbank investors absorb funds already in existence, but may lead to increased savings or divert funds from investment in other ways, such as mortgages on houses.

It follows that most of the Treasury's efforts to influence economic trends through debt management involve questions concerning maturities of securities to be offered and investor groups to be tapped. In general, long-term issues relate more to nonbank investors, while short-term issues relate more to commercial banks. Sales to individuals used to be largely undertaken through savings bonds but, with highly attractive rates on market issues selling at substantial discounts below par, individuals have recently purchased them or new issues at high coupon rates.

What the Treasury does *not* do may be news, because th omission of certain maturities from new offerings can be ' great importance to the money and bond markets. For example, in the early 1960s, at a time when the Administration felt that there was considerable slack in the economy with an unemployment problem, it avoided putting upward pressure on interest rates in the bond and mortgage area by reducing offerings of new Treasury bonds that might have tended to make the bond market heavy. Instead, it put out more Treasury bills to reinforce the Federal Reserve's program to push short-term interest rates up for balance of payments reasons.

The mechanics of Treasury offerings of bills have been discussed in an earlier section. The important thing to note here is that the Treasury bill auctions each week are a major event in the money market. If the Treasury increases the volume sold and the bill rate moves up in the weekly auction, the entire money market may be affected. Contrariwise, if the Treasury reduces the volume of the weekly bill offering, the money market may experience a better tone and interest rates on short-term securities in general may decline somewhat.

Moreover, it is not too strong a statement to say that *all* Treasury financing is of great significance to the money market. Treasury issues occupy such an important place in our financial structure that it is unwise to assume that there is any stone wall between the short-term issues and the intermediate and long-term issues.

Treasury financing decisions obviously involve a large element of judgment. I have noted certain Treasury powers in feeding and starving markets. It may also price securities generously or skimpily in relation to existing issues. These decisions always carry some element of risk, for they affect the appeal of the issues to buyers. Treasury officials have to try to get just the result they want, and they do this after consultation with commercial bankers, investment bankers, and others.

Since income tax payments by individuals are heavier in April than in other months and corporate payments tend to be larger in March, April, and June, the Treasury usually runs a deficit during the first half of each fiscal year beginning July 1 (even when the full year is in balance), and offerings of securities for cash tend to be concentrated in the July–December period. Usually the maturities of the new issues, such as Tax Anticipation bills, are set for March, April, and June when the seasonal expansion in tax receipts makes it possible for the Treasury to pay off such issues without any refunding.

Refunding operations present many alternatives to the Treasury. It may offer new securities in exchange for maturing issues or may offer a new issue for cash. In the latter case, the offer gives the holder of the maturing issue no preference or "right" in the allotment of the new issue (but he may tender his holdings in payment and be subject to the same allotment as new investors). An exchange offering involves careful pricing by the Treasury to avoid giving too large a yield, in comparison with outstanding issues of similar maturities, which might attract speculators, or overly tight pricing that might lead to excessive attrition in which holders refuse the exchange offering and demand cash on maturity. A large amount of attrition may indicate that a refunding offering has failed and thus embarrass the Treasury, which must pay out more cash than expected. For example, in February 1969, the Treasury experienced a large attrition on a refunding offer for maturing bonds. In the progressively tightening money market, many investors preferred cash to the fifteen-month and seven-year notes offered in exchange.

From time to time the Treasury also engages in advance refundings, in which an exchange offering is made for an issue not yet due and the holder of the outstanding issue is given the option of either accepting the new issue or holding on to his present security. In market parlance, junior advance refundings are offerings of medium-term issues in exchange for issues that mature in less than five years; senior advance refundings are usually defined as offerings of long-term securities in exchange for issues that mature in more than five years. Those within a year are usually called pre-refundings. The money market is very interested in advance refundings and pre-refundings because they shift the maturity structure of the debt: they reduce the volume of issues outstanding in the nearer maturities and increase the volume outstanding farther out. Thus, a junior advance refunding can significantly reduce the volume of securities that will be moving into the money market area in the next five years. Advance refundings take advantage of the fact that the current holder of a security may have bought it originally because he liked a longer maturity; thus the refunding enables him to extend his holdings back to the desired maturity range without having to go through the market.

The investor usually considers many factors in deciding whether to accept or reject an advance refunding offer. He would consider whether or not the maturity of the securities offered fits into his investment program or objective. For example, if a

118

corporation held a nine-month note which was eligible for refunding into a seven-year note, the treasurer would probably decide not to make the exchange. Perhaps he had bought the note as a liquid investment when it had only eleven months to run and the new seven-year note would be considered too long a maturity for liquidity purposes. Another investor who bought the note when it was issued more than four years earlier might consider the outlook for interest rates. If he thought interest rates would be lower in nine months when the note matured, he would exchange for the seven-year note to insure receiving a more favorable rate of interest. If, on the other hand, he thought interest rates were likely to move higher, he would not exchange but would wait until maturity when he would hope to receive a better offer. Another investor might decide to accept the offer because the coupon rate on the new issue was above that on his present holding and he was interested in obtaining a higher rate of income now.

The Treasury also has certain powers with respect to coordinating issues of Government agencies. If a number of agencies all issue securities on an uncoordinated basis, the total market impact can be much worse than if they are carefully planned in sequence. From time to time it is argued that it would be better to have a larger volume of borrowing by the Treasury in its own issues than to have the market peppered with small amounts from several Government agencies. This is particularly true because some of these agencies put out the kind of securities that are in the money market area—those with maturities up to two years—and therefore compete with Treasury issues.

The evolution of what are called Treasury Tax and Loan Accounts in commercial banks provides another interesting example of adaptation to meet market needs. In the great borrowing drives of World War I, the Treasury found it convenient for commercial banks to act as sales offices for Liberty Loan Bonds, collecting the funds from the public on behalf of the

Treasury. For convenience, the Treasury permitted any commercial bank to place such funds in a Treasury deposit account in that bank which was then called "The War Loan Account." The Treasury would "call" these funds as needed, transferring them to the Federal Reserve Banks so that checks could be written against them. It became clear that this arrangement was not only a convenience to the Treasury, it was also of considerable help to the Federal Reserve System inasmuch as it served to smooth out the flow of funds from commercial banks to Federal Reserve Banks, an important consideration when we realize that the net result of such a shift of funds is that bank reserve positions will be tightened, only to be eased again as the Treasury spends the funds held in the Federal Reserve Banks.

Since World War II, the War Loan Account has been changed into the present Treasury Tax and Loan Account and acts as a vehicle for receiving various Treasury funds, including proceeds from both sales of securities and most taxes payable by individuals and corporations. A commercial bank is usually permitted to pay for new Treasury issues by crediting the Tax and Loan Account (except when the amount of an issue is small or when the proceeds are being used to redeem a maturing issue). The Treasury is thus "paid," but no money leaves the bank until calls are made. In contrast, the Treasury does not permit payment for weekly Treasury bills to be made through the Account because the new bills generally replace maturing issues. However, payment for Tax Anticipation bills, which represent new cash raised, usually in a large amount, is generally permitted through the Tax and Loan Account. Banks are generally heavy buyers of such issues because they have the use of the deposits until they are withdrawn by the Treasury. After subscribing to the issue, a bank may sell it within a short time to other investors, such as corporations. Even if the sale price is less than at the time of the bidding, a bank may still earn a net profit on the employment of the funds retained for a short period in the Tax and Loan Account. The Treasury expects to get a

120

lower rate by such bank participation and is also more certain that the issue will be a success.

Following is an example I worked out in 1968 on the profitability to a bank of subscribing for a Treasury issue for which payment could be made through credit to the Tax and Loan Account. It is assumed that the bills were sold immediately at a slight loss.

Tax Anticipation Bills

1.	Subscribed for	$100,000,000 par value
2.	Per cent allotted by the Treasury	52.2%
3.	Allotted	52,200,000 par value
4.	Cost @ 98.791	51,568,902
5.	Proceeds from sale @ 98.789	51,567,858
6.	Loss on sale of bills	1,044
7.	Average daily balance in Tax and Loan Account	31,704,000
8.	Less: reserve required on balances in Tax and Loan Account	5,231,000
9.	Average daily available balance	26,473,000
10.	Earning credit on average daily available balance at Federal funds rate of 4.22% for twenty-two-day balances held	67,355
11.	Less: FDIC assessment on balances	561
	Loss on sale of bills	1,044
12.	TOTAL NET PROFIT	$ 65,750

A $65,000 profit may seem rather small at first glance, but remember it was earned in twenty-two days. This works out at an annual rate basis to $1,089,200.

In the management of its cash funds, the Treasury has the power to arrange the distribution of cash balances as between commercial banks and Federal Reserve Banks. If a greater proportion of Treasury cash is shifted to Federal Reserve Banks by "calling" for payment of funds from the Tax and Loan Accounts in commercial banks, the reserve position of commercial banks is made tighter since the transfer from commercial banks to

Federal Reserve Banks is effected by charges against the banks' reserve accounts. Contrariwise, a relative shift from Federal Reserve Banks to commercial banks, by not calling so fast on the Tax and Loan Accounts or by redepositing funds in them, produces an easing effect at commercial banks. The particular power here is obviously limited since the Treasury does not have an infinite amount of funds with which to maneuver, but at times this power may be useful.

THE PUBLIC DEBT LIMIT

As noted earlier, one of the Treasury's objectives of debt management is to minimize difficulties caused by the public debt limit. Living within this limit is a continuing problem to the United States Treasury. It is interesting to note how the idea of a debt limit developed. Up until World War I, the Congress used to approve *each* security issue to be sold by the Treasury. When World War I broke out, it continued this policy for a while but it soon became evident that the Treasury needed more flexibility. Congress was not always in session and it was difficult to get precise amounts for individual issues put into legislation at the proper times. Accordingly, in 1917 the Congress shifted from authorization of individual issues to a system of granting the Treasury blanket authority to have a given amount of public debt outstanding.

At first, changes in the debt limit were rare, but the limit has been changed twenty-eight times in the last seventeen years. In late 1966, the margin was so close that the Treasury was apparently afraid it might accidentally breach the limit, as for example through sales of savings bonds (which are decentralized across the country). For convenience, small Treasury borrowings from the Federal Reserve were used when Treasury checks were presented for payment in excess of Treasury balances at Federal Reserve Banks. In the form of "Special Certificates," they represented overdrafts and made it possible to avoid the use of larger public offerings of securities.

In the fiscal year 1967, the debt limit problem caused the Treasury to substitute marketable issues for special nonmarketable issues * held by certain Government trust funds. The special issues were then retired, thus reducing the size of the debt. The purchase of marketable issues required cash, and the Treasury drew down its balances in banks in order to accomplish it. When the public debt limit was raised, the trust funds sold the issues they had purchased in the market and once again acquired special issues from the Treasury.

One of the results of the pressures of the public debt limit has been that the Treasury, the Budget Bureau and the President at times have had to adopt various gimmicks to artificially reduce the budget deficit. These have been employed by both political parties when the need arose. Since the essential need at such a time is to reduce expenditures, the devices have usually taken the form of finding methods to get the public to finance certain types of expenditures.

Treasury officials have always lamented the need to adopt gimmicks of this kind and have consistently urged that a more realistic debt limit be set to fully take care of discrepancies in the flow of tax funds as against the volume of expenditures. Their argument is that the Treasury did not set these figures and that the figures are simply the result of cumulative Congressional actions; therefore Congress should be realistic and permit the Treasury to sell whatever debt has to be issued as a result of all the Congressional fiscal actions and not ask the Treasury to stand on its head to try to hold down the public debt by subterfuge.

As described in Chapter 3, one gimmick used in the past in order to operate within the debt limit was the sale of certain loans of Government agencies, either directly or indirectly through the sale of PCs—participation certificates—in a pool of assets.

I am sure that most citizens assume that the idea of a debt

---

* Described later in this chapter.

Topless Ceiling*

On Capitol Hill the members of the House and Senate are once again playing their favorite version of fiscal fun-and-games. It is called raising the debt ceiling.

In its present form the legal ceiling on the Federal debt was established in 1941 at $65 billion. As need developed during World War II this limit was repeatedly raised. In 1946 the figure was set at $275 billion.

The Republicans, while in control of Congress in 1954, introduced a new variation to the game. The existing ceiling was established as "permanent," but at the same time was breached by a "temporary" increase. For more than a dozen years the raising-the-debt-ceiling game has been played with the new variation.

Last month President Johnson asked Congress to raise the "temporary" ceiling to $336 billion, since otherwise it would drop to the "permanent" ceiling, now fixed at $285 billion. The House complied, but the Senate Finance Committee decided it would be too boring simply to agree. Instead, it reported out, and the Senate yesterday approved, a bill to make the $336 billion figure asked by the President a permanent rather than temporary ceiling.

At first glance this might seem a sensible step. But it is not, because under the rules of this peculiar game temporary increases are easier to obtain than permanent increases, and everyone knows the Treasury will need to raise the limit once again come summer.

A visitor from another planet might regard a ceiling that has to be raised once or twice a year as no ceiling at all. A visitor might instead view it as an administrative nuisance for the Treasury Department, a waste of time for Congress, and an incitement to cynicism for the general public. But that is not how the debt limit is regarded on Capitol Hill. There it is taken very, very seriously. In Congress, everything has a ceiling except nonsense.

* The New York Times, February 22, 1967.

limit is sensible and forces fiscal discipline on the Government. While it may have this tendency to some degree, it also results in an awkward situation at times because the Congress tends to be inconsistent in authorizing expenditures in excess of taxes and the allowable increment in the public debt. In other words, Congress enacts tax legislation that at any given time will raise a certain amount of money. If the expenditure figure exceeds the tax figure, the public debt must go up. What happens if the public debt is already at the ceiling? Does the Government cease to pay its bills? The question has never been tested but on several occasions the Treasury has been faced with an inconsistency in having to carry a bigger deficit than the amount it could add to the public debt under the existing authority. In theory I believe that the Secretary of the Treasury would have to cover out of his own pocket any securities sold above the debt limit. A favorite Treasury story goes as follows: The then Secretary, a wealthy man, on asking the question as to who would be liable, was told, "You are." He replied, "If we ever go over, make sure it is in the hundreds of millions so that coming to me for the pay-off is obviously ridiculous."

Time after time the Treasury has asked Congress to enlarge the limit and Congress grudgingly has gone along, although usually it has refused to give the Treasury the full amount requested. Also, Congress has frequently put in a temporary increase, with the public debt limit reverting to a lower figure at a later date. At the end of 1971, the statutory debt limit was $430 billion and the amount subject to the debt limitation was $421 billion; there was thus a leeway of $9 billion.

One of the gimmicks used to keep within the debt limit, the sale of PCs, is no longer available because of the adoption in 1968 of a unified budget. This represented the implementation of one of the recommendations of the President's Commission on Budget Concepts, which was charged with the responsibility of suggesting a new and simpler Federal Budget. The unified budget now essentially consists of two parts: a receipt-expenditure account and a loan account. These two accounts constitute the "total" budget; the surplus or deficit is the difference between receipts on the one hand and expenditures plus net lending on the other. Net lending is the difference between loan disbursements and loan repayments.

The new budget format differs from the old cash budget in only a few major respects. It excludes "negative" expenditures, which are reductions in budget outlays associated with receipts from the sale of Government assets. Since 1967, sales of PCs are no longer regarded as asset sales because the Government in fact retains ownership of the pool of loans against which the certificates are issued. PC sales are now regarded as a means of financing budget deficits rather than a reduction in expenditure.

One big omission was the failure to clear up the status of Government corporations. This permitted Fanny May, Federal Intermediate Credit Banks, Banks for Cooperatives, and the Export-Import Bank to escape the budget.

INTEREST RATE CEILING

The 4¼% limit on the interest rate that may be paid on Treasury bonds also goes back to World War I. When the Congress stopped approving individual bond issues, it set a flat rate limit as a kind of policy in lieu of the authorization of individual bond offerings. The First Liberty Bond Act, in April 1917, set a 3½% ceiling on new bonds; the Second Act, in September 1917, increased this to 4%; and the Third and Fourth Acts, April and July 1918, set a 4¼% ceiling. The 4¼% ceiling has held ever since on all new Treasury bond issues.

Most money market technicians consider the 4¼% limit to be an unrealistic restriction on the Treasury. Thus since 1965, with the 4¼% interest ceiling below the going rate in the market, the Treasury has been unable to offer long-term bonds. In a period in which inflationary pressures are prevalent, it usually would make sense for the Treasury to do some of its financing in the form of intermediate or long-term bonds in

126

order to act as a dampening force by attracting money away from the marketplace. If the going market rate is 6% or more, however, there is no point in talking about offering a bond at the 4¼% ceiling rate. No one would buy it. Therefore, the effect is the same as prohibiting the Treasury from selling bonds in periods of tight money. Many requests have been made of Congress to correct this problem but Congress so far has found it expedient to do no more than permit certain exceptions. Thus the definition of Treasury notes was changed from five years to seven years; and in 1971 Congress authorized the Treasury to sell $10 billion of bonds without regard to the 4¼% ceiling.

Federal Agencies

A number of Federal agencies are of active interest to the money market: the Federal Land Banks, the Federal Intermediate Credit Banks, the Federal National Mortgage Association, the Banks for Cooperatives, Federal Home Loan Banks, the Export-Import Bank, the Farmers Home Administration, the Federal Housing Administration, and several others. Some of these agencies were established as long as fifty years ago by Congress to undertake various types of financing operations which would facilitate the extension of credit to farmers, homeowners, and others. Most of the other agencies were organized in the 1930s to provide financial assistance following the banking crisis. Their operations vary considerably—from the Federal Home Loan Banks, which may make loans to member institutions, numbering more than 5,000 thrift institutions throughout the country, to the Banks for Cooperatives, which may make loans to eligible cooperative associations owned and controlled by farmers.

As noted earlier in this chapter, the Treasury has assumed a more important role in coordinating the issuance of Federal agency obligations to avoid unfavorable repercussions on the money and bond markets generally. It also has to coordinate agency financing with its own direct financing.

The Treasury's Role As an Investor for Government Investment Accounts

In the last generation, the Government has found that it is convenient to undertake many functions through its trust funds, or what are more formally called Government Investment Accounts. As they have a money market significance, it is necessary to touch on them briefly here. The investment accounts include the Federal employees' retirement funds, the Federal Old-Age and Survivors Insurance Trust Fund, the Railroad Retirement Account, and the Unemployment Trust Fund, which collect the taxes imposed for retirement and unemployment insurance and pay out the benefits. There is also the Highway Trust Fund, which receives the special taxes imposed for this purpose and pays out the benefits to the states through the 90% payment for new highways based on a formula that requires state and local governments to provide only 10% of the cost. The idea of the trust fund is to set up a special mechanism that receives all taxes levied for a particular purpose and thus avoids commingling with funds that are available for general Treasury use. It means that the funds are earmarked for a particular purpose and expenditures are made only from the earmarked funds.

The important point for our present purpose is that these funds accumulate huge amounts of dollars that have to be invested. The Treasury Department is the manager of these investments. This responsibility gives the Treasury some additional opportunities that may be helpful in the overall job of managing the public debt. This is true even though the largest part of the total investments held by the trust funds are in so-called special issues. These special issues are nonmarketable securities issued by the Treasury to particular trust funds on

128

the basis of specifications, including interest rates, laid down by Congress in the various statutes governing the activities financed by these trusts. For example, in the case of the Federal Old-Age and Survivors Insurance Trust Fund, special issues are authorized at an interest rate equal to the average market yield on marketable U.S. securities with a remaining life to maturity of over four years.

Some of the trust funds are invested in public marketable issues. This gives the Treasury, acting as agent for the trusts involved, the opportunity to prop a weak market if it wishes. On occasion, the Treasury has put as many dollars into the market in support operations as the Federal Reserve. On rare occasions the Treasury has gone into the market on its own to support a situation. Even so, the use of trust fund monies for such purposes by the Treasury is not a common occurrence; in practice the Treasury is reluctant to use these powers.

In the latter months of 1971, U.S. Government accounts held $106.5 billion of Federal securities, of which $18.5 billion were marketable issues and the balance of $88 billion were special or nonmarketable issues.

Corporations: Some Lend, Others Borrow

"Frisbee, what's our cash position?"

"Well . . . err . . . err . . . uhh . . . you see, boss. Well, right now we haven't got any cash."

"Wonderful, Frisbee. You're the best treasurer this company ever had." [1]

CHAPTER 9   In recent years corporations have become very active participants in the money market both as investors and as borrowers. In this chapter we will cover non-financial corporations and finance companies.

The flow of funds in a modern corporation is a complex proposition. Corporate treasurers have developed systems of control of these funds and arrangements for advance planning of the flow of funds that enable them to use their money very efficiently. They try hard to manage their cash positions in such a way as to maximize earnings. In so doing, they endeavor to carry demand deposits in banks in the right amounts to pay incoming bills, quarterly dividends, etc., and also to reimburse the banks for services rendered and provide compensating balances for lines of credit. If funds available exceed what they consider necessary for these purposes, the treasurers will try to invest the excess in the money market in order to obtain a maximum return for the length of time they expect the funds to be available. If funds are short, they may arrange to sell short-term investments or replenish cash through bank loans or long-term financing. Some corporations issue commercial paper through dealers specializing in this market. Finance companies issue similar paper, but, in the case of large companies, the paper is placed directly with investors instead of through dealers. It is a continuing job of careful management. Some corporations are continuously active in the money market, investing liquid funds over and above the cash held in banks, while others may be in the money market only intermittently.

Corporations As Investors in the Money Market

The major motivation of corporate treasurers in investing in the money market is to utilize short-term investment funds so as to obtain a maximum return without sacrificing needed liquidity.* This was not always so. For example, in the Great Depression, interest rates were so low that corporate treasurers piled up large cash positions in the banks in the form of demand deposits. When interest rates rose after the war, however, treasurers began to look at their funds much more carefully; as interest rates increased even more in the 1950s and then went to new peaks in the 1960s they tried diligently to see that their excess cash funds were hard at work. In many corporations one man was designated as the one responsible for seeing that the maximum rate of return was received on short-term funds. Total corporate liquid assets have been rising more or less steadily ever since the end of World War II. There have been large shifts in the composition, however, as certain categories have become more attractive than others.

Demand deposits and currency rose steadily to a peak in the 1959–62 period and then began a decline which accelerated as interest rates rose in recent years.

* Demand deposits also provide liquidity but the principal purpose of such deposits is proper management of the corporate cash needs, including compensating bank balances.

132

In the 1950s, U.S. Government securities—largely Treasury bills—dominated short-term investments of corporations. At a peak of $25 billion in 1959, holdings of Governments were many times the small amounts of commercial paper and time deposits held. (This was prior to the introduction of negotiable CDs.)

There were substantial shifts after CDs were introduced in 1961. Time deposits (mostly CDs) increased sharply, declined, and then rose again, depending on whether Regulation Q interest rate ceilings made CDs attractive or unattractive in relation to other types of investments: from less than $4 billion in early 1961 to $24 billion in 1968, time deposits went down to $14 billion by the end of 1969, and back up to a new high of more than $27 billion in 1971.

In addition, open market paper, namely, commercial paper and bankers' acceptances, rose strikingly to $29 billion, exceeding all other types of investment in mid-1970, but then slipped to $19 billion by late 1971.

Another dramatic expansion occurred in holdings of municipal issues which spurted to more than $11 billion in late 1971. The rise reflected corporate purchases of high-quality short-term tax-exempt notes which became available in increasing volume at more attractive yields, after adjustment for differences in tax status, than on other short-term instruments.

Meanwhile, holdings of U.S. Government securities were cut by more than half from the 1959 peak to about $12 billion in late 1971.

The corporate treasurer, of course, is interested not only in the American market but very frequently in foreign markets. Many American corporations have become international in scope. They need funds abroad because their foreign operations are important. But, even if they did not, they are alert enough to move short-term funds abroad for investment when rates are more attractive than they are at home unless free movement is discouraged, as in recent years, by voluntary or mandatory restraint programs to reduce the country's balance of payments deficit.

For years it was understood in money market circles that when the rate on British Treasury Bills rose to much more than ⅜% or ½% over the American counterpart (adjusted for foreign exchange hedging costs), corporate treasurers and some banks would seek to move funds abroad in order to obtain higher yields. More recently, especially in 1971, corporate treasurers have also been tempted by rates on Euro-dollars abroad that have been higher than on various money market instruments in the United States. Similarly, for a long time, there was quite an incentive to invest short-term funds in Canada through New York banks or brokers or through New York agencies of Canadian banks.

Corporations As Borrowers in the Money Market

As borrowers, corporations have shown increasing activity in the money market through the issuance of commercial paper and the use of bankers' acceptances. Finance companies have been issuing their obligations in the short-term market for a long time.

The use of commercial paper has risen steadily over the years. New companies have entered the market for the first time and previous issuers have tapped the market more frequently and in larger amounts through commercial paper dealers. The substantial expansion in the volume issued has received its impetus from the favorable rate compared with bank loans and the desire to expand financing options.

Moreover, some corporations have set up "captive" finance companies which in turn have issued paper directly to investors in the short-term money market. A company like General Motors Acceptance Corporation sells its notes to investors and is willing to tailor them to the exact maturity that investors may wish. Thus, one investor may say that he can take $10 million with a maturity of forty-eight days and another may have $1 million to invest for seventy-two days. GMAC tries to accommodate such investors, and the investor in turn feels that he has a very productive investment completely tailored to his own needs. GMAC has no hesitation in arranging these tailor-made maturities since the aggregate results are satisfactory.

Corporations and some unincorporated enterprises also borrow in the money market through the medium of bankers' acceptances. As explained in Chapter 4, a typical bankers' acceptance originates through an import or export of merchandise. An importer requires credit to finance the shipment and he asks his bank to "accept" the draft received. When the bank so stamps the draft, it becomes an obligation of the bank and accordingly is readily accepted as a high-grade credit instrument. Sometimes banks hold such acceptances for their own short-term investments but frequently they sell them to dealers who specialize in handling them or directly to other investors.

Corporations have customarily borrowed in the money market when their needs for funds were short-term and when the costs of borrowing through the use of commercial paper and bankers' acceptances were less than alternative borrowing from their banks. In periods of tight money, such as in 1966 and 1969, many corporations have turned to the money market when their banks, because of restrictive Federal Reserve policies, were unable to meet all their credit needs.

Managing Tax Funds

The timing of money market activities by corporations either as investors or borrowers varies tremendously from one company to another. One problem common to all, however, is arranging for payments of Federal income taxes. Even here there are differences between corporations on a calendar year basis and those on a fiscal year basis.

The Treasury has found that corporate tax payments are so heavy in March, June, September, and December, and more recently in April, that it usually issues Tax Anticipation Bills that corporations can buy and use for payment of taxes. We have noted that interest on these tax bills usually runs to a maturity date about seven days beyond the tax date, so that a corporation turning them in for taxes gets some break in receiving interest beyond the fifteenth of the month when tax payments are due. The money market is, of course, vitally concerned with these arrangements, and any changes in corporate tax rates and payment dates are of considerable significance. For example, the requirement that corporations make tax payments on estimated current income under the program of accelerated payments had important effects on corporate finance and repercussions in the money market.

Now that corporations are on a current tax basis, they are no longer faced with the burden of paying more than 100% of one year's taxes in a single year, as they were in the years when the Treasury was accelerating corporate taxes to get them from the old system of paying taxes with a one-year lag. However, corporate liquidity is still low, despite the restructuring of capital by many corporations in recent years through new financing. The present tax schedule provides less leeway in making payments than the old system and corporations will undoubtedly have to plan more carefully in order to meet their tax liabilities. The money market offers many instruments to facilitate such planning and more and more corporations will undoubtedly accumulate funds in Treasury bills, particularly TABs, RPs, commercial paper, and bankers' acceptances. All of these instruments provide maturities at or near the tax dates.

Government Securities Dealers: They Make The Market

CHAPTER 10   Dealers in Government securities are a real focal point in the money market. As dealers they make a market in Government securities, which means that they are ready to buy or sell any issue in which a customer is interested. In order to perform this function, dealers frequently carry substantial inventories on which they stand to make or lose money as security prices change. Since they require large amounts of money to carry their inventories, they have developed an uncanny ability to round up funds all over the country from corporations, state and local governments, smaller banks, and other investors, as well as money center banks, and, in effect, have acted as financial intermediaries.

There are two kinds of Government securities dealers, namely, certain commercial banks and certain firms known as nonbank dealers. Nine commercial banks and eleven nonbank dealers, which report regularly on their activities to the Federal Reserve Bank of New York, constitute the central market for buyers and sellers of U.S. securities all over the country.

The nonbank dealers* are particularly active in mobilizing funds to carry their inventory positions from corporations and other entities all over the country. Bank Dealers are not all active in this way because the financing of their inventories is blended into the money operations or position of their own banks.

Making a Market in Government Securities

Government securities dealers play a major role in connection with the marketing of the public debt and in maintaining a secondary market in Treasury securities after the securities are issued originally by the Treasury. It is interesting to note that the Treasury did not decide that Government bond dealers should be brought into the picture. Rather, the function of these dealers evolved as the public debt increased in size and as the profit potential for taking on the task became evident. It is a good example of how the money market generates institutional changes as they are needed.

The dealer structure evolved rapidly in the 1930s when the public debt began to increase substantially as a consequence of substantial deficits in the Federal budget. Then in the 1940s, war financing increased the public debt even more rapidly, so that by 1945 it was more than fifteen times as large as it was in 1929 when the Great Depression began. One result of this big increase was considerably more buying and selling of Government securi-

---

* A remarkable lack of similarity characterizes the structural organization of the nonbank dealers. For example, one (Merrill, Lynch, Pierce, Fenner & Smith) is the largest and most active member firm of the New York Stock Exchange; two other important houses (Salomon Bros. and First Boston Corporation) are leading factors in the underwriting and trading of corporate and municipal securities, doing business with institutional clients. Discount Corporation of New York and A. G. Lanston & Co. confine their operations to Government and Federal agency obligations, the former also being active in the market for bankers' acceptances and both dealing in bank certificates of deposit.

ties, and such volume required a marketplace where buyers and sellers could arrange transactions.* The Government securities dealers began to provide this service and grew in importance as the public debt rose and more transactions in Government securities occurred.

In making a market in Government securities, several dealers issue quotation sheets each night listing the price (and yield) at which they are willing to buy or sell—in reasonable amounts— each issue of Government securities. The spread between bid and asked helps the dealer make a living as no commissions are charged. If the quotations on the sheets issued by the various dealers are compared, there is a fairly good consistency, but they are not necessarily identical. The listing of quotes is a dealer's best appraisal of the market at or near the close of the day but it is not a guaranteed statement as to the basis on which he is willing to do business. This is a negotiated market, and the dealer will always reserve the right to change the price if he sees fit. Nevertheless, the listings at the close of trading are an important indication of the prices and yields on Government securities at that time. On odd-lot transactions (under $100,000 of Treasury bills and under $50,000 of other issues) where the spread between bid and asked prices does not cover costs, dealers now usually have an odd-lot service charge.

It is important to understand that the role played by dealers in the Government securities market is not a mere mechanical one which perhaps the words "making a market" might suggest. Collectively, the Government securities dealers assure that there *is* a market—an active, usable one in which buyers and sellers

---

* Government bonds are officially listed on the New York Stock Exchange but there has been no trading since 1962 because buyers and sellers do not choose to use this market. While a small amount of trading occurred prior to that time, it represented only a fraction of the total volume. Over the years buyers and sellers found that dealers in the over-the-counter market provided a much broader base for trading than brokers dealing on the Stock Exchange. Thus, we have another example of the resiliency of the money market in that investors made decisions which built up the dealer structure. No Government agency was involved in the decision.

may have confidence. Thus, for example, the holder of a one-year Treasury bill knows that he will be able to sell it if he wants to at any time simply by putting it on the market. He always has a good idea of the price and yield prevailing by following the dealers' quote sheets or asking the dealers for quotations during the day. Sometimes there are erratic movements in the market, such as occurred in the late 1960s, 1970, and 1971. In one week in mid-1967 rates went up almost 1%, but this is not typical. Usually, the movements in the market are within much narrower bounds, at least in the case of short-term securities. This continuity is very important, for it means that the liquidity for which short-term securities are being held will in fact be there when the investor wishes to have it.

Perhaps the matter could be summed up by saying that the dealers virtually guarantee that there will be an actively operating market with reasonable quotations for buyer or seller at any time. Their ability to function in this way depends to a large extent on their judgment in managing their inventories and their confidence that commercial banks, the Federal Reserve, and the Treasury will make sensible decisions in managing their parts of the complex forces which intermingle in the money market. This is all the more important in view of the magnitude of the market in which they operate: during 1970, for example, dealers traded about $625 billion of Government securities, about two-thirds as large as the Gross National Product. More than $500 billion of trading in 1970 was represented by Treasury bills and other issues maturing within a year.

From the foregoing we can see that the Government securities dealer is a kind of buffer* for commercial banks and other in-

* ". . . one important aspect of the dealer's role in the United States money market is to serve as 'buffer of last resort' for the principal banks. . . . banks' use of the Government securities dealers has the effect, most of the time, of reducing the extent to which the money market banks turn to the 'lender of last resort' (that is, the Federal Reserve) for help in meeting the net residual effects which converge upon them from reserve shifts among the banks of the country and from any decided swing in liquidity preference for the country as a whole. One part of the

vestors since he ordinarily acts for his own account when he buys and sells securities. If the load is too great, of course, the dealer will back away and the situation will translate itself into shifting prices of securities.

The Federal Reserve Bank of New York is in very close touch with Government securities dealers in order to keep its finger on the pulse of the market. The Fed wishes to know which way market pressures are going. It wants to know through the dealers what the various kinds of pressures are and whether the dealers are able to raise the funds they are trying to find. At times, markets may become overly tight and the Federal Reserve may not only buy securities in an effort to improve bank reserves but also may make RPs to dealers in order to improve the money market tone.

Managing Security Positions for Profit

All dealers have an obvious need to maximize profits and minimize losses in handling their inventories. Mismanagement and poor market judgment can cause failure. It follows that the Government dealers are diligent, thorough students of factors affecting the money market. The dealers are centers for collecting facts and figures and appraising possible future developments of significance to the money market. Thus, because of self-interest, they are well informed and helpful to their customers in passing along some of the information they keep at their fingertips.

Moreover, the objective of protecting their inventories gives them a certain stabilizing function in the Government securities

---

dealer's 'buffer' role is his standing readiness to take short-term Government securities in some volume at a reasonable price whenever banks or others are trying to obtain funds on balance by selling them. At the same time, banks that have been lending to the dealer to help carry his previous holdings may find they need funds, and so the 'buffer' absorbs pressure from the other side as these lending banks either raise their rate or perhaps call back their loans." (Robert V. Roosa, "Federal Reserve Operations in the Money and Government Securities Markets," p. 16.)

market. In theory, if prices seem to have worked a little too high, dealers are likely to sell as a countermove; if prices seem to be a little low, dealers are likely to buy a little more aggressively in anticipation of an upward move.

Over the long run, the theory just described probably works out, but dealer activity may also intensify a price movement just beginning if the dealers sense that the movement will go considerably further and, in an effort to maximize profits, they take appropriate steps by selling in a declining market or buying in a rising market. Later on in the particular price movement, the stabilizing theory is likely to be reasserted as dealers take counteraction because they feel the move has gone too far. Accordingly, the volume of dealers' inventories of U.S. securities has varied materially, ranging, for example, from an average daily volume of $1.5 billion in mid-1966, when money was tight, to $4.2 billion in December 1966 and to $5.3 billion in the third quarter of 1968 when it was thought that easier money conditions were developing. Even in 1969, when interest rates were rising rapidly, dealers' inventories averaged $2.7 billion. They began to rise as interest rates declined in 1970 and reached a peak of $5.8 billion early in 1971. With the volume of daily transactions ranging from $2 to $4 billion, this means that dealers' inventories are turned over approximately every one to two days.

Dealer inventories thus are enormous, both in absolute amounts and in relation to their capital. Because of the fact that most of the twelve or fifteen leading dealers in U.S. Government and Federal agency obligations are either diversified investment banking firms or major commercial banks, it is difficult to estimate the total capital employed in the Government market per se, but a rough guess would be about $150 million, perhaps a bit more. The figure would vary from time to time depending on market activity and the willingness of the dealers to take positions.

Based on typical margins* of about 5% for longer-term obli-

* Meaning use of own funds with remainder borrowed.

142

gations, 2% to 3% for intermediate issues, 1% for coupon debt maturing within a year and fractions of a percent for Treasury bills, the available capital enables dealers to borrow substantial amounts of funds in order to carry very large trading and investment positions when they so desire. Part of the funds consists of advances under repurchase agreements with corporations, banks and others and these often involve narrower margins than is the case with direct bank loans. With the heavy weight in bills, total borrowing can easily run to several billion dollars. The actual range of daily borrowings in recent years has been from a low of slightly under $2 billion to more than $7 billion.

Mobilizing Funds to Finance Inventories

I have noted that Government securities dealers show ingenuity in raising needed funds from first one source and then another as opportunities and needs develop. There is an obvious continuing need to finance inventories, which at times may be heavy. Nonbank dealers, of course, do not have the facilities that bank dealers have to finance inventories. Thus, they are major borrowers of short-term funds, tapping money market banks, nonbank investors, including corporations,* and out-of-town banks. Increasingly, a large volume of funds is being borrowed from nonbank investors,† particularly during periods when bank loan funds are scarce. Early in 1971, when the money market was approaching its low in interest rates for the year, U.S. Government securities dealers were borrowing an average daily total of $7.2 billion, of which $2.5 billion had been obtained from commercial banks in New York City, $1.9 billion from out-of-town

---

* The Canadians have a nice term for this type of activity: the "country banking system," which includes corporations and other nonbank investors who make loans to dealers.
† Note that this is another example of the money market adapting itself to new needs. The old system only gave the alternatives of either money market loans from banks or positive action to reduce inventories.

banks, $600 million from corporations, and $2.2 billion from other sources. In contrast, when interest rates were near their peak in October 1969, dealers were borrowing only $2.2 billion a day on the average. Commercial banks supplied about $850 million, corporations $520 million, and other sources about $850 million.

Funds obtained from corporations and other sources, as noted earlier, are frequently in the form of an RP under which the dealer sells an obligation, usually a short-term Government security, for a short period with an agreement to buy it back at a stated time and price. Such a transaction is in effect a short-term loan to the dealer even though in a legal sense the security has changed hands. The willingness of corporate treasurers and others to provide funds by purchasing RPs has the advantage of bringing the necessary funds into the market to carry dealer inventories, even though the time period is short. Corporations have found dealers' loans a convenient vehicle for short-term investment because the maturity can be tailored to meet the need for the temporary investment of funds accrued for taxes, dividends, etc., due on a specific day.

Banks feel that they have a kind of moral obligation to finance the "box" (basic portfolio) of dealers for whom they clear, *i.e.*, the monetary and physical mechanism to expedite the transfer of securities from seller to buyer. Otherwise, dealers' loans tend to be on an impersonal basis, with no implied commitment that the banks will take care of all the dealers' needs no matter what pressures there may be on their own money position. The dealers remain free to get the funds from whatever source they consider desirable. The banks remain free to use their funds in whatever way they wish, taking on loans from dealers if it is in their own best interest and turning them down or quoting a rate above the market if they see fit to do so in order to discourage such loans. The point, therefore, is that competitive forces in the broad range of the entire money market determine the ebb and flow of bank loans to dealers.

Making a Market in CDs

When the commercial banks first began to issue negotiable certificates of deposit, some of the nonbank dealers in Government securities set out to perform the important function of making a secondary market for CDs. The advantage of this was that the owner of a negotiable CD could sell it to a dealer or a dealer's customer. CDs began to be quoted by dealers in this secondary market. This, of course, provided liquidity to the holder of CDs and made the instrument more useful to the money market. Concurrently, the offering of such paper in the secondary market by dealers made another instrument available to buyers of short-term investments. For example, a CD with an original maturity of 180 days might be turned over when it was only ten days short of maturity.

Dealers' quotations on CDs in the secondary market are available just like quotations on other securities. Typically, the quotes on the CDs of the largest banks for similar maturities are very close to one another, but CDs issued by smaller banks usually sell on a higher yield basis than CDs of the larger, better-known money market banks.

In 1966 and 1969, when money conditions were extremely tight and there was considerable attrition in the volume of CDs outstanding at major banks, the secondary market in CDs practically dried up. Subsequently, on both occasions, the secondary market became an active market when monetary conditions eased. It is interesting to note that the dealer function in providing a market for negotiable CDs is another illustration of the way the money market develops what is needed from time to time.

Other Participants:
Domestic and Foreign,
State and Local Governments

CHAPTER 11   There are several other important participants in the money market. These include state and local governments, stock brokers and dealers in municipal and corporate securities, foreign central banks and governments, other foreign investors, including New York agencies of foreign banks, and other domestic investors. Obligations issued by state and local governments are commonly called tax-exempt securities because they are exempt from Federal income taxes and from income taxes of the state in which they are issued.

In this book we are not interested in the total debt operations of state and local governments, since many of these occur in the bond market rather than the money market. However, we should note that the total debt of state and local governments has been rising steadily ever since World War II. The total of such debts, which was $14 billion at the end of World War II and $47 billion in 1957, crossed the $100 billion mark during 1966 and is estimated at about $143 billion at the end of 1970. The problem seems to be that the tax structure imposed by state and local governments does not cause collections to rise as fast as their expenditures. The services required of state and local governments keep expanding and the basic costs of providing them keep rising. Hence, these governments are in a kind of chronic crisis. They are constantly offering new long-term bond issues and are continually using short-term borrowings in the money market to carry them for periods of temporary need.

For example, in New York City, tax anticipation notes are issued in order to carry the City during the slack period prior to the collection of major taxes around October and April. Many state and local governments issue such tax anticipation notes. Some of them also issue bond anticipation notes. These provide funds temporarily needed pending the completion of a long-term bond offering. An example of this would be the sale on June 10, 1969, of $81 million New York State Transportation Capital Facilities Bond Anticipation Notes maturing March 13, 1970.

We refer to short-term state and local government borrowings as being part of the money market, but many of them are arranged locally rather than occurring in the main New York or other large city money markets. Such temporary borrowings are commonly arranged with local banks and, while in a technical sense the securities acquired by the banks are negotiable, there is really no market in which to sell the issues. Hence, they are more nearly equivalent to a bank loan than a security. However, the money market is affected because the banks in turn may have to obtain funds in some form in order to carry the issues. Thus friends of mine in Syracuse, New York, tell me that new issues of short-term tax-exempt notes placed directly with banks added to the general problem of tight money in 1969 and caused the local banks to lean more heavily on Federal funds and other borrowing sources.

State and local governments also supply some funds to the money market: they buy short-term U.S. Government and agency securities to improve earnings on liquid funds; they have also placed funds in bank CDs. Pension funds of state and local governments are also major buyers of securities but these are

148

largely concentrated in longer-term industrial and utility bonds and more recently in a limited amount of stocks.

Stock Brokers and Dealers in Municipal and Corporate Securities

The term "brokers' loans" refers to loans to stockbrokers who borrow to finance their own holdings of securities, as well as the funds they advance to customers who are purchasing securities on margin.

In the 1920s, stock market credit rose to a very high level and was financed by "call loans." This was perhaps the largest money market instrument at the time. As a group, brokers continually needed large amounts to finance their own and their customers' activities and they obtained the funds each day from any source that was willing to make loans. They paid whatever rate was required in accordance with the availability and demand for funds. The market thus would sometimes show rather violent changes as the supply–demand situation changed; rates would sometimes rise to very high levels as a squeeze in availability of funds relative to demands occurred. In 1929 call loan rates got up as high as 20%.

In today's money market, stock market credit is a much smaller part of the total picture. Margin requirements are now set by the Federal Reserve Board and for some time they have been high enough to keep stock market credit from zooming to the level of the 1920s. Requirements are changed from time to time: from November 1963 to June 1968, for example, buyers of stock were required to put up 70% cash on every dollar of stock purchased. They could borrow (*i.e.*, margin) only 30%. From June 1968, when the requirement was raised to 80%, they could borrow only 20%. On May 5, 1970, the margin requirement was lowered to 65%, and on December 6, 1971, to 55%. In the aggregate, customers owed brokers about $5 billion during the latter months of 1971, or the equivalent of less than 1% of the aggregate value of all stocks listed on the New York Stock Exchange. An exactly comparable series is not available for 1929 but total brokers' loans at that time reached a peak of $8.5 billion, which represented about 10% of the value of all stocks on the New York Stock Exchange.

Moreover, brokers now do their financing on a somewhat improved basis as compared with the 1920s. The call loan of the twenties has been replaced today by brokers' loans from banks, and brokers know much better where they stand. Banks can, of course, cut down on the volume of credit they are willing to make available to brokers, but they are likely to do this on a more orderly basis than before. Rates on brokers' loans do indeed fluctuate in accordance with changing supply and demand situations. At the peak of the money tightness in 1969 rates on brokers' loans were raised above the prime rate, with some banks charging a varying spread above the prime, depending on the volume of loans above a certain level or in relation to the brokers' deposit balances.

Dealers in municipals and corporate securities sometimes require a large amount of money to carry inventories, particularly if it is a time of heavy new offerings. Thus, suppose that a $100 million State of California offering that has just been made is moving rather slowly. There are many dealers involved, they are scattered all across the country, and most of them will require temporary financing. While not all such financing is covered in the money market in New York City, a substantial part of the total borrowing of the major dealers will tend to be in this market. The loans required will be short-term and will tend to be overnight loans made largely by commercial banks.* We say that the money market will require these loans because dealers and brokers are participating in money market activities.

---

* On tax-exempt new issues the financing is frequently in the form of warehousing the securities with the bank members of a syndicate and these show on the banks' books as temporary investments rather than loans.

The commercial banks operating in the money market feel a certain sense of obligation to take care of the credit needs of brokers and dealers, although the obligation is certainly not the same thing as the moral commitment to take care of a business customer who has a line of credit. Rather, it is a working relationship from day to day in which the bank seeks to take care of its broker and dealer customers up to a point beyond which it would be difficult or imprudent to provide accommodation. It is a common practice for banks to borrow in the Federal funds market to take care of money market loans, and more than one bank has gone to the Federal Reserve to borrow funds to finance these loan demands.

Foreign Central Banks and Governments

Since World War II, foreign central banks and governments have accumulated a large amount of funds in the United States. In large measure, this is a counterpart of the deficit in our international balance of payments over the years. The funds held here generally represent official holdings of foreign exchange reserves and under normal conditions are more or less stable. In addition, these central banks and governments traditionally wish to keep their investments in the New York money market in fairly short maturities in order to be sure they are liquid. In September 1971, foreign central banks and governments held about $35 billion in short-term dollar assets.

Many years ago some of the foreign central banks and governments asked the Federal Reserve Bank of New York to act as their agent to make investments in short-term money market securities, largely Treasury bills. The Federal Reserve has maintained this activity on a continuing basis ever since for quite a number of countries. The total dollar amount held in custody by the Fed for foreign account was about $21 billion in September 1971.

151

In addition, these foreign central banks and governments have been carrying substantial deposits in money market banks. Some of these are in demand form but, as interest rates rose in recent years, a larger amount was accumulated in time deposits, thus roughly paralleling what was taking place with funds of American corporations. The large commercial banks realized a long time ago that if they did not make time deposit facilities available to these customers, their funds would be concentrated in Treasury bills and other securities. Thus, as discussed in Chapter 5, the funds would not flow into the commercial banks and funds already there might leave. Accordingly, during the 1950s the large banks used certain time deposits for these foreign accounts. This was before the corporate negotiable CD was developed in 1961. The instruments used for these foreign accounts were nonnegotiable CDs or open accounts,* but, when the negotiable CD came along later on, this too was used. In the next half-dozen years, a growing proportion of the total volume of time deposits held by foreign central banks and governments took the form of negotiable CDs.

Legislation enacted in 1962, and subsequently renewed, provided for the exemption from the rate ceiling limitations of Regulation Q of time deposits of foreign governments, monetary authorities, and international institutions of which the United States is a member. At the end of September 1971, foreign central banks and governments held $1.4 billion of demand deposits and $2.4 billion of time deposits in American banks. The balance of short-term funds, amounting to $31.2 billion, was invested in U.S. Treasury bills and other short-term paper.

The usual objective of foreign central banks and governments is to arrange United States deposits and investments to obtain maximum income from these accounts while maintaining their short-term maturity structure in order to insure their true liquidity potential. The money market is interested in all of these

---

* Balances in such accounts receive interest if maintained to maturity, under terms specified in agreements between customers and banks.

activities of foreign central banks and governments in holding funds in the United States, partly because of the impact of these holdings on money market conditions and partly because of the possibility that the foreign owners might begin to withdraw them.

Other Foreign Investors

For a time foreign central banks and governments dominated the activity of foreign investors in the American money market. However, beginning in the 1960s other foreign investors assumed a more prominent position. These investors consist primarily of foreign commercial banks and corporations. With the substantial deficit in our international balance of payments, dollars were accumulated not only by foreign central banks and governments but by foreign commercial banks and corporations. Some of these dollars were invested in United States Treasury bills, some took the form of demand deposits in commercial banks, and some found their way into time deposits of commercial banks. Then, in 1968 and 1969, a substantial volume of dollar funds were withdrawn from foreign central banks by foreign commercial banks under the stimulus of the high interest rates available in the Euro-dollar market. This trend was reversed in 1970–71.

In late 1971, the total amount of liquid assets held here by foreign commercial banks amounted to about $12 billion. Other foreigners, largely foreign corporations, held an additional $4 billion.

New York Agencies of Foreign Banks

From a money market point of view, New York branches of foreign banks really should be thought of as being in approximately the same situation as American banks, since they have similar functions and operate under similar rules and regulations. Foreign agencies in this country, however, are quite different from branches. They are not able to accept deposits but they can make arrangements for deposits to be sent to their home offices. If these deposits are denominated in American dollars, the agencies in New York can arrange for the investment of these deposits in American dollar assets for their home offices. Frequently these take the form of money market loans, that is, loans to Government securities dealers or to other dealers and brokers. The evidence is not complete but it would seem that on occasion the total loans of these foreign agencies have been very large.

Other Domestic Investors

Thrift institutions such as mutual savings banks and savings and loan associations are participants in the money market to varying degrees, depending on the size of their liquidity positions. They will seldom hold short-term securities in proportionately as large amounts as commercial banks, however, since their main emphasis is on long-term mortgage loans.

Insurance companies are also active participants in the money market at times, but they seldom have large volumes of funds invested in short-term maturities for long periods of time. Typically their participation is confined to temporary holdings while awaiting completion of some long-term transactions.

Pension funds may hold short-term investments for a variety of reasons, such as temporary investment while awaiting receipt of a long-term investment, or holding a buying reserve if changes in market prices are considered likely. Some banks arrange cooperative pools of short-term paper for the short-term money of the pension funds they administer.

For many years, individuals were not active participants in the money market. This was probably because there had been a strong trend toward institutionalizing the funds of individuals: they had largely used financial intermediaries to do the investing for them.

It is interesting to note, however, that in the recent periods of tight money and high interest rates a reverse process has taken place. Thus, in 1959 when the Government issued the "Magic Fives," individuals bought substantial amounts because the 5% rate was a magnet. Thrift institutions lost deposits as individuals shifted funds into this Government security. Again in 1966 when interest rates reached the highest levels in a long period, there was a further tendency on the part of individuals to make their own investments in various interest-bearing securities and to finance their purchases by withdrawing funds from thrift institutions. PCs became quite attractive when they were issued at rates above 6%. Individuals also bought more Treasury bills and other short-term issues than they had been accustomed to buying for many years. The shift of funds was called disintermediation because it involved the withdrawal of funds from financial intermediaries, such as thrift institutions, for direct investment. Much stronger trends developed in 1968 and 1969 when market rates rose to new highs which attracted much attention. The reversal of rates toward lower levels in 1970 and 1971 brought heavy reintermediation of funds to savings institutions. However, individuals were quite attracted by the 7% Treasury bond offered in the summer of 1971, the first issue sold under the $10 billion exception to the 4¼% interest limitation on Treasury bonds.

The Larger Universe

PART IV

Major Forces Affecting the Money Market: Sometimes They Swamp It

CHAPTER 12   I have often mused over the fact that everyone is a captive of his situation. The Chairman of the Board of a large corporation is a captive, at least partly, of a larger situation: to some extent he is a captive of his competitors and the marketplace, and the Board of Directors is his boss, and so are the stockholders. Perhaps, also, he is a captive of forces stemming from Government. Even the President of the United States, as powerful as he is, is controlled by forces emanating from the public, from Congress, and from around the world.

In a similar way, the money market may be a captive of forces from outside. We may talk of supply and demand in the money market as shaping the forces that determine prices and yields, and we may talk of competition among different instruments in the money market and among various institutions, and all this will be true. But the money market may be a captive of larger forces at times that may push it suddenly and decisively in some new direction, and may even swamp it. One example in the 1965–70 period was the Vietnam War, which brought with it enormous pressures on the economy and on the money market.

For a different kind of example, look at the emergence of the Euro-dollar market, which grew so rapidly in the last ten years or so that it found a life of its own which in certain ways confounded central banks and extended our money market to an international basis. Also, consider the growth of multinational corporations which cross international boundaries at will and add new dynamism to the world's money markets.

National Economic Policy

For more than a generation, theories have been evolving as to the proper role of Government in smoothing out the business cycle and promoting stable economic growth. In the 1930s, the Great Depression raised many questions about what Government could do, and John Maynard Keynes wrote extensively in developing new theories about the cause of economic stagnation. In 1946 Congress enacted the "Employment Act," which stated that "it is the continuing policy and responsibility of the Federal Government to use all practicable means . . . to promote maximum employment, production, and purchasing power." This act also created the Council of Economic Advisers to perform the functions of economic analysis and appraisal called for in the act and to advise the President.

As time has passed and experience has been amassed, economists and Government officials have gained understanding and insight into economic problems and also into the impact of monetary and fiscal policies and other measures as remedies to economic difficulties. Everyone now recognizes that the Government can help smooth out fluctuations in the business cycle through appropriate monetary and fiscal policies. It can provide a stimulus to the economy when there is unemployment and introduce a drag when there is excess activity accompanied by inflationary tendencies. If the economic furnace is not warm enough, the Government can shovel in monetary and fiscal fuel. If the economic furnace is too hot, the Government can take contrary action to cool it off by withdrawing some of the monetary and fiscal fuel. It is generally considered appropriate to have Government deficits during economic slumps, but these should be followed by a surplus during periods of strong economic activity.

There is a body of thought, commonly known as the "New Economics," whose adherents propose that Government intervene actively and frequently in the economic process, using monetary and fiscal programs and also an "incomes policy" which sets guidelines for wage negotiations, usually based on the average increase in the productivity of the country. Advocates of the New Economics maintain that through "fine tuning" the economy can be controlled and directed to the desired and proper goals.

As is so often true, it seems to be a good deal easier to enunciate the theory than it is to develop the appropriate degree of action in practice. Perhaps this is because in a democracy there are always important differences in point of view, and these are bound to be injected both into appraising the state of the economy at any given time, as well as into prescribing the proper policies for that particular situation. It would take a different kind of book [1] to delve deeply into these questions but we can stop long enough to consider some of the criticisms. One is that the net result over time is inflationary because the tendency is to push the New Economics harder when there is slack in the economy than when some restraint should be exercised. Some of the policies tend to be one-sided, in that it is easier politically for Government programs to be turned on than off. Moreover, in the past a deficit in a boom period was almost certain to be financed very heavily by short-term issues in the money market because interest rates in the long-term market were higher than the 4¼% ceiling on new Treasury bond issues.

In any event, the money market is vitally affected by the

practice of national economic policy. Thus, the initial impact of monetary policy, as we have seen, is to a very large extent felt in the money market and, as we shall see later on, is transmitted to the bond market, the mortgage market, and the stock market, through linkages between short-term issues and long-term issues and other factors.

Similarly, fiscal policy affects the money market, directly and indirectly, in a very penetrating way. Large Government deficits during economic slumps require large financing activities in the money market and, in theory at least, surpluses in the Government budget later on bring repayments of Federal debt.

A short digression on the so-called full employment budget is in order here. This is not really a budget in the usual sense but rather an attempt to measure the deficit that would exist if the economy were operating at full employment levels (that is, a 4% unemployment figure). The full employment budget concept thus adjusts for the feedback effect of economic activity on the budget. When the economy is sluggish and profits and incomes are weak, Federal tax receipts lag, typically leading to budget deficits (as in fiscal 1971). Conversely, when the economy is booming, tax receipts surge and budget surpluses should accumulate. The full employment budget represents an attempt to measure the effect of the Federal budget on the economy, and its suitability. When the full employment budget is in surplus, the impact on the economy is restrictive; when it is in deficit, the impact is stimulative.

In any event, we may say that the entire program of the Government in the economic area has either a direct or indirect impact in the money market. To follow this through, let us consider various stages of the business cycle in the thirteen years ending with the Nixon wage-price freeze in 1971. An enormous amount of change occurred in these years in the money market, so much, in fact, that it is an ideal period of history in which to examine the creative processes which the money market always exhibits as challenges arise. We will start with a recession, go to

162

a recovery, then a boom, and finally we will close with a mixed economy showing both slowdown and inflation.

Our procedure will be to consider first the economic theory characteristically describing such periods. What should we logically expect of each period? Then we will trace through what actually happened in a selected period. As will be seen, the theory and practice will not always be consistent and there will be some large surprises.

Some duplication of other chapters will inevitably occur, but this will help to provide the proper emphasis on important matters.

The Recession Syndrome

THE THEORY

Let us consider first the supply of credit in the money market in a recession of the type we have seen since World War II. By recession I mean a relatively small setback in economic activity in contrast with the Great Depression of the 1930s, which was a major downturn and lasted for several years. In a recession, the Federal Reserve System will usually be stepping up its purchases of securities in order to improve the reserve position of member banks, with a view to adding to credit availability and ultimately stimulating economic activity. If the Federal Reserve System buys $1 million of securities, there will be an equivalent increase in bank reserves; the rule of thumb today is that banks will be able to expand their holdings of securities and loans by somewhat more than ten times. Thus there is a multiplier effect on the supply side and commercial banks generally will be eager to put money to work. Banks will usually wish to restore their liquidity positions because in the previous boom phase they had to draw hard on liquid assets to meet the demands for loans and the typical squeeze on deposits. Banks may also wish to increase their liquidity in order to prepare for the next round of loan expansion and for possible deposit losses because they are not too sure that all of the demand and time deposits flowing in will stay with them.

Now let us turn to the demand for credit in the money market in a recession. Corporations will be less aggressive in their borrowings because sales are slack and inventories are being worked off rather than being accumulated. Finance companies will need less credit as consumer spending slows up. Demands for funds through the use of bankers' acceptances will also weaken because imports tend to decline in such a period, although exports sometimes hold up fairly well. To the extent interest rates decline, some borrowers will issue long-term bonds to pay off bank loans and commercial paper issued earlier on a temporary basis when rates were high. Commercial banks will probably be less eager to issue CDs because they do not need the funds for immediate use. On the other hand, the Treasury will usually require considerably more short-term credit because a larger deficit will occur. More money will be paid out on Government spending and lending programs and less money will come in from taxes than before. Treasury borrowing in recessions is usually concentrated largely in short-term issues because it is feared that long-term borrowing might draw in private funds that would otherwise finance housing and other capital outlays.

Interest rates in the money market will turn downward as the supply of credit moves ahead of demand. The downswing may be sharp, especially if expectations regarding business activity become very bearish.

THE PRACTICE—1957–58, AND A BIG SURPRISE

The 1957–58 period may be taken as an interesting illustration of the effects of change in the money market during a recession. With the benefit of hindsight, we may say that the recession started during the third quarter of 1957. On the supply side of credit, the Federal Reserve started easing bank reserve positions late in 1957 and pursued an easy money policy until mid-1958. During the nine-month period ending in June 1958, the Federal Reserve expanded its Government security portfolio by close to $2 billion and it reduced reserve requirements against net demand deposits by 1% to 2% for different classes of banks. Free reserves of member banks—that is, excess reserves less borrowings at Federal Reserve Banks—moved from a deficiency of more than $450 million to a surplus of close to $500 million, despite a substantial expansion in bank credit. Commercial bank deposits expanded by $12 billion, with the increase about equally divided between demand and time deposits.

On the demand side, bank loans increased slightly less than $2 billion in the nine months ending June 30, 1958. More than three-fourths of this increase was represented by loans on securities; business loans declined $1.4 billion. With business loan demand disappointing, banks were willing to take on security loans, particularly in response to a relatively heavy demand for such loans in connection with a Treasury refunding operation in June. They increased their portfolio of U.S. Governments by about $7 billion and added about $2.5 billion to their holdings of State and local securities during the nine-month period. About one-third of the purchases of U.S. Governments was in the form of notes, reflecting the emphasis in Treasury financing and suggesting that, with substantial excess reserves, banks had little need to add to their liquidity in the form of bills and certificates which were nearly unchanged over the period. The Federal budget shifted from a surplus of $3.2 billion in fiscal 1957 to a deficit of $2.9 billion in fiscal 1958.

There were four reductions in the Federal Reserve Bank discount rate from November 1957 through April 1958, bringing the rate down from 3½% to 1¾%. The ninety-one-day Treasury bill rate declined from 3½% to less than 1% and the prime rate was reduced in two steps from 4½% to 3½%. Yields on long-term bonds declined by more than ½%.

165

There are many surprises in the money market,* and a big one occurred in June 1958 in connection with a Treasury refunding operation. The story is an interesting one. In late May, the Treasury announced a refunding offer of two issues (1¼% certificates due May 15, 1959, and 2⅝% bonds due February 15, 1965) in exchange for 2⅞% notes maturing on June 15. At the time there was little feeling that the end of the recession was in sight. As often happens when two Treasury issues with widely differing coupon rates are offered at the same time, one of them seemed to have more speculative potential for quick profit than the other. There was quite a surge to buy the maturing issue in order to attain the rights† to exchange into the 2⅝% bond. Some purchasers hoped to make a quick profit by buying heavily on margins of 5% or even less. In other words, buyers planned to subscribe to the issue, borrowing 95% or more of the funds required, and to sell it within a matter of a few days, hoping to make a profit of perhaps half a point or more. Percentagewise, the rate of return on their own cash investment could be quite high because of the leverage provided through the heavy use of borrowed funds. The larger the amount of borrowing relative to direct personal investment, the greater the return even on a small price increase, as shown below:

	5% Margin	3% Margin
Cash invested	5%	3%
Borrowed	95	97
Total—price paid	100%	100%
Gain if sold at 100½:		
As % of price paid	0.5%	0.5%
As % of cash invested	10%	16.7%

* It is well to be alert to surprises in all the financial markets. When things begin to look certain—in the money market, the bond market, or the stock market—beware, a change may well be in the making!
† The rights accorded to a holder of a security to subscribe to issues offered in exchange for that security.

Thus, on 5% margin, one-half point would bring a 10% profit to the investor; on 3% margin, the profit would be 16.7%. If a 10% to 16% profit does not seem large, remember that it was expected to be made in a short period, so the gain on an annual rate basis would be very large.

It soon became clear that, with so many speculators in the new 2⅝% issue, there was a large supply of bonds overhanging the market. As the days passed, evidence that the economy would soon improve began to unfold, suggesting that interest rates might move upward.

The price of the new bonds in the market began to sag as the speculators began to sell and, with so many more sellers than buyers, the issue went below par. Some of the borrowed funds proved to be from temporary sources. One large corporation was reported to have advanced funds to speculative buyers on the expectation they would be repaid within a few days, as the funds were earmarked to make a dividend payment. But the borrowers did not wish to sell out the securities when the loans were due because of the loss they would realize. One substantial borrower from banks held on for weeks hoping to avert loss but the market continued to deteriorate so that he was asked from time to time for more margin to cover the reduced value of his collateral.

It was clear that a bad technical situation had developed in the market and all eyes were on the Federal Reserve to see whether action would be taken to ameliorate the strains that were beginning to show. The Federal Reserve did do some buying of the 2⅝% issue but, to avoid putting additional reserves in the market, it made compensating sales of Treasury bills in substantial amounts. The result was that the market was disappointed and prices of other Treasury bonds sagged.

By August, further evidence had accumulated that recovery from the recession was under way. Thereafter, the Federal Reserve moved steadily to a less easy monetary policy and some sizable losses were taken by sellers of Treasury bonds, not only on the new June issues but on other issues as well. In retrospect, it was clear that the business recovery would have brought about changes in the market in any event, but they occurred earlier because of the June speculative situation, and the telescoping of these two events provided a dramatic chapter in Treasury financing.

The Recovery Syndrome

THE THEORY

In a robust recovery after a recession, the Federal Reserve is expected to take steps toward restricting the supply of credit. At first, the Fed may buy less Treasury securities in its open market operations but at a later stage it will often switch to a policy of selling securities or not replacing maturing obligations. As a result, commercial banks will find the growth in their reserves diminishing, followed possibly by a decline in reserves, with a correspondingly high-leveraged effect on their ability to extend credit in the form of loans and securities. (It makes no difference in this context whether the Fed sells securities to member banks or to others, because in effect the checks of buyers will be debited by the Federal Reserve to the reserve accounts of member banks.)

On the demand side, some corporations will begin to increase their borrowings, both from banks and in the commercial paper market, as needs arise to rebuild inventories. Finance companies will borrow more and consumer loans will expand as consumer spending rises. There frequently will be a gain in imports as the recovery proceeds and this will lead to a reduction in the country's trade balance, as well as to a rise in bankers' acceptances outstanding. The Federal Government may find that its receipts are rising as economic activity improves and logically should begin to cut back on expenditure and lending programs. The result should be a smaller deficit with a reduction in Treasury borrowing in the money market.

Interest rates will tend to rise, reflecting these changes in the supply and demand situation. The rise in rates may be quite pronounced if expectations are that there will be a substantial business improvement.

THE PRACTICE—LATE 1958

As the recovery picked up speed in the summer and fall of 1958, after the big surprise in the Government bond market, the Federal Reserve proceeded to tighten monetary conditions in accordance with the theory just described. Free reserves dropped steadily from the peak of $547 million reached in July. By September they were down to $95 million and by the end of the year there was a net borrowed reserve position of $41 million: for the country as a whole, then, the amount of borrowings by borrowing banks exceeded by $41 million the amount of excess reserves held by others, mostly smaller banks.

As would be expected, both short- and long-term rates rebounded sharply. The ninety-one-day Treasury bill rate rose from less than 1% to about 2¾%. The discount rate was raised from 1¾% to 2½% in two steps and was accompanied by a rise in the prime rate of banks from 3½% to 4%. Yields on long-term bonds rose about ½%, wiping out most of the preceding decline from the highs in late 1957.

During the last six months of 1958, bank loans increased $2 billion, with about two-thirds concentrated in business and agricultural loans. Security holdings of commercial banks increased $1.4 billion; U.S. Governments by $1.1 billion; and other securities by $300 million. Unlike the theory just described, the Government deficit was increasing during this period and most of the funds were obtained through short-term financing. In addition, the Treasury called an outstanding short-term bond issue through an advance refunding operation. These financings were reflected in the banks' Government security portfolios, which showed a reduction of $3.8 billion in bond holdings and an increase of $4.9 billion in their holdings of bills, and certificates, and notes.

THE PRACTICE—1961–62 PERIOD AND BEYOND

Now let us turn to another case, that of 1961–62, in which recovery lagged; this development was reflected in a slower response by the Federal Reserve in terms of monetary policy. The sixties had opened on a note of slight recession, the outcome of a number of restraining factors, such as the very tight monetary policies of 1959, policies so tough that total bank credit was held to practically no growth for the year; a dramatic shift of the Federal budget from substantial deficit in fiscal 1959 to a surplus in fiscal 1960; and a steel strike in 1959. The low point of the recession was in February 1961.

The last half of 1961 was a period of recovery and the industrial production index moved up steadily, reaching a new high at the end of the year. Monetary and fiscal policies were directed toward promoting recovery and stimulating growth in the economy. This was the year that the negotiable CD was initiated and the volume rose modestly at first but gained a fair amount of momentum toward the end of the year.

A prolonged period of recovery then emerged that continued at a moderate pace for several years. Industrial production and employment kept rising with only the most modest interruptions. There was unusual price stability. Just enough slack was present in the economy to keep price pressures from accelerating, but there was also some uneasiness that economic growth was deficient. Some were concerned about the fact that teenage unemployment remained large, although employment was rising reasonably well among married men. Also, unemployment among minority groups was high. Hence, the argument was that monetary policy should be kept fairly easy in order to stimulate the economy with the hope of putting these unemployed resources to work.

Many economists believed at that time that fiscal policy was a little too tight and that monetary policy ought to be a little easier in order to provide the right compensation. The term "fiscal drag" was popularly used at this time to describe fiscal policy which tended to keep the economy from reaching full employment. Actually, the progressiveness of the Federal tax structure is a form of fiscal drag in the sense that tax collections rise in percentage terms faster than Gross National Product. When the combined effects of the Government's tax structure and expenditure program keep the economy at less than full employment, fiscal drag is occurring.

Two actions to reduce taxes took place in the early sixties. In 1962, the investment tax credit and more rapid depreciation arrangements were adopted by Congress to stimulate business capital outlays. In 1964, Congress reduced taxes across the board to encourage economic growth. These tax reductions were not only helpful to the economy but they seemed to demonstrate that the theory of Government fiscal action to stimulate the economy in periods of weak business was workable.

Looking back at the period, the recession that ushered in the 1960s was fairly easily turned around by Government action in the monetary and fiscal areas. In statistical terms, the recession was over by February 1961. But, as we have noted above, the aftermath saw continuing Federal action in the effort to bring down unemployment and to raise the level of economic growth. If there was a surprise in this period, it was the remarkable stability in wholesale prices and in long-term interest rates. In the three and one-half years from the middle of 1961 to the end of 1964 industrial production rose by about one quarter, unemployment declined from 4.9 million to 3.7 million, the money supply rose from $144 to $160 billion, and Gross National Product, in constant dollars, rose from $493 to $588 billion. Yet in this same period there was practically no change in the level of wholesale prices and increases in short-term interest rates were tolerable. For example, during the three-and-one-half-year period, the discount rate was raised 1% and other open-market rates increased by roughly the same amount, but there was no change in the prime rate or in long-term rates. No wonder then that people were saying that a remarkable job was being done in national economic policy to produce true economic growth without inflationary price pressures and painful interest rate increases. The bold new tax reduction in 1964 contributed to the euphoria, and the Federal Reserve followed a consistently easy monetary policy. However, this euphoria was soon to be overtaken by a real jolt as we shall see below in discussing the boom syndrome.

The Boom Syndrome

THE THEORY

As recovery proceeds into boom, supply and demand factors will become intensified. The supply of credit in the money market will be severely tightened: first, because the Federal Reserve System will typically be following an intensified tight monetary policy in attempting to restrain economic activity. The money market will note that the Federal Reserve has raised the discount rate perhaps several times and has been conducting its open market operations so as to force banks into a tighter reserve position; second, there will be the multiplier effect as this action is carried through the reserve position of member banks in the usual multiple fashion i.e., as securities are sold by the Federal Reserve, bank reserve positions will go steadily down. After having used all the other alternatives available to them, banks may find themselves borrowing at the Federal Reserve banks as a last resort.

Meanwhile the demand for credit will zoom, pressing ever harder against supply. Commercial banks, of course, will endeavor to raise all the funds they can through CDs, Federal funds, and other sources because of loan demand and the continuing pressure on their reserve position. Corporations will need tremendous amounts of funds, in spite of the fact that profit levels will be good, because of the need to finance larger amounts of receivables, expanded inventories and the customary higher expenditures for plant and equipment. Practically all borrowers will find that it has become more difficult and expensive to raise funds from banks or the bond market so there will be a natural desire to turn to the money market, if at all possible, for temporary accommodation. Sales of commercial paper will continue to rise throughout such a period. Bankers' acceptances generally will be used more heavily, not only because of the large volume needed for international trade, but also because more domestic trade is financed through this route when banks are tight.

The borrowing needs of the Federal Government should sharply diminish in a boom period. As we have noted earlier, most economists would agree that there should be a surplus in the Federal budget to act as a restraint on the economy and to balance out earlier deficits during periods of economic weakness.

As the recovery period proceeds into boom, interest rates in the money market will be very firm and may rise in a continuing series of steps. Expectations of coming events, such as tighter money and escalating interest rates, will increase the demand and reduce the supply of funds as some borrowers will be motivated to borrow early to avoid still higher rates and some lenders will delay transactions because they anticipate that waiting will be profitable.

THE PRACTICE—1966–69 AND SOME SURPRISES

The 1966–69 period is certain to go down in economic history as a period of boom. Gross National Product expanded $244 billion, or almost 35% from the last quarter of 1965 to the fourth quarter of 1969—a period of four years. More than half of the expansion, however, represented inflation. The rise in prices reduced the growth in Gross National Product, in real terms, to $97 billion, or 15%. Industrial production rose 17% over the same period. Personal income expanded by more than one-third. However, an important part of these gains was lost by the increase of 25% in consumer prices. In fact, the rise in the cost of living exceeded the increase in average weekly manufacturing earnings. The only serious interruptions in the progress of economic indices to ever new high levels in this period occurred in late 1966 and early 1967, following efforts of the fiscal and monetary authorities to brake an overheated economy and slow down the rate of inflation. The uptrend was resumed, however, and the boom finally peaked out in November 1969. A period of recession followed but with surprising continuing inflation.

By late 1965, following the period of unusual growth with price stability, the Federal Reserve Board took steps to move toward a tighter monetary policy as signs of overheating began to appear. The Vietnam War had escalated sharply about the middle of the year. The first real signal was December 6, 1965, when the Board of Governors approved an application by the Federal Reserve Bank of New York for an increase in the discount rate from 4% to 4½%. The Board was by no means unanimous; four of the seven members voted for the increase and three voted against it. The Administration in Washington let it be known that it did not approve and for a time there was debate in political circles and in the press concerning the higher discount rate. Regulation Q ceilings were also increased.

Early in the calendar year 1966, there was considerable discussion about whether or not a tax increase was desirable. Those arguing for a tax increase, including many officials of the Federal Reserve System, felt that Government spending, particularly for Vietnam, was not only rising but likely to increase still further at a time when the economy was already operating at near-full employment. Those opposed seemed to feel that the size of the increase in Federal spending was uncertain, that inflationary pressures were not developing on a large enough scale to be serious, and that it was desirable to push the economy still further in order to create as many jobs as possible for the less fortunate in our society. The Administration in Washington sided with the school opposing a tax increase and Congress took no action on taxes.

After some hesitancy early in the year, the Federal Reserve System moved toward progressively tighter monetary policies throughout the first two-thirds of 1966. Net borrowed reserves grew to close to $500 million. Some banks were criticized at the discount window for repeated borrowings. The Fed failed to raise Regulation Q ceilings despite the rise in open market interest rates which made CDs progressively less attractive to corporations.

By the summer of 1966, the economic pot was boiling and the demands for credit were intense. Interest rates were rising sharply, reflecting a demand for funds which clearly was excessive in relation to supply at a time when the Federal Reserve was turning the screw toward a tighter monetary posture. Some observers feared a money panic, and "precautionary" borrowing made the picture worse, as some corporations sought loan commitments to be sure they would have funds available regardless of how tight money became.

In the spring and summer, thrift institutions ran into severe competitive pressures as highly attractive rates appeared on securities offered in the market. Withdrawals rose and new money inflows stopped for all practical purposes. Soon thrift institutions virtually ceased lending money on mortgages, and new housing starts were cut back severely. Both savings institutions and the home building industry began to put pressure on Congress, with the result that some Congressmen spoke out against the Federal Reserve as the agency responsible for the trend in interest rates.

Commercial banks, especially in money centers, were under pressure of very heavy demands for loans. Aside from CDs,

175

deposits held up fairly well, partly through success in selling smaller savings certificates to individuals. However, these small savings certificates carrying a rate of 5½% were drawing some funds from thrift institutions paying 5%, so moves were started in Congress to set interest rate ceilings on certain deposits by law rather than by Federal Reserve action under Regulation Q. The idea was to reduce the ceilings to cut into the power of commercial banks to attract small savings, but the Federal Reserve resisted these moves and Congressional action was never taken. However, Congress raised the maximum permissible level of reserve requirements on time deposits from 6% to 10%, with no change in the minimum of 3%, and urged the Federal Reserve to use the new authority to move against the growth of certain types of time deposits in commercial banks. In addition, Congress broadened the basis for setting interest rate ceilings, and established rate ceilings for insured nonmember banks, mutual savings banks, and savings and loan associations under authority granted to the FDIC and the Federal Home Loan Bank Board. Subsequently, the Fed reduced the maximum rate on deposits of less than $100,000 from 5½% to 5%.

The year 1967 saw a series of startling developments: the Vietnam War increased Government spending considerably and the Treasury deficit rose to $14 billion for the calendar year. Such a deficit was of course inconsistent with the theory described above for a boom period—the Treasury was providing a greater stimulus to the economy, when in fact it should have shifted to a policy of restraint. The Administration did ask for an increase in taxes but Chairman Mills of the House Ways and Means Committee proposed that there be cuts in spending to match any increase in taxes. The Administration and Mr. Mills were unable to get together on this plan, so Treasury borrowing rose considerably and the credit markets once again became quite congested. Interest rates rose further and, in fact, rates in the bond market returned to and in many cases exceeded the levels of the credit crunch of 1966.

Monetary policy had moved in the direction of ease late in 1966 and early in 1967 in spite of the overexpansionary fiscal policy. Business in general—and construction in particular—was in a temporary slump caused by the credit crunch of 1966. Presumably, the Federal Reserve was hoping that the fiscal impasse could be resolved without the need to tighten monetary conditions prematurely.

Wage increases were proving to be quite inflationary. In the early sixties, the Administration had endeavored to get business and labor to follow a set of guidelines in the field of wage increases. Thus in the 1962 Report of the Council of Economic Advisers it was suggested that wage increases in any year be limited to the average annual increase in the productivity of all industry in the preceding five years. This worked out at 3.2% until 1966, when the guidelines were broken by a wage settlement in the airlines industry which called for an increase of more than 4%. Administration officials deplored the crumbling of the guidelines but offered no new benchmark, and in 1967 the Council suggested no specific figure.

Even after the airlines wage contract in June 1966 called for an increase beyond the recommended guidelines, there were several episodes in which moral suasion was used by the Administration in endeavoring to hold down prices. In September and December 1967, for example, the steel industry was denounced by Administration officials for raising prices. Appeals were made to all industries and labor unions to halt the wage-price spiral. Meanwhile, the international balance of payments situation also continued bleak for the United States and there were various expressions of concern that the dollar might be undermined by speculators.

The Federal Open Market Committee voted on December 12, 1967, to move "slightly beyond the firmer conditions in the money market that have developed." [2] There was a temporary, partly seasonal, improvement in the money and bond markets at the beginning of 1968, but by early spring it was clear that

177

another decisive move toward monetary restraint was in process. The domestic economy was showing new signs of overheating and the balance of payments deficit seemed worse than ever, as evidenced by a sharp increase in the deficit in the fourth quarter of 1967. Unemployment dropped to 3½% and consumer prices were rising at an annual rate of approximately 4%, the largest rate of increase since the Korean War period. The combination of the Vietnam War and peak private demand was above our capacity to produce. Meanwhile the domestic fiscal impasse continued. The Administration persisted in its request for a tax increase, so that fiscal policy would be more appropriate in the circumstances. Seemingly endless Congressional delay finally gave way and a 10% surcharge on income taxes, together with a $6 billion cut in expenditures, was approved in June 1968.

Then came a big surprise. It was widely expected that the tax surcharge would have a fast restraining effect on business activity, but it did not. The Federal Reserve moved quickly to ease monetary conditions to cushion the expected tax impact, but reversed itself in December when inflationary conditions did not lessen. The Treasury bill rate moved as if it were on a roller coaster. At 5¾% in May just before the tax surcharge was enacted, the ninety-one-day bill rate slid to under 5% in July, with the expectation of a slowing up in business, then rose to 6¼% at the year end as business activity kept on a strong inflationary track. As 1969 opened, all interest rates were at new highs and the Federal Reserve was back again trying to tighten money because the tax increase had not exerted any obvious restraining bite on the overheated economy.

The year 1969 brought a real crescendo to the money market. Inflationary expectations rose to a new peak, and it proved surprisingly difficult to cool the economy through monetary and fiscal measures. Interest rates rose early in the year and then kept moving irregularly higher so that by the end of the year most interest rates were higher than ever before recorded. I am sure that no one predicted such record rates, and, if they had, they would not have been listened to.

From a money market point of view, the year 1969 breaks down conveniently into two parts. The first part runs to perhaps mid-May. At a meeting of the Federal Open Market Committee on December 17, 1968, Federal Reserve policy had shifted toward restraint. Fed spokesmen later characterized the shift as a policy of "gradualism" in the monetary effort to control inflationary pressures. While gradualism was never officially abandoned, it is clear that a period of tougher monetary policy began in late May and carried through the balance of the year.

The term "gradualism" was used by representatives of the Administration and the Federal Reserve System, I believe, to reassure people that, although tighter money was being employed as an active weapon against inflation, there was to be no repeat of the credit crunch of 1966. Rather, there was to be a kind of persistent "turning of the screw" in an orderly fashion to bring on the remedial corrections needed. Net borrowed reserves, which were approximately $500 million when the program of gradualism began in January 1969, rose rather steadily to about $900 million in the spring, and then exceeded $1 billion in May. The discount rate was 5½% at the beginning of the year and was raised to 6% in April 1969. The prime rate began the year at 6¾% and was raised to 7% in January and 7½% in March. But the Treasury bill rate did not follow this pattern. The ninety-one-day bill rate opened the year 1969 at 6¼%, moved sideways for a time, and then drifted downward to the 6% area in the spring. It was about this time that some forecasts were being made that the Treasury surplus in the second quarter would be sufficient to bring the bill rate down still further and thus lead the money market into generally easier conditions. These forecasts proved to be wrong, however, in spite of the fact that the Treasury did have a surplus. More important, the economy showed no signs of slowing at this time, whether measured by industrial production, employment, Gross National Product, or price levels. In fact, price increases seemed to accelerate.

From about mid-May 1969 the Federal Reserve System said less about gradualism and a good deal more about its determina-

179

tion to cool the economy and break the back of the inflationary expectations so generally held. Commercial banks were feeling the pinch where it really hurt—in deposit losses—because the Federal Reserve refused to increase the ceiling rates on time deposits under Regulation Q,* even though the rate on three-month Treasury bills had risen sharply to 8% by the year end. Under the extreme pressures of 1969, the 6¼% ceiling on six-month CDs was hopelessly below the level necessary to attract funds. A continuing outflow of money from CDs hurt the money market banks in particular. In New York the decline was particularly sharp. Starting with $7.5 billion CDs in mid-December 1968, the figure at the end of September was down to approximately $2 billion, a decline of two thirds. By the end of 1969, the volume had moved up to $2.7 billion, reflecting new CDs issued to foreign governments, central banks, and certain international entities (none of which are subject to Regulation Q), which more than offset continued attrition in CDs issued to domestic customers.

The pressure on banks showed up in many ways. The prime rate was raised to a record-breaking 8½% early in June. The banks bought Federal funds whenever they could get them, at rates running as high as 11%, and they vastly stepped up their efforts to buy Euro-dollars through branches in Europe. The rate on Euro-dollar deposits rose to as high as 13%. Such short-term borrowings at rates well above the prime rate were obviously terribly painful to money market banks, and earnings were sharply curtailed. But the Federal Reserve kept moving doggedly along to make the tightening even more effective.

The situation boiled down to this: With the arbitrary action taken to squeeze down CDs by hopelessly low ceiling rates, banks were forced to look for alternate sources of funds. As they used their ingenuity to develop these, the Federal Reserve kept run-

---

* New levels had been set in April 1968 which seemed to place the ceilings on a more realistic basis than those in effect in 1966. Rates were raised to 5½% for maturities of thirty to fifty-nine days, 5¾% for maturities of sixty to eighty-nine days, 6% for maturities of three to six months, and 6¼% for maturities six months or more.

ning right along and tried to close them off or make them more expensive. Consider these actions:

1. Euro-dollars—In July 1969 the Fed took steps to close what was considered a loophole by defining checks used in settlement of Euro-dollar transactions by member banks with their foreign branches as deposits subject to reserve requirements. The use of these checks had previously avoided reserve requirements for overnight borrowings.

2. Euro-dollars—A reserve requirement of 10% was imposed, effective in October 1969, on Euro-dollar funds used, and on loans transferred to foreign branches, over and above the average base level in the four weeks ending May 28, 1969. This was later raised to 20%.

3. Loan Participations—As of August 28, the Fed classified bank loan RPs with nonbank investors as deposits subject to reserve requirements and to Regulation Q, unless they were collateraled by U.S. Government or agency securities. This was directed at the practice of some banks in selling participations in their loan portfolios to corporate investors.

4. Commercial Paper—In late October, steps were first proposed to eliminate the use of commercial paper by bank affiliates; this, in the last half of 1969, had proved a useful device for obtaining bank funds. In January 1970, additional steps were proposed in this area which would apply reserve requirements against commercial paper issued by bank holding companies to finance their banks. These threats became reality later in 1970 when a 5% reserve requirement was imposed on funds obtained by banks through commercial paper issued by holding companies or affiliates.

Fiscal policy in 1969 was once again not making the contribution that theory called for. Only after a long hassle in Congress and a lot of political maneuvering to link the extension to the tax reform bill was the 10% surcharge, enacted so grudgingly in 1968, extended again in 1969 at a 5% rate to expire June 30, 1970. Fortunately, the fiscal year ending June 30, 1969, showed a surplus of about $3 billion in the Federal budget. While this was a great improvement, I do not feel that it was enough. In my judgment, the budget should have been running a surplus of perhaps $10 to $15 billion, considering the inflationary situation.

While 1969 brought a crescendo to the money market, it certainly illustrated that the money market is a viable, creative mechanism. The players on the demand side and those on the supply side of the money market were all skillfully doing their part, even if at times they felt swamped by the speedy parade of new developments.

In terms of economic theory, the developments of 1969 were causing some rethinking to be done. Once again, fiscal policy was proving hard to deliver restraint in accordance with the doctrine of the New Economics. The so-called Monetarist school of economists was gaining converts fairly rapidly at the expense of the New Economics group. The Monetarists were saying that the Federal Reserve all along had been severely at fault: first, by being overly generous in creating money over a long period, and second, by overreacting when they did tighten in 1966 and 1969. As 1970 opened, the economy was slowing and critics of the Federal Reserve were charging more strongly than ever that the Federal Reserve was overdoing restraint, while the System's defenders were contending tight money had to be continued until inflationary expectations were sharply reduced.

The Mixed Syndrome—Economic Slack with Inflation

THE THEORY

There is a big gap here. I am afraid that in a meeting of a hundred economists, central bankers, and Treasury officials, there might be fifty different theories enunciated. It is a subjective matter, largely to decide which is the lesser evil, inflation or unemployment. To put it another way: What is the trade-off between inflation and unemployment? I think the difficulty of resolving the question is leading more people to propose the use of an incomes policy to suppress inflationary tendencies. The theory then becomes something like this: Use monetary and fiscal policy to combat unemployment; use the incomes policy to suppress inflation. Critics say this suppresses symptoms, not causes, and only leads to more trouble later on.

THE PRACTICE: THE 1970–71 AGONY

Following the 1965–69 boom, a picture emerged in which economic slowdown occurred along with continuing high inflation. It was possible to look at many business indicators and conclude quite clearly that there was recession. Indeed, the National Bureau of Economic Research, which has been the semiofficial agency dating recessions, ruled that a recession started in November 1969 and ended in November 1970. Nevertheless, prices did not weaken as one might expect in a period of economic decline. On the contrary, many of them kept on rising. Thus the consumer price index rose from 112 to 119 during the twelve months labeled recession. Within the consumer index, the housing component rose from 114 to 122, the medical component from 115 to 123, and the transportation component from 108 to 116.

This situation created consternation in economic circles. Which symptoms should be treated—those of recession or inflation? In Government, there was some tendency to opt for having the other agency take care of the problem. Thus there was a tendency for the managers of fiscal policy to suggest that monetary policy should be eased to stimulate employment, while holding fiscal affairs unchanged to avoid contributing to inflation. Some Federal Reserve people argued that fiscal policy should be used to stimulate the economy but no further expansion in monetary policy was desirable because of the inflation problem. Neither school really knew what to do because of the lack of hard facts on the trade-off between unemployment and inflation. There was much talk about developing an incomes policy to provide guidelines to hold down labor union pressures for wage increases. The Chairman of the Federal Reserve Board argued that some form of temporary incomes policy could be helpful but the Administration said that it was opposed to this approach.

Both monetary policy and fiscal policy were expansionary. The deficit in free reserves, which had been $1 billion in 1970, fell to zero by April 1971, and a surplus appeared. Money supply (demand deposits plus currency) rose substantially, mostly following a 6% or better growth curve. Regulation Q interest rate ceilings were first raised and later suspended altogether on shorter maturities. In the fiscal year 1971, the *actual* Federal budget deficit on a unified basis rose to $23 billion (from $3 billion the preceding year). In contrast, the unified *full employment* Federal budget for fiscal 1971 had a small surplus of $2.5 billion. This discrepancy showed clearly how a sluggish economic performance at levels well below full employment held down actual Government tax receipts.

The money market and the bond market were buffeted by volatile shifts in sentiment in this mixed economy. The Treasury bill rate dropped from the 8% high of December 1969 to about 3¼% in the spring of 1971 and then started rising again, passing 5% by mid-1971. Offering rates on new long-term bonds fell substantially, then rose sharply. For example, the rates on new issues of Aaa telephone issues bobbed up and down dramatically: in mid-1970 an issue was sold to yield more than 9%; by early 1971 a similar new issue was sold at under 7%; by mid-1971, such an issue was being sold at over 8%. The bank prime rate dropped from its peak of 8½% to 5¼% and then rose to 6% by mid-1971; the discount rate first fell from 6% to 4¾%, then was raised to 5%.

The most agonizing part of the 1970–71 experience was that

rapid price growth and sluggish economic growth appeared determined to coexist side by side for some time. Part of the problem was that inflationary pressures were more intense and of longer duration in the second half of the 1960s than had been experienced in many decades. As a result, strong inflationary expectations were formed by workers and businessmen alike.

Even after the excess demand pressures on the economy eased in the 1970 environment, the wage cost pressures continued to intensify as unions sought to make up for purchasing power lost under earlier contracts. In an effort to ease the squeeze on profit margins, companies responded whenever possible with more price increases. The lesson of this experience is that once an economy is thrown out of balance (the surge in government defense spending in 1965–66 being the factor that kicked the already fully employed economy over the edge in this case) it is extremely difficult to bring it back on a course of sustained non-inflationary economic growth.

By early 1971 the stage was set for a slowing in the rate of price increases with a substantial 6% of the civilian labor force unemployed and only about 70% of our economy's productive capacity in operation. Unfortunately, all indications pointed to the fact that progress in actually bringing down price advances would be painfully slow. High unemployment and rapidly increasing prices had existed side-by-side in earlier postwar recessions but only temporarily during periods of transition from excessive inflationary pressures to eventual slower price rises. The problem with the 1970–71 experience was that the transition period was considerably more drawn out than earlier, thus leading to impatience, uncertainty, and growing frustration.

Finally on August 15, 1971, the President abruptly cleared the air with his bold new economic program including the temporary wage-price freeze, new tax and expenditure recommendations, and action to improve the balance of payments position.

Throughout the 1970–71 period, the money market again proved its resilience. With somewhat greater Federal Reserve

185

emphasis on a target growth rate in monetary aggregates and somewhat less emphasis on stabilizing money market conditions, there were unexpectedly large swings in interest rates, but the money market continued to accommodate borrowers and lenders without any great difficulty.

Interest Rate Controls and the Money Market: Lessons From Recent Experience

This chapter is taken from a paper I presented to the International Monetary Conference at Hot Springs in May 1970. It is presented here, with minor editorial revisions, because it highlights the way interest rate controls backfired and caused malfunctions seriously affecting the money market during the recent boom.

CHAPTER 13   Our financial markets have undergone major stresses and strains in recent years. The capacity of participants in the money market generally and the banks in particular to adapt to rapidly changing circumstances has been remarkable. It is important, however, to try to pinpoint the sources of stress, with a view to modifying them in a way that will allow our financial system to operate more effectively. What lessons from recent financial experience might we pass on to the President's newly formed Commission on Financial Structure?

Efforts to curtail inflationary pressures have placed a heavy burden on our financial markets. Two major problems have arisen: 1) credit has become scarce relative to total demands and 2) the allocation of credit among competing uses has been uneven, with major shortages evident in the housing and state and local government sectors. The shrinkage in the credit total relative to demand is the by-product of an extended period of monetary restraint. It is a necessary step in the effort to cool off inflationary pressures. The distortions in the allocation of credit are, on the other hand, a source of major concern.

This analysis will focus on the role played by interest rate ceilings and other rate rigidities in the credit allocation problem. The money market and banks are the primary objects of interest, but other market sectors will also be examined. Among the questions raised by recent financial developments are: What have been the effects of Regulation Q bank time-deposit interest rate ceilings on money market banks in particular and the money market participants in general? Were the Federal Reserve's main objectives in using Regulation Q achieved? Have interest rate ceilings and rigidities in the money and capital markets seriously undermined the market mechanism in the credit allocation process? What budget posture should the Federal Government assume in periods of heavy private capital demands?

Regulation Q Backfires

The credit allocation problem is closely related to the Fed's active use of Regulation Q as a policy tool. One of the Fed's primary objectives in using Regulation Q was apparently selective in nature, namely, to reduce the proportion of total credit extended to big business. The Fed's logic seemed to be that the rate of growth of bank business loans could be curtailed if somehow the Fed could make it more difficult for big banks (which make the bulk of the business loans) to lend to big business.

Large negotiable certificates of deposit (CDs) in big banks are especially sensitive to rates paid relative to rates on competing money market instruments. Regulation Q ceilings on large CDs were held rigid by the Fed and, as monetary restraint pushed market rates on competing instruments above CD ceiling rates, CD holders let them mature and placed the proceeds elsewhere. By squeezing large CDs out of big banks, the Fed felt it could slow the rate of business spending on one hand, and lessen the credit squeeze on sectors typically hit hardest by tight money—housing, State and local governments, and small business—on the other.

The flaw in the Fed's Regulation Q plan was that major business borrowers were not deterred from seeking funds even after being refused credit by their banks. Business was able to finance a high rate of plant and equipment spending by turning to nonbank sources of credit. The increase in business credit was actually larger in 1969 than in 1968, but the proportion of business credit extended by banks declined as the CD pinch intensified.

More generally, when market rates rise above Regulation Q ceilings, there is a corresponding drop in the bank share of total credit extended. This pattern was evident in the second half of 1966, early 1968, and most strikingly in 1969. Since the banks are the point of contact for Fed monetary policies, one would expect even without Regulation Q that a general policy of restraint effected through a squeeze on bank reserves would result initially in a drop in the bank share of the total credit flow. The point is that the decline in the bank credit share is apparently intensified by the operation of Regulation Q over an extended period. As a direct result of Regulation Q, nonbank credit channels are opened up, refined, and given a greater role that may be of lasting importance. One unfortunate by-product is that the disciplines of bank lending are lost and the quality of credit declines. Both bank credit departments and bank examiners scrutinize bank loans, but nonbank credit transactions, such as the sale of commercial paper by one corporation to another, are not subject to such supervision. Thus, the Fed loses touch with not only the quantity but the quality of a substantial share of credit in the periods when Regulation Q ceilings are at work this way.

Controlling Business Credit and Spending

The Fed's use of Regulation Q to force a CD runoff stimulated the rapid development of a highly efficient system in which corporations with short-term funds to lend purchased the commercial paper of corporate borrowers. This credit extension process short-circuited the commercial banking system and made it possible for credit-financed business spending to be larger in volume and longer in duration than would otherwise have been the case. The Fed, in its use of Regulation Q, thus compounded the credit allocation problem that it had set out to correct.

An obvious question which arises at this point is whether or not there was any way of curtailing the rapid expansion of business credit and spending which occurred in the recent boom. Certainly the Regulation Q experience suggests that indirect attempts at controlling business credit and spending are probably doomed to failure. What about imposing direct credit controls on businesses themselves? Such controls might be supplemented with additional taxes on business profits to insure that both external and internal sources of funds used to support business spending will be curtailed.

While such an approach would be more likely to curb the share of credit going to business and restrain business spending than the back door CD runoff approach, it does raise important questions typically associated with direct selective controls. Why, for example, should the effort be to try only to restrain business credit and spending and not consumer credit and spending? Indeed, should not the direct controls be applied across the board to all major demand sectors? But if it is agreed that controls be widespread, aren't we faced with an overwhelming administrative problem? Finally, if the direct credit controls on business alone should drastically curtail its spending, aren't longer run anti-inflationary policies threatened by restrictions on additions to productive capacity?

A related issue concerns the apparent insensitivity of business spending to high interest rates. The inflationary expectations of the business borrowers should be (but often are not) taken into account in this connection. If business borrowers expect that the price of their new plant and equipment will rise at a 4%

annual rate, an 8% nominal interest rate on funds borrowed to finance this spending is, after subtracting expected price appreciation, reduced to an effective real rate of 4%. Moreover, if business borrowers choose to issue bonds or some related form of debt involving interest payments which can be subtracted from taxable income, the effective borrowing rate must be adjusted downward still further to take into account tax savings. It is this adjusted borrowing rate which should be used in measuring the interest sensitivity of business spending.

Market Response to Regulation Q

Money market participants adapted quickly to the stresses and frictions caused by Regulation Q ceilings. Money market banks, which carried the brunt of the Regulation Q–induced CD runoff, were stimulated to seek out other sources of funds. Many of these banks began to bid aggressively for the Euro-dollar funds; Federal funds purchases were increased; repurchase agreements with corporations and others were relied upon more heavily; loan participations with nonbank customers were introduced; bank holding companies and affiliates began to sell commercial paper; and some banks sold subordinated notes.

The Fed reacted with a patchwork of regulations on the sources of funds that banks had so creatively sought out. Marginal reserve requirements were imposed on Euro-dollar borrowings. Both rate ceilings and reserve requirements were applied to loan participations entered into with nonbank customers. The Fed at one point threatened to place rate ceilings on bank-related commercial paper offerings. It subsequently proposed, instead, to place reserve requirements on bank-related commercial paper. Neither of these proposals for bank-related commercial paper have been carried out, but the uncertainties they created in bank decisions on sources of funds linger on. Finally, the Fed has proposed new regulations governing the maturity and minimum denomination of bank-subordinated notes. (Subsequently the Fed did place reserve requirements on bank-related commercial paper and adopted new regulations on bank issues of short-term notes.)

Corporate participants in the money market were not as encumbered as banks in adapting to Regulation Q stresses. The shift of corporate borrowers to nonbank sources of funds is evidenced by a rise in commercial paper outstanding from approximately $10 billion in early 1966 to roughly $30 billion in early 1970 (excluding bank-related paper). Corporate Eurodollar borrowing and lending has been still another form of adaptation.

It is clear that even the small saver in bank and nonbank financial institutions is not insulated from the market adaptation process. As rates on money and capital market instruments rose higher and higher above rates that financial institutions could legally pay, the small saver was induced to shift his funds from savings accounts to market instruments. The pace of disintermediation by the small saver picked up sharply in the second half of 1969 and into early 1970. The Fed's purpose in restricting rates banks pay to small savers has been to protect savings and loan associations and small banks who can't turn over their portfolios rapidly. These institutions are caught in a cost squeeze when rates are rising rapidly.

A basic question concerning overall market response to Regulation Q is whether the resulting stresses pushed money market rates higher than might have been the case had Regulation Q not been operative under similar conditions. Opinions on this issue will vary, but a strong case can be made for the fact that interest rates probably rose higher because of Regulation Q. Both banks and business borrowers had to turn to unfamiliar sources for funds. In each case rates paid to attract funds were probably higher than if market forces had been operating to allocate funds through normal channels. Regulation Q thus impaired market efficiency while at the same time failing to help accomplish the Fed's selective credit goal of curtailing business credit expansion.

Other Interest Rate Rigidities

From our recent monetary experiences we have learned that the interest rate structure is full of rigidities. We have just examined Regulation Q in some detail, but we should not overlook the fact that there are many other examples of rate rigidities.

A good case in point is the prime rate. The prime rate was adjusted upward five times during the late 1968–early 1969 period as monetary restraint took hold. But the final adjustment from 7½% to 8½% in June 1969 raised such a political furor that the prime rate was held at the 8½% level despite the fact that the rates on Euro-dollars and on other marginal bank funds continued to rise throughout the rest of 1969 to levels far above the prime rate.

Greater flexibility in the prime rate would have been desirable during this period and will continue to be so in the future. A prime rate more closely tied to the cost of bank funds (on both the up side and down side of rate movements) would be desirable. Perhaps a prime rate supplemented by a cost of funds marginal rate on a larger body of loans can be developed. All this would seem to conform more closely to Fed Chairman Burns' recent observation on bank lines of credit. He has noted that "If bankers were to limit their commitments to totals they felt sure they could finance in periods of tight money, and if they charged at least as much for commitment takedowns as they themselves were paying for additional funds, I suspect that some of our nation's battles against inflation would be easier to win." *

* Reference: Arthur Burns, "The Federal Reserve and the Banking System," Remarks before the 59th Annual Meeting of the Association of Reserve City Bankers, April 6, 1970, Boca Raton, Florida, p. 8.

An even more inflexible rate has been the Federal Reserve discount rate. This rate remained far below other money market rates during most of 1969. As a result, the emphasis at the discount window was on nonprice items including Fed scrutiny of borrowing bank's balance sheets. Until the discount window can be modified along the lines proposed by Governor Mitchell's committee some time ago, bank suspicion of Fed discount window administration will persist. The result is a less efficient money market mechanism for bank reserve adjustments.

Other sources of rate rigidities are rate ceilings in the mortgage area. State usury laws, for example, set mortgage rate ceilings at 7½% in New York and 8% in New Jersey. FHA and VA mortgage rate ceilings are currently 8½%. (Subsequently the FHA and VA mortgage rate ceilings were lowered to 7% in easier financial conditions.)

Private investors tend to lose interest in mortgages in periods when rates on new corporate issues and other competitive market instruments rise above mortgage rate ceilings. Each time rates on new bond issues rise above rate ceilings on FHA and VA mortgages and conventional mortgages, net private lending in the mortgage market weakens. The decline in net mortgage purchases by private investors was most pronounced in 1969.

The declines in the flow of private funds into mortgages during periods of tight money and rising rates reflect not only the operation of mortgage rate ceilings but savings deposit rate ceilings as well. As noted earlier in this analysis, the saver disintermediates by shifting funds from time and savings accounts to market instruments when market rates rise above time and savings deposit rate ceilings. The institutions hit hardest by disintermediation just happen to be the ones that account for the bulk of the private mortgage lending, namely, savings and loan associations, mutual savings banks, and commercial banks.

When private mortgage lending falls off, Federal agencies tend to come to the rescue by issuing their own debt at competitive market rates and rechanneling the funds in one way or another into the mortgage market. Agency activity has accelerated, as evidenced by the fact that new mortgage credit provided by the U.S. Government and Federal agencies was roughly $2 billion higher in 1969 than in the previous tight money year, 1966. Similarly, Federal Home Loan Banks (FHLBs) rechanneled roughly $3 billion more credit through savings and loan borrowings in 1969 than in 1966.

The point is that, if rate ceilings had not interfered with the market credit allocation process, it might never have been necessary to resort to stop-gap agency financing. Agency support for the mortgage market is artificial and transitory. The FHLBs have gone to the point of asking Congress for a subsidy to cover the margin by which the rate they pay for funds borrowed in the money and bond markets exceeds the rate at which they relend the funds to savings and loan associations. If Congress decides on major subsidies to the FHLBs as a way of propping up the mortgage market, the question raised is: Why should this agency channel funds only through savings and loan associations rather than through all major mortgage financing channels?

Measures to Overcome Credit Shortages

Public policy makers are today greatly concerned with whether the financial structure is capable of allocating a sufficient amount of credit to housing, State and local governments, and other socially desirable uses. We might well ask whether mortgage and State and local government borrowers will ever get their fair share of credit in periods of monetary restraint when they are kept from bidding at competitive rates for funds by state usury ceilings and other types of rate control.

Real Estate Investment Trusts (REITs), recently established by a number of banks and insurance companies, are an innovation which helps channel funds into the credit-starved mortgage area.* In the case of banks, the REITs represent a new "off balance sheet" activity which has much promise. It is possible that banks can, through such activities, keep customers who might otherwise be attracted to other marketable securities.

A number of measures to direct credit into the areas of funds shortage have been proposed. Governor Brimmer has recently proposed that marginal reserve requirements be imposed on various types of bank loans and investments. This proposal would be aimed at inducing banks to purchase more mortgages and municipals (presumably carrying, under the Brimmer plan, low marginal reserve requirements or perhaps none at all) at the expense of business and consumer loans (presumably carrying high marginal reserve requirements).

There are several questions regarding this proposal. First, would not the plan represent another link in the regulatory chain that tends to undermine the market system for allocating credit? Would the plan be needed if rate ceilings were removed, allowing mortgage borrowers and municipalities to bid for credit market funds at competitive rates? Might not the plan hurt anti-inflation policies (as discussed earlier in connection with direct business controls), if the incentive for banks to direct funds away from business loans results in a sharp curtailment of additions to productive capacity? Finally, would not the proposal have to be applied to all lenders, not just banks, to influence the credit allocation process? In other words, would not the regulatory focus have to be on the overall debt creation process?

---

* Real Estate Investment Trusts raise funds by issuing long-term bonds and shares of beneficial interest. These issues are packaged in small denomination units, typically $2,000 or less. A $2,000 unit issued by the REIT might, for example, be equally divided between fixed interest coupon issues ($1,000) and shares of beneficial interest ($1,000). The shares of beneficial interest are linked to the earnings of the trust. The funds acquired by the REITs are invested in first mortgages, income yielding real estate, real estate equity investments, and other related assets which qualify under real estate investment trust provisions of the Internal Revenue Code so as to exempt the trusts from Federal income tax on the income which they distribute to their shareholders.

Another recently proposed method of allocating a larger proportion of credit into mortgages involves forcing pension funds to direct a specific quota of funds into the mortgage market. The threat behind this proposal is that pension funds might lose their tax-exempt status if they don't comply. This plan has all the pitfalls of any system of selective controls. Any required amount of pension fund mortgage financing would necessarily be arbitrary. Who is to decide the appropriate amount? How would such a program be administered and enforced?

There is, finally, a long-standing proposal in Congress that the Federal Reserve should channel funds into the housing area by purchasing mortgage paper. Fed officials reject this plan on the grounds that their open market purchases are for the purpose of increasing total bank reserve and credit flows rather than to selectively influence where the credit goes. In this regard, the Fed argues, any purchases of mortgage paper would, other things being equal, have to be offset by sales of Government or agency holdings so that there would be no net reserve effect.

Blame for High Interest Rates

The often-expressed view is that some kind of bank greed is responsible for high interest rates. The facts show, however, that many banks don't do so well in periods of tight money and high rates. In the case of many of the larger money market banks in particular, profits have been off in the final quarter of 1969 and so far in 1970. In the second half of last year these banks were paying a substantially higher rate for borrowed funds than that received on new loans at the prime rate.

A generally conservative stock market valuation of banks, as reflected in modest bank price-earnings ratios, also suggests that banks may not have things as good as the general public thinks. This valuation probably reflects, in large part, the fact that banks bear the brunt of monetary restraint. This fact is often overlooked in the heated debate over banking practices and structure.

The general level of interest rates is determined not by what banks alone do but by the interaction of the overall demand for and the supply of credit. Heavy credit demands by business and others in the face of recurring monetary restraint has played a significant part in pushing interest rates to record highs. Individual banks, being one type of market participant among many, must pay a competitive rate for funds or they won't be able to attract the raw material essential for their lending activity. Today this may apply more to the larger money market banks than to the smaller regional banks. But in the future, as markets become more refined and integrated, the principle will apply increasingly to all banks.

General inflationary expectations have also contributed to the surge in interest rates in the past five years. Because of the persistence of rapid price growth over the past five years, a substantial inflationary premium is built into current market rate levels. Banks stand to benefit along with the general public if inflationary pressures are eventually brought under control and price growth expectations are adjusted downward.

Banking's image is hurt by the fact that competing thrift institutions have political appeal stemming from the fact that they deal almost exclusively with housing and the small saver. There is currently a need to identify banks more closely with the same areas. REITs may help in this identification process.

Changes Ahead for Banking

Banking in the years ahead will change markedly in character. Demand deposits will continue to decline proportionately as a source of bank funds as money balances are managed more efficiently with an eye to the opportunity costs of high interest rates in the money market. The gradual development of instantaneous means of electronic payment will also contribute to the proportionate decline in demand deposits. (There also may be competition with savings institutions using payment systems like checks.)

At the same time the rate of demand deposit turnover will rise sharply as monetary receipts and payments are more closely coordinated. This trend is already underway. Over the decade from 1959 to 1969, for example, the annual rate of demand deposit turnover for New York City banks (heavily influenced by financial transactions) rose from 61 to 145.7. For banks outside New York City, demand deposit turnover increased from 27.7 to 49.2 over the same period.

Banking of the future will depend still more on the intermediation process, that is, on bidding for funds at competitive rates in one set of markets and lending these funds out at a reasonable mark-up in rates in another set of markets. This intermediation process, will, of course, be inhibited to the extent that controls such as Regulation Q prevent banks from bidding at competitive rates for funds.

Finally, there will be greater bank use of "off-balance sheet" activities, such as managing REITs or mutual funds, brokering commercial paper, or selling computer and financial counseling services. It is quite possible that banks can help the small saver earn a fair rate of return through REITs or mutual funds. Banks might also act in the role of brokers in matching corporations with surplus funds with corporations in need of funds. In selling computer and counseling services, banks can take advantage of economies of scale in equipment and staff already in operation as a part of their internal operations and customer services. Each major activity could conceivably be financed with its own specialized debt independently of bank deposit-loan operations.

Future Financial Demands

We can expect heavy demands on our financial markets in the decade of the 1970s. There will be heavy business borrowing to finance improvements in productive capacity necessary to increase efficiency and cope with high labor costs. Business will face consumer demands inflated by a shift in the age distribution of our population in favor of the high-spending (low-saving) 20- to 35-year-old age category. Adding to the pressure will be the financing of sharply accelerating housing demands (amounting to an estimated 2.6 million units per year in the 1970s versus a current housing start rate of 1.2 million units per year). The financing of rapidly increasing state and local government spending will also add to demands. State and local government spending on pollution control alone is likely to be significantly higher in the 1970s than in earlier decades.

How do we insure sufficient savings to meet the heavy capital demands of the 1970s in order to avoid accelerating inflationary pressures? It is essential that the Federal Government steer a budget course in the decade ahead far different than in the 1960s. Federal budget deficits occurred in every fiscal year but two in the 1960s, climaxing with a highly inflationary $25 billion deficit in fiscal year 1968. The Federal budget swung into a more restrictive surplus posture in fiscal year 1969, but, according to estimates, the surplus is eroding quickly. The Federal Government must, in the years ahead, insure that its expenditure growth is curtailed and receipts exceed expenditures by a comfortable margin except in periods of real economic weakness.

The financing of a string of large Federal budget deficits in the years ahead, should they occur in a high demand economy on top of heavy private credit needs, would spell trouble for our financial markets. If the Fed monetizes net new Treasury debt by "even keeling"—pumping new reserves into the banking system and allowing credit and money to expand enough to absorb the new Treasury debt at going money market rates—inflationary fiscal and monetary policies would exist side by side as they did in the late 1960s. High interest rates and distortions in the allocation of credit under our system of rate ceilings would result. If, on the other hand, the Fed begins to focus more on controlling the rate of growth of monetary aggregates, as now appears to be the case, a large Federal budget deficit in the face of a restrictive monetary policy and slow growth in money and credit would pit the Government against private borrowers in an intensive struggle for scarce funds. In these circumstances, Treasury financings may be threatened by disorderly market conditions as was the case in May 1970.

Perhaps the most promising way of insuring an adequate savings flow would be to give the small saver a greater incentive to save in the 1970s. Currently the small saver is being discriminated against: 1) Regulation Q and ceilings on rates paid by nonbank intermediaries limit the return he earns on savings and time deposits; 2) he receives below market rates on U.S. Savings Bonds; 3) he pays a penalty fee on odd-lot securities transactions; 4) the minimum denomination of Treasury bills and certain agency issues was recently raised from $1,000 to $10,000 to keep the small saver out; 5) a study prepared for the New York Stock Exchange has proposed a 160% fee increase in small-scale stock transactions. The point is that the small saver is today penalized in one way or another in virtually every financial form in which he might choose to save. Future policy must be reversed, giving the small saver more convenient savings options, higher interest rates for his savings, and perhaps even tax incentives to save.

Conclusions

The principal lesson we have learned from our recent financial experience is that the operation of rate ceilings and conventional rate rigidities create more problems than they solve. When such controls as Regulation Q and mortgage rate ceilings come into play, they inevitably cause severe distortions in credit flows. An ever-expanding patchwork of additional controls is required in the attempt to correct these distortions in the allocation of credit. The Fed's string of regulations on Euro-dollars and other sources of bank funds coming on the heels of the Regulation Q–induced CD runoff is a case in point. Similarly, the shortage of mortgage credit produced by mortgage rate ceilings has led to stopgap agency financing efforts along with a wide range of proposals to force arbitrary amounts of funds into this area.

If interest rate ceilings and rigidities were relaxed and rates in all market sectors responded more freely to credit supply and demand pressures, we could rely more on the market mechanism to allocate credit. In periods of prolonged inflationary pressures and heavy financial demands, such as we are now experiencing, we could expect that interest rates would be at high levels as they now are. But in the absence of rigid rate ceilings, mortgage borrowers and others currently short of funds because of rate ceilings would at least have the opportunity to bid competitively for their fair share of funds at the going market rates.

We have found, in the final analysis, that rate ceilings, rather than insuring low cost funds for certain groups of borrowers, act to cut off the supply of funds to these groups in periods of inflation and high interest rates. The current strains on our financial markets, one hopes, will eventually ease. The point is that rate ceilings provide no shortcut to lower interest costs. Lasting rate relief will come only after inflationary demand and cost pressures are reduced.

Linkages Between the Money Market and other Markets: Interest Rates and Institutional Ties

CHAPTER 14   Powerful linkages connect the money market, the bond market, the stock market, and the mortgage market. Yet these linkages are elusive, they function in different ways from time to time, and their operations defy accurate predictions.

One of the most important linkages is provided by interest rates: the relationship of interest rates in the money market to interest rates in other markets. We will consider this first, examining the historical trends of short-term rates and long-term rates and then studying the meaning of yield* curves which show the relationship of yields to maturities. Finally, we will consider institutional ties between the money market and other markets.

* The annual rate of return on a security when held to maturity.

Short-Term and Long-Term Interest Rates

HISTORICAL RELATIONSHIP

The chart that appears below compares short- and long-term interest rates over a long period of time. I call this a dipper chart. The short rate started quite high in the 1900s, forming a handle,

INTEREST RATES

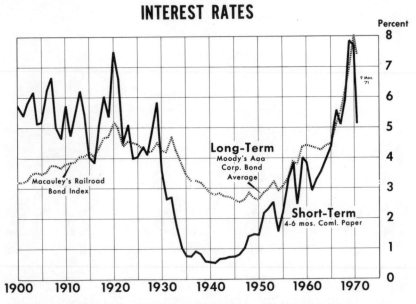

Source: Board of Governors of the Federal Reserve System. Averages of monthly figures.

then dipped almost to zero in the Great Depression of the 1930s, and finally recovered to the 1920 level in the late 1960s. Note that the short rate shows the greatest swing over this entire period. The long-term rate dropped from about 5% at the beginning of the 1920s to a low of nearly 2½% at the end of World War II and since that time has risen spectacularly. The situation in 1970 was thus similar to, although higher than, that

204

in 1920. We will comment on the meaning of this relationship later in connection with a discussion of yield curves.

SHORT-TERM RATES SHOW LARGER SWINGS IN YIELD, BUT LONG-TERM ISSUES SHOW LARGER SWINGS IN PRICE

Short-term rates characteristically show wider swings than long-term rates. In terms of price, however, the amplitude of swings works opposite to interest rates: long-term securities show the greatest swings in price for a given change in rates. To understand this, let us compare the price action of several 6% issues of varying maturities. First, we will take a one-year issue with a 6% coupon. If we assume that the yield on a one-year issue rises in the market to 7%, the price of the issue, according to the bond tables, will drop to 99.05. On the other hand, if the yield drops to 5%, the price of the issue will rise to 100.96. In other words, there is a swing of about one point in price as the issue goes from a yield of 6% to either 7% or 5%. This is logical enough because a change of one percentage point in rate over one year ought to come out to about one point in price. The reason the amount is not exactly one point is because of the impact of compound interest: the bond yield tables are computed on the basis of reinvestment of the semiannual coupon payments, and the base on which the rate is applied is not par (100) but the amount invested (99.05 or 100.96 in the examples above).

Now let us take a five-year 6% issue and make the same assumptions about changes in market yields. If such an issue goes to a 5% basis, the price will rise to 104.38; if it goes to a 7% basis, the price will drop to 95.84. Notice that the change in price approaches five points, which would be expected by taking the difference of 1% in rate and multiplying it by five years. Once again the reason the amount is not exactly five points in price is the compounding principle on which the bond tables are based.

Now, if we go to a ten-year issue, we find that a 6% coupon issue will rise to 107.79 on a 5% basis, or drop to 92.89 on a 7%

basis. Here the compounding effect is becoming more important, since the swing in price is about eight points on either side of par, even though we are talking about ten years times a one point difference in yield. For a twenty-year maturity, a 6% coupon issue would rise to 112.55 on a 5% basis, or drop to 89.32 on a 7% basis. A thirty-year maturity with a 6% coupon would rise to 115.45 on a 5% basis, or drop to 87.53 on a 7% basis.

So the principle is clear: short-term rates fluctuate more widely than do long-term rates, but long-term issues swing in price more than short-term issues with a corresponding change in yield in the market. Obviously, then, the chances of capital gain or loss are larger as maturities are lengthened.

The buyer of a security is thus faced with the need to decide whether he wants to be safe by buying a short-term issue which falls due when he expects to need funds, or wants to be venturesome by going into a longer issue where he will risk substantial capital losses but will have the chance of making substantial capital gains. Of course, if the buyer of the short-term issue expects to reinvest again and again at maturity, he is taking a risk of declining rates of return by postponing his more permanent commitment.

People sometimes talk about the "interest rate" whereas there are many interest rates—rates differentiated by maturity and by differences between the kinds of debt, risk, and other factors. But there is some fluidity among different interest rates. When I am queried about this fluidity, I usually ask the questioner to think for a moment about the connection between the market prices and yields on a one-year Treasury issue and a two-year Treasury issue. Buyers may much prefer the one-year maturity (some corporations hate to go longer), but if there is a great distortion in the spread between the one-year issue and the two-year maturity, some buyers will shift to take advantage of it.

Dealers in particular will tend to buy the issue which looks cheap and sell the one which looks dear, an operation similar to arbitraging. In fact, that term is frequently (but not quite accurately) applied to these transactions. Similarly, there is a connection between the rates on a two-year issue and a three-year issue and so on along the line to the longest issue. This means that there is a connection, however uncertain, between short-term issues in the money market and long-term issues in the bond market.

The Yield Curve

Now let us put a spotlight on the interest rate structure for one day to show the relationship of yields for various maturities. I have chosen December 31, 1960, to show conditions during a period of easy money. (Later on, we will look at a chart when money conditions were much tighter.) The chart presented here is a "yield curve" based on market yields of outstanding United States Government securities for that day. The horizontal scale shows the years in which various issues of U.S. Government securities mature, and the vertical scale shows the level of interest rates, that is, the market yields to maturity. The plotting points are located by reading along the horizontal scale to the proper maturity date for a given U.S. Government issue and then reading up the vertical scale to the market yield for the issue. A line is drawn through these dots to form the yield curve.

Of course, the shape of this curve keeps changing from day to day, depending on conditions in the money and bond markets. The chart for December 31, 1960, reflected conditions during a period of slight recession. As has been true of such periods, there was a fairly steep upward slope in the yield curve at that time. The shortest issues of Treasury bills were yielding about 2.20% but the rate was about 2.65% for the one-year issue. Then, there were successive increases at two years, three years, four years, and so on, with the yield curve leveling out in the longer maturity range.

An investor at that time could study the yield curve to assist him in selecting securities. Some issues may seem out of line.

For example, the 11/15/64 note offered a higher yield than the curve, and therefore appeared to be a better buy than adjacent issues. But other issues, such as the 2/15/66's, yield less than the curve and may be considered to be somewhat high-priced. If we look at the longer maturities on the yield chart, we find

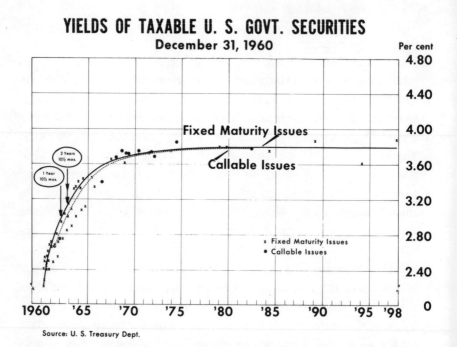

YIELDS OF TAXABLE U. S. GOVT. SECURITIES
December 31, 1960

Source: U. S. Treasury Dept.

that the issue maturing in 1995 is yielding only about 3.60%, while the yield curve at that point is around 3.80%. The third longest issue, due in 1990, is yielding about 3.85%, compared with the curve of about 3.80%. Examination of these details suggests that the 1995 issue is overpriced and the 1990 issue looks relatively more attractive. Variations of this kind, however, can sometimes be explained by differences in coupon rates, call periods,* size of issue, and other factors which have lasting effects. For example, most of the issues maturing after 1980 are

* That is, the period during which an issue is subject to call by the issuing agency for payment prior to maturity.

favored and sought after by trustees for estate tax purposes (they are accepted at par in payment of estate taxes). Buying in particular has been concentrated in the 1995 issue because it carries the lowest price. It has therefore sold for many years at yield levels below the yield curve. In addition, temporary supply and demand conditions sometimes cause quirks.

An experienced portfolio man would be watching these yield curves and might also keep charts showing spreads from day to day between issues of comparable maturity. A comparison of such charts could throw very definite light on which issues appeared to be better buys at any given moment.

Portfolio men know that it is of the greatest importance to use the tool of marginal analysis. The significance of a small change may be enormous as a new development takes place. For example, if supply and demand in a farmer's market are equal at one hundred bushels, we have equilibrium. But suppose that there is one bushel less, so that ninety-nine bushels have to meet one hundred bushels of demand. The change is small but one less bushel at the margin may cause significant repercussions in the market. Prices may go up by sizable amounts simply because each buyer tries to protect his position now that there is a shortage. Contrariwise, if the supply rises after a bit from ninety-nine bushels to 101, while demand stays constant at a hundred bushels, the difference may be like that between night and day. A position of shortage has suddenly shifted to a position of excess supply. Surprisingly large changes in price occur under such conditions in many markets and in the money market in particular. Continuing study of yield curves helps pinpoint changes that are occurring.

So much for variations from the December 31, 1960 yield curve. Let us now turn to the question of whether this would have been a good time to buy long-term bonds. We will not use the benefit of hindsight, but rather attempt to reason the way someone at that time would have been forced to do. The question we are trying to answer is whether it would be wise to buy a long-term bond (after all, it would yield more than short-term

209

issues) or whether there might be considerable risk in the current level of the market, in which case it might be better to invest temporarily in a short-term issue (even at a lower rate of return), hoping to buy a long-term bond later on after the price had declined.

Since this was a period of slight recession, the experienced investor knew that one reason the yield curve was so steep was that investors were showing more willingness to buy short-term issues than long-term issues. He knew, too, that the Federal Reserve was following a fairly easy money policy which generally meant that it was buying short-term issues to improve the banks' reserve position and that banks in turn were also buying short-term issues to invest some of the new funds made available to them. There must have been some investor reluctance to move out into the long-term issues because of the fear that a price decline would occur later on.

Suppose then we consider purchase of a thirty-year issue to yield 3.85%. This issue has a 3½% coupon and a price of 93.80. Thirty years to maturity is a long period, and we know that if interest rates were to rise it would take only a small change in the level of yields to produce a large change on the downside in price. A glance at a table of bond values would show the price on a twenty-nine-year maturity (that is, one year later) at various assumed yield levels:

Yield	Price
3.90% = 93.09
4.00% = 91.46
4.25% = 87.57

An increase in yield from the original 3.85% to 3.90% a year later would mean a loss in price of .71 points; 4% would involve a loss of 2.34 points, and 4.25% would mean a loss of 6.23 points.

So we have the question of deciding whether to take 2.65% on a one-year issue, 2.90% on a two-year issue, or reach for the 3.85% on the thirty-year issue (or something in between). This

Practical Workout of Net Return
on Treasury Issues Purchased in 1960 Recession and Held One Year

	One-Year Issue	Two-Year Issue	Thirty-Year Issue
1. Market yield—All coupons 3½%	2.65%	2.90%	3.85%
2. Purchase price	$100.83	$101.16	$ 93.80
3. Premium or discount (d) to be amortized	$.83	$1.16	$6.20(d)
4. Years to maturity	1 yr.	2 yrs.	30 yrs.
5. Annual amortization of premium or accretion of discount	$ − .83	$ − .58	$ + .21
6. Book price [1] after one year	$100.00	$100.58	$ 94.01
7. Assumed market yield after one year	—	3.50%	4.25%
8. Computed market price after one year	$100.00	$100.00	$ 87.57
9. Capital loss	0	$ − .58	$ − 6.44
10. Annual return: Coupon interest	$ 3.50	$ 3.50	$ 3.50
Amortization of premium	− .83	− .58	
Accretion of discount			+ .21
	$ 2.67	$ 2.92	$ 3.71
Capital loss (from above)	0	− .58	− 6.44
Net annual return	$ 2.67	$ 2.34	− 2.73
11. Net rate of return on original investment	2.65% [2]	2.31%	− 2.91%

[1] The term "book price" refers to bondholders' records of cost as adjusted for amortization of premium or accretion of discount.

[2] Computed by dividing net annual return of $2.67 by purchase price of $100.83.

calls for a comparison of the difference in yield between these issues and the possible losses which might occur if interest rates should rise and prices decline. Let us assume that we are optimistic about the business outlook and expect a much higher yield curve one year later with interest rates as follows: 3¼% for a twelve-month maturity, 3½% for a two-year maturity, and 4¼% for a twenty-nine-year maturity. We can then calculate the results for the three issues. The comparative figures for a hundred-dollar investment, assuming coupons in each case are 3½%, are worked out in the table on page 211.

This table shows that the two-year issue would work out with a return of 2.31%, compared with the market yield of 2.90% because a capital loss would offset part of the yield. The thirty-year issue would give a return of minus 2.91% because a capital loss would amount to well over the entire original yield of 3.85%. The one-year issue, however, would have no capital loss, so the yield of 2.65% would be realized.

Clearly, the higher yield in buying either the two-year issue or the thirty-year bond, as compared with the one-year issue, would therefore not materialize if the anticipated decline in the bond price takes place at the end of a year in which rates rose. Buyers who expect this prefer short issues to long-term bonds and are pushing the shorter maturities to higher prices. They are willing to take lower yields while they wait to invest on a longer-term basis. If interest rates do rise, they do not want to get stuck with the longer issues, so they feel safer with a lower yield on short issues until the rise in interest rates has materialized.

Borrowers will also understand this. Many borrowers will try to borrow through long-term issues, even though short-term rates are lower, because they think long-term rates will rise later on.

Riding the Yield Curve

Now let us look more closely at the short-term issues on December 31, 1960. Compare the yield on the curve at one year of

2.65% with the higher yield of 3.15% for a maturity of 2 years 10½ months. (See double arrow on chart on p. 208.) A portfolio manager who wanted a one-year investment might decide to buy the 2 years 10½ month issue and plan to sell it a year hence on the theory that he would get a higher net return than the 2.65% on the one-year issue. This is known as riding the yield curve, *i.e.*, from 2 years 10½ months maturity to 1 year 10½ months. Our investor would, of course, be gambling that the yield curve would be basically unchanged at the end of a year (unlike the example we considered just above). He could read the curve to see what a 1 year 10½ month issue would yield if the curve were unchanged: the single arrow on the yield curve shows a reading of a 3.00% yield for a maturity of 1 year 10½ months. The results of his speculation would work out as follows:

Assumption: Purchase on 12/31/60 of 4⅞ % note maturing on 11/15/63 at a price of 104.70 to yield 3.15%.

Question: What would net return be if yield curve remained unchanged at the end of one year so that 1 year 10½ month maturity would yield 3.00%?

1. Purchase price		$104.70
2. Premium to be amortized	$4.70	
3. Years to maturity	2.89 yrs.	
4. Annual amortization of premium		− 1.63
5. Book price at end of one year		$103.07
6. Computed market price of issue at end of one year		
at yield of 3.00%		$103.39
7. Capital gain		$ .32

8. Annual return: Coupon interest	$4.875	
Amortization of premium	−1.63	
Net income	$3.245	
Capital gain	+ .32	
Net annual return	$3.565	
Net rate of return on original		
investment of $104.70	3.405%	

The calculations show that riding the yield curve for one year would give 3.405%, because of a modest capital gain on top of the original yield, compared with 2.65% for a one-year issue. It would thus be profitable, if the assumption proves correct that the yield curve would not change.

Now let us see what actually happened. To illustrate this, consider the yield curve for the end of December 1961. Yields generally moved upward during the year and the yield curve became somewhat less steep. Let us see how the investor riding the yield curve for one year would have fared with his investment in a 2 year 10½ month maturity. The curve for December 31, 1961, shows a reading of 3.46% (see arrow) for an issue due in 1 year 10½ months. Sale at this yield would produce a net return of 2.593%.

1. Purchase price		$104.70
2. Premium to be amortized	$4.70	
3. Years to maturity	2.89 yrs.	
4. Annual amortization of premium		− 1.63
5. Book price at end of one year		$103.07
6. Market price of issue at end of one year at yield of 3.46%		$102.54
7. Capital loss		$ − .53

8. Annual return: Coupon interest	$4.875	
Amortization of premium	− 1.63	
Net income	$3.245	
Capital loss	− .53	
Net annual return	$2.715	
9. Net rate of return on original investment of $104.70	2.593%	

The 2.593% net rate of return would be lower than the expected return of 3.405% as calculated previously. It would also be lower than the 2.65% yield on a one-year issue on the December 31, 1960, curve. In short, the gamble of riding the yield curve would not have paid off.

Riding the yield curve is obviously speculative because the expected profit can turn into a loss if the curve should shift to a higher level with a change in monetary conditions. In theory, the curve can be ridden at any maturity area but the risk rises as longer maturities are used because of the greater price swings.

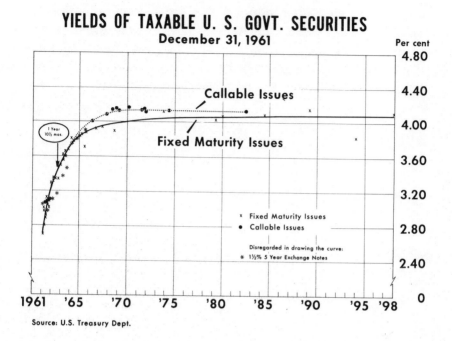

YIELDS OF TAXABLE U. S. GOVT. SECURITIES
December 31, 1961

Source: U.S. Treasury Dept.

It is very important to weigh the risks when attempting to ride the yield curve. If monetary policy becomes easier after a security is purchased, security prices will rise, but if monetary policy becomes more restrictive, security prices will decline and the whole basis for the transaction will become invalid.

The Humped Yield Curve of Tight Money

Consider now the yield curve for September 30, 1969. It looks quite different from the one we have just been considering. There is a peak at the beginning and then a long downward slope. The yield for a one-year issue is about 8.05%, the yield on a two-year issue about 8.13% and the yield for a twenty-nine-year bond about 6.40%.

215

This type of yield curve is characteristic of periods of tight money and high interest rates. It reflects not only restrictive monetary policies but also variations in the supply of new issues in the various maturity ranges. The Treasury could not issue bonds because of the 4¼ % rate ceiling and had to limit its direct financing to notes with a maximum maturity of seven years. The

YIELDS OF TAXABLE U. S. GOVT. SECURITIES
September 30, 1969

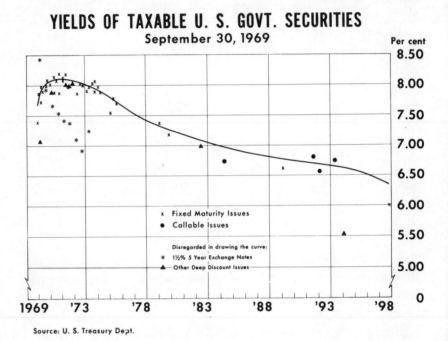

Source: U. S. Treasury Dept.

added volume of short-term maturities contributed to higher short-term rates.

I like to think of a curve like this as a skeptical curve about business in the year ahead. It seems to say quite clearly that investors do not believe it: they do not believe that conditions causing interest rates to be so high will continue. If they did, they would be satisfied to buy short-term issues to obtain the higher yields and would avoid longer-term issues; this action would tend to knock long-term market prices down (and interest rates up) until the yield curve became more or less flat. Instead, to a degree, they are buying the long-term bonds partly because they are attractive in yield and partly because they do not expect market losses later on; rather, they expect market gains whenever business does weaken. Long-term borrowers are holding back on offering bonds with long maturities and are paying higher rates for short-term money, in the expectation of refunding these short-term loans at lower rates later on.

On September 30, 1969, the attitude of many investors was that the monetary situation was in a temporary bind. The Federal Reserve had been following a tight monetary policy because of the overheated economy with strong inflationary expectations. Bank liquidity was severely impaired. To many, it certainly looked like the kind of situation which would not continue for very long. Moreover, if investors considered the whole situation as temporary, they would be expecting the yield curve to drop down all along the line, sooner or later, and would expect capital gains to occur in bonds. Remember that the longer bonds would show the greater gains. This means that if investors did buy short-term issues and expected the yields to be available on renewal when the short-term issues ran out, they would not only be wrong on that count, but would then find that they missed the capital gains potential occurring as bond prices rose.

Preferences for Short Issues

Now let us stop to review some of our findings about interest rates. We pointed out that when the yield curve has a sharp upward slant some investors are saying that they think interest rates are going to rise, so they are reluctant to buy long-term bonds and are emphasizing the purchase of short-term issues even though the interest return is well below the return on long-term issues. Using the terminology of John Maynard Keynes, this might be called the "speculative" demand for short-term issues.* In the 1930s the urge for liquidity was so strong that investors were willing to earn next to nothing temporarily on short-term holdings rather than take the risk of long-term investments at historically low rates of return. Also the money market at that time was clearly attracting investors from all sectors of the economy who were saying that they preferred to hold short-term issues rather than invest in plants and equipment or spend for other purposes. The money market was thus a great reservoir of liquid funds which investors were satisfied to hold, in spite of the lack of return, because they were simply unwilling to make other commitments at the time.

We have seen, however, that in 1969 there was a downslope in the yield curve and that this indicated the opposite kind of a situation. Some investors were saying that they expected interest rates to go down. They were buying long-term securities rather than short-term securities even though the latter had higher returns. The reason had to be that they did not expect short-term rates to stay where they were and therefore felt that it was desirable to lock up some funds at the unprecedently high interest rates in the long-term market. The speculative motive for liquidity, in other words, was low in their minds at this time.

How about borrowers? Were they reacting in a thoroughly consistent way with this diagnosis? The financial press reported almost daily that borrowers canceled long-term borrowings because they did not want to lock themselves in at the high rates involved in long-term issues. They were expressing the opinion that interest rates would go down later on and that temporary borrowing was better than permanent borrowing while they awaited a more suitable time for funding their obligations. Of course, many borrowers disagreed or found that short-term borrowing was not feasible and went ahead with long-term borrowing even though rates were high.

* The asset choice posed by Keynes was actually between money and long-term bonds. But the speculative demand for short-term issues to take advantage of swings in rates on longer-term issues is analogous to the speculative demand for money.

Here we see that the money market is interlinked inevitably, not only with the bond market, but also with the economic decision-making process of consumers, lenders, and all other segments of the economy. Let anyone assume that it is better to borrow or invest short-term for reasons of confidence or expectation of change in the future, and the money market is involved. Contrariwise, if the assumption is that investing or borrowing should be done in long-term maturities, the money market will be affected as action moves to the bond market.

Yet in the end, there is a certain amount of segmentation in the market. Some investors, lenders, and savers do typically confine their operations to either the short-term market or the long-term market. For example, the insurance companies generally are not important investors in the short-term market but concentrate their buying in the long-term market. Typically, corporations managing their cash position will stick to short-term instruments including short-term Government issues, CDs, etc., as we have noted.*

But, as moods change because of economic and psychological developments, even the typical investor will alter his habits. Thus, in the 1930s, long-term investors held massive amounts of short-term investments because of their fear of the future. And in 1969, some typical long-term borrowers were borrowing in the short-term market or were leaning on bank loans because of their unwillingness to commit themselves to long-term debt.

In recent years, there has also been a pronounced shift on the part of pension funds away from investments as a rule in long-term bonds to stocks. Pension funds do not buy many short-term instruments and therefore are not heavy investors in the money

---

* Banks are motivated to hold short-term issues partly because of liquidity needs and partly because some supervisory authorities impose higher bank capital requirements for securities with longer maturities. Thus the formula used by the Federal Reserve Bank of New York calls for bank capital of 5% against U.S. Government issues of more than five years maturity as against zero for shorter issues. Requirements against municipal issues are 5% for issues due in less than five years and 12% for longer maturities.

market. But they have held large amounts of bonds which of course have suffered tremendous price declines as interest rates have risen in recent years. There has thus been real disenchantment with holding bonds and a trend to purchase and hold equities, because equities have in general done very well over the last twenty years. There has been some swing back to bonds, however, as overheating in the economy has been reduced and bond prices have begun to firm.

Linkages between the Federal Reserve, the Money Market, and the Bond and Stock Markets

In the chapter on the Federal Reserve, we noted that the monetary authorities like to operate in the money market because of close links to that market and its links to other financial markets. Let us examine the series of links which would operate in a period of increasing monetary restraint.

1. The Federal Reserve would sell off some of its holdings of U.S. Government securities, thus tending to reduce bank reserves.

2. Dealers in Government securities would react by endeavoring to reduce inventories.

Expectations of dealers (and other market participants) concerning future money rates and securities prices can be strongly influenced by such action on the part of the Federal Reserve. If market participants feel that this move by the Federal Reserve is the start of an effort to tighten monetary conditions, they would begin to anticipate the effects of such a program on securities prices, and would start to reduce their inventories of securities in an attempt to prevent future losses. The result would thus be a kind of reinforcing of the downward effect on market prices (rise in interest rates) which had begun as a result of Federal Reserve sales. All maturities of securities could ultimately be affected.

Linkages between various markets are facilitated because some

220

dealers are in other lines of business as well as making a market in Government securities. Bank dealers in Government securities have close connections with all markets pertinent to commercial banking activities. The nonbank dealers also have antennae which reach out into many markets, since they are active in such diverse instruments as CDs, bankers' acceptances, Government agency issues, corporate bonds, municipal bonds, and stocks.

3. Commercial banks would be tightened by the reduction in their reserves induced by the Federal Reserve.

The sale of securities by the Federal Reserve would create reserve deficiencies initially at those banks whose Federal Reserve accounts were reduced as their customers paid for the securities. The reduced availability of bank reserves might induce these banks to cut back on the financing of dealers' holdings of Government securities or other loans. These banks might also attempt to sell securities or attract more funds through CDs, thus competing more aggressively with other money market securities. Alternatively, they might step up efforts to raise funds in the Euro-dollar market.

4. The increase in short-term interest rates would tend to spread out to other interest rates.

There is a definite although variable connection, not only between different maturities, as we have noted, but also between different types of security issues. This relationship originates from the fact that buyers can shift from one type of security to another if they wish. For example, if the yield on Government securities gets out of line with corporate issues, some buyers will consider shifting from one to the other.

It follows that Federal Reserve action, or any other development in the money market, affects interest rates and tends to set up some chain reaction across the entire span of interest rates, both across the range of maturities and the range of qualities. Thus, a rise in the bill rate in a period following a recession might have an upward rate impact that spreads throughout the short-term money market and on out to rates on long-term Government bonds, corporate bonds, and municipal bonds, and to mortgages.

5. *Long-term borrowers would tend to borrow less.*

When the rates on bonds rise, this would tend to discourage some borrowers from selling new bonds to raise funds,* and it might also discourage them from undertaking certain projects because the costs would now be too high, after taking account of the higher interest rates. It is often argued that corporations are not affected by higher interest rates because the projects they wish to undertake are so important and so carefully analyzed through financial budgeting that the interest cost effects after taxes and consideration of inflationary prospects are small and therefore any given rise is of little significance. While this is undoubtedly true in a great many cases, it is also an oversimplification because some projects are always on the edge of being postponed or canceled, and they will be the first to be hit by higher interest rates.

High rates tend to cause deferment of some projects of municipal governments and home builders, although the former may borrow short in the form of bond anticipation notes rather than postpone vitally needed facilities. Many municipal governments do postpone construction projects when interest rates rise, however, sometimes simply to await lower rates and sometimes because of established legal ceilings on rates. Buyers of homes may postpone a purchase, buy smaller homes, or not buy at all because required debt service must be kept within their capability.

* An exception to this generalization occurred in 1966–67. After the credit crunch, corporations borrowed heavily in the bond market, despite rising rates to record high levels, in order to bolster their financial positions. Liquidity had dropped sharply due to heavy capital expenditures and accelerated tax payments. Corporations funded short-term debt and restructured their capital to place themselves in a better position to meet another crunch if it should develop. A similar trend developed in 1970–71. In addition many corporations expected such heavy needs for new funds over the years ahead that they decided against any deferment of financing.

6. *Long-term lenders would tighten their operations.*

Customers who are turned down by commercial banks often go to other institutions to seek credit. A reserve squeeze on the commercial banks would therefore tend to sop up the funds of other lenders. There is thus a constant spreading of the symptoms from commercial banks to other institutions and from the money market to other markets. Also, if it is difficult to find enough funds to meet loan demands, there would be a persistent need by investors to liquidate securities. As market prices decline on securities, capital losses (whether "realized" by sales or not) would develop, so that nonbank institutions, which might *not* have been tight until recently, would find that they are becoming reluctant to sell to raise funds because they do not wish to take the resultant losses.

7. *The restraining impact of financial conditions on important business and consumer demands would, in turn, tend to depress business sales, production, employment, and profits.*

A tightening of money and rising interest rates would be expected to slow business activity generally with important effects on production and employment and on profits. The business and consumer mood would probably be much less exuberant and lead even to broad pessimism.

8. *The stock market would probably weaken as economic activity drops off and profits are hurt.*

Stock prices might decline at the first hint of or in anticipation of such a course of events. Also when money is tight, yields on money market instruments and bonds would rise (prices fall). This in turn would make stock prices seem relatively higher (yields lower) and stocks might be sold. Moreover, if money is tight, it would be more difficult to get loans to purchase stocks and the carrying costs would rise.

In the foregoing remarks, the emphasis has been on the effects of tightness of money. But it is clear that the reverse is also true. Purchases of securities by the Federal Reserve tend to have opposite effects to what has just been described. Dealers would be encouraged to buy securities with the hope of profits ahead. Bank reserves would be increased and banks would seek to put more funds to work. If the commercial banks are easy, it would be transmitted to the entire money market and the built-in linkages would carry this ease to the bond market and to the stock market. Bond prices would tend to rise for all maturities and interest rates generally to decline. Long-term borrowers would tend to borrow more. Long-term lenders would tend to open up their lending and investing activities. Economic activity would show an upturn and probably send the stock market moving up.

Sometimes the Federal Reserve System itself provides a strong direct link between the money market and the bond market when it engages in open market operations in intermediate- or longer-term issues. One purpose of such an action may be an attempt to ameliorate a disorderly bond market. Another may be to put bank reserves into the bank system at a time when it is necessary for reasons associated with the international balance of payments to avoid buying short-term issues with attendant downward pressure on bill yields.

Federal Reserve Policy: The Monetarists vs. the Navigators

CHAPTER 15   In Chapter 6 we described the tools used by the Federal Reserve to control the money thermostat. I think the idea of a thermostat is useful in this context, but it may oversimplify. In fact, there is of course no one thermostat; rather there are a group of financial and economic barometers and thermometers. And there is a raging argument over which ones to emphasize, or even to rely on exclusively, in setting policy.

The Monetarists have a simple idea: look at one dial only—namely, money supply—defined in a specific manner (discussed later). They want money supply to grow at a steady predetermined rate. They do not want the Fed to jiggle money growth on the basis of all those other dials, like money market conditions, interest rates, business conditions, the impact of fiscal policy, inflation problems, banking and credit developments, balance of payments problems, etc., largely because they think the effort to do so creates more problems than it solves.

The Fed, on the other hand, is pragmatic; it looks at many dials and from time to time changes their relative importance.

This is because it emphasizes the need for some discretion in managing matters. As I know of no commonly accepted name for this approach it will be convenient to coin a term, "the Navigators," for it. The image here is of navigators on a sailboat constantly adjusting the sails to arrive at the desired destination in the best shape possible.

The money market has a vital concern with the controversy between the Monetarists and the Navigators primarily because interest rate volatility is much greater under one theory than the other. Governor Rasminsky of the Bank of Canada stated it this way before a Parliamentary Committee: "Very large fluctuations in interest rates and probably in exchange rates would have to be accepted as a price for obtaining relative smoothness in the growth of the money supply." [1]

The Monetarists' Case for Steady Growth of Money

Professor Milton Friedman of the University of Chicago has long contended that steady growth in the money supply would yield better and more predictable results than irregular growth resulting from Federal Reserve discretionary management.[2] This proposal is founded upon two basic tenets: (1) changes in the money supply are the primary determinant of changes in economic activity, and (2) the Federal Reserve can effectively control changes in the money stock over a period of time. Friedman asserts, in effect, that the Federal Reserve will contribute best to a steady growth in economic activity by stabilizing the rate of growth in the money supply.*

As Chairman of the Joint Economic Committee, Senator Prox-

---

* The Monetarists seem to believe this could be as automatic as the supply of currency in circulation. Before 1913 the supply of currency was relatively fixed and demand fluctuated. Now the supply fluctuates with demand depending on business and individual need. What was once a major problem in monetary policy is no longer a concern of the monetary authorities.

mire once proposed a modified steady growth program. He urged the Federal Reserve to maintain the growth of the money supply between 2% and 6% annually on a quarter-to-quarter basis and said that if it is below or above that range, the Fed should provide an explanation for Congress. The argument is, it would seem, that this would give some room for discretionary management but would tend to eliminate extremes. After debate, the Joint Economic Committee backed the Proxmire proposal.

Why 2% to 6%? Presumably the figures relate to growth of GNP. Real growth of GNP (ex price inflation) over annual periods has typically been in the range of 2% to 6% in the postwar period, except in recessions. It rarely exceeded 6% except in the Korean and Vietnam periods. Critics of the Federal Reserve sometimes contend that growth in the money supply above 6% is almost certain to be inflationary because it will exceed the potential for real growth in GNP. On the other side, the argument for a 2% minimum probably stems from critics' charges that the Federal Reserve is sometimes too tight and thus helps to bring on recessions. The point is that wide swings in the growth rate of the money supply are held to have a destabilizing effect on economic activity.

The Navigators' Case for Discretionary Management

We have seen in earlier chapters how the Federal Reserve reacted in policy decisions to changing domestic and international conditions. An ever-unfolding vista of changes gives substance to the Navigators' case for discretionary management of money. One of the basic rules, as William McChesney Martin, Chairman of the Federal Reserve Board from 1951 to 1970, has said many times, is that the Fed should lean against the wind. Thus, if the economy is sluggish, the Fed should take more expansionary steps; if inflationary pressures are paramount, the Fed should take more deflationary actions. The late Professor Jacob Viner of Princeton University, a long-time adviser in Washington, once told me that in his opinion the Fed should be so flexible that each day it would decide what it should have done yesterday and thereupon proceed to do it.

Let us enumerate some of the traditional arguments cited by the Navigators' school. Perhaps the most important factor is that there is a constant ebbing and flowing of money market pressures reflecting changes in business activity, Federal budget deficits, balance of payments problems, and psychological and other factors (*e.g.*, shifts in expectations of real growth, shifts in the political climate, etc.). The Navigator would argue that efforts to follow rigid and unyielding rules for money supply growth in the face of sudden shifts in winds and currents in the money market would result in sharp destabilizing swings in interest rates that would severely impair the functioning of the financial markets. The only answer, according to the Navigator, is to try to cushion the effect of such swings on interest rates. When business activity or psychology drops off sharply and threatens to send interest rates into a downspin, the Navigator would act to slow down monetary growth in order to lessen the downward pressure on rates. Conversely, when a surge in business activity and related credit demands threatens to push interest rates sharply higher, the Navigator would act to speed up the rate of growth in money and credit. The Navigators' approach to monetary management differs from the Friedmanite approach in that, in the short run at least, swings in growth of money will be wider and swings in interest rates will be narrower.

Note, however, that Friedman's monetary school contends that the arguments just cited are irrelevant. Friedman's group says that efforts to correct such matters through discretionary money management have not been successful; they have simply introduced new problems. There are many complications anyway: e.g., there will not be a close relationship between the Federal deficit and the money supply if the deficit is financed out of savings rather than by the creation of new money.

Then there is the question of money definition. The basic
definition of money supply is private demand deposits (less
items in process of collection) plus currency outside banks. A
broader definition brings in time deposits of commercial banks
only and this was chosen by Professor Friedman and Anna J.
Schwartz, largely for convenience, in an authoritative study
published a few years ago.[3] The choice of definition may bring
different statistical results, as George Garvy and Martin R. Blyn
bring out clearly in their "The Velocity of Money."[4] A chart in
that study shows that velocity of the money supply as customarily defined (demand deposits plus currency) doubled during
the twenty years ending in 1968, while velocity of the money
supply defined very broadly—including time deposits of thrift
institutions as well as commercial banks—was virtually unchanged. The significance of this would seem to be that, as
interest rates rose, depositors economized on demand deposits
and currency and increased their appetites for time deposits
generally.

It is not surprising, then, that Federal Reserve Governor
Dewey Daane should point out "that money demand can be
partly a by-product of changes in institutional patterns of money
uses—which the Federal Reserve must always take into account,
and which illustrate that no single set target for money supply
increases is desirable."[5] Such changes are reflected in variations
in the velocity of money.

There are also continuing statistical problems. In 1969, for
example, the money supply (narrow definition) series was revised twice: first to correct for the downward bias produced,
under previously employed accounting and reporting procedures,
by the growth in cash items generated by Euro-dollar transactions of the large banks; second, to make the periodically scheduled benchmark adjustments in order to correct previous estimates of the deposits and vault cash of nonmember banks, as
well as new seasonal factors. In 1970, the series was revised
again: the usual corrections to new benchmark levels and

229

seasonal adjustments and a sizable revision to correct for a downward bias that had developed with the sharp expansion of payments flowing through United States branches, agencies, and affiliates of foreign banks and of Edge Act * corporations which were being cleared through New York banks. The effect of these revisions was to raise the level of the money supply, indicating a greater growth than had previously been estimated.

Special factors too may suddenly arise. Consider the second quarter of 1968 when the money supply rose rapidly at an annual rate of almost 9%. This was just prior to passage of the tax increase-spending restriction bill at the end of June 1968. Such an expansion was hardly characteristic of an avowed policy of restraint, and charges were being made that the Federal Reserve had been overly easy in providing reserves. However, there is considerable evidence that a major cause of the increase in the money supply was the extremely high volume of trading in stocks and the "fails" in deliveries which occurred when sellers did not deliver stocks on time to buyers. Higher deposits resulted as charges against them were delayed by bottlenecks.

Senator Proxmire, I suppose, would say his formula is flexible enough to meet the problems noted, since the Federal Reserve can go outside the 2–6% limits if necessary or if it makes a mistake, but must then explain the circumstances to Congress.

An Emerging Compromise

It is interesting to review directives of the Federal Open Market Committee (FOMC) in recent years as new emphasis was gradually given to monetary and credit aggregates in the formulation and conduct of open market policy. Up until 1966, the Committee's operating instructions to the Manager of the System Open Market Account usually called for achieving specific

* Banking corporations organized by U.S. banks specifically to finance and stimulate foreign trade and for similar purposes.

money market conditions until the next FOMC meeting. For example, a typical directive read: ". . . system open market operations until the next meeting of the Committee shall be conducted with a view to maintaining about the same conditions in the money market that have prevailed since the last meeting of the Committee." [6]

As the Federal Open Market Committee was meeting every three or four weeks to set policy for the Manager of the Open Market Account, a given market tone was noted as a key objective. The traditional *modus operandi* was that the Account Manager watched the market tone and provided or absorbed reserves necessary (through open market operations) to help maintain or achieve the desired objective. The market tone was evidenced by the rate on Federal funds, the volume of member bank borrowings at the discount window, net free or borrowed reserves, and at times the three-month Treasury bill rate.

Beginning in mid-1966 through February 1970, there was added to the directive noted above a so-called proviso clause, which sometimes read "provided, however, that operations shall be modified in the light of unusual liquidity pressures or of any apparently significant deviations of bank credit from current expectations." [7] Such expectations represented the staff's estimate of the growth in a selected aggregate, usually the bank credit proxy, that would result from specified money market conditions. The bank credit proxy is the best currently available indicator of the volume of bank credit, although it is measured from the liabilities side of the banking balance sheet. It is based on total member bank deposits subject to reserve requirements adjusted to include nondeposit liabilities such as Euro-dollar borrowings and commercial paper issued by bank holding companies or affiliates. The Committee thus considered each time whether market conditions and interest rates should be given less attention, with greater attention being directed to growth of the monetary aggregates.

Then in March 1970 the emphasis changed again, when the

directive read ". . . the Committee desires to see moderate growth in money and bank credit over the months ahead. System open market operations until the next meeting of the Committee shall be conducted with a view to maintaining money market conditions consistent with that objective." [8] Subsequent directives of the FOMC have occasionally somewhat altered the relative emphasis on monetary growth vis-à-vis market conditions, but there is no doubt that monetary aggregates are much more important than a few years ago. This is quite a concession to the Monetarists, even though it does not go all the way to looking only at one dial, as I mentioned earlier, and does not imply that a fixed, steady rate of growth should be sought.

But the issue remains. The Monetarists are not satisfied—in 1971 they contended for a time that money supply was rising too rapidly. Some other critics in the Administration felt it was not rising rapidly enough. Various correlations between monetary growth and economic activity were cited, leading Chairman Burns to refer to some of the critics of the Federal Reserve as the Great Simplifiers.[9]

In any event, the Fed is still struggling with its many dials, including those on interest rates and market tone. Press reports say that in the summer of 1971 a Federal Reserve Board Economist* reported that the money supply had to be permitted to grow faster than 6% in the first quarter of the year or there would have been a swing above 17% in short-term rates. He also said that for social as well as political reasons it was impossible to accept astronomical rises in interest rates. So, we may say that interest rates remain a key aspect of the issue.

In the final analysis, it is important to stand back and view the Monetarist debate with perspective. I am a great admirer of Milton Friedman. He always argues with skill that free markets do a better job than Government regulators in making essential decisions bearing on the allocation and use of economic resources. However, the case can be made that regulating money

* James L. Pierce, paper delivered on June 25, 1971, at Konstanz University.

is different than regulating railroads or widgets; Allan Sproul, the former President of the Federal Reserve Bank of New York, once said that "money will not manage itself."

It is encouraging that there is emerging at the Fed a consensus view which represents a compromise between the Monetarists' approach and the older Federal Reserve practice which focused on money market conditions and involved a considerable amount of short-term rate fixing. Due in large part to Professor Friedman's influence, more attention is being given to monetary aggregates. This is as it should be. Money may not be the only thing that matters, but most people would agree that it does exert a very important impact on the general course of economic activity. Thus, in practice, the Fed is feeling its way toward a more flexible approach in its discretionary management.

Attitude of the Money Market

Did the money market prefer the old managed system which had tended to create wide swings in money growth but provided more stability in interest rates between changes in Federal Reserve posture than we have had thereafter? I am not sure. After all, the swings in Federal Reserve attitude were sometimes so violent that shock tremors were felt by all money market participants. In the late summer of 1966, tight money threatened to immobilize the money market. In 1969, some reactions to tight money were worse, while others were less violent. So the traditional system was sometimes very hard on the money market.

I was deeply impressed with the resiliency of the money market both in those periods and more recently as the Fed has endeavored to place more emphasis on monetary growth. I am confident that the market will be able to handle future developments whatever they may be. After all, the Fed may go further toward the Monetarists or it may retreat toward its old approach. Perhaps it will do both—at different times—as it becomes ever more sophisticated in its job.

New Perspective on CDs:
Some Major Questions

CHAPTER 16   The creation of negotiable CDs for corporations brought forth not only a new market instrument for banks, but also a controversial one. In earlier chapters we have described how the CD was developed and how it operates in the money market. Now it is time to consider some of the major questions which have been raised about CDs. Some economists question whether the banking system really can grow through the use of CDs. Also, some observers ask whether they do not attract primarily what is known as "hot money." Some people also ask whether they are really profitable to banks. Let us consider these questions in some detail in order to try to provide new perspective on CDs.

Can the Banking System Grow through CDs?

Whether the commercial banking system can grow through CDs is a question which is both important and complex. It is important because the thesis favoring the CD has been, as we have noted earlier, that it provides banks with an opportunity to compete with money market instruments and thus to take over at least some of the lending that occurs by corporations to other corporations in the money market. At first blush it would seem that the very fact that CDs have grown so rapidly, except when the Federal Reserve has blocked them, is proof that some funds have been brought in from the money market.

But here we come to the complex part of the question. There are quite different points of view, largely theoretical in nature, as to how much the banking system can in fact grow through CDs. To explore this, let us first consider the orthodox analysis of the question:

> The banking system can grow through the use of CDs only to a limited extent—namely, by shifts from demand deposits to CDs. Such shifts permit an expansion in total deposits because reserve requirements against CDs are below those required against demand deposits. At today's requirements in large city banks of 17½% on demand deposits and 5% on large CDs there would be an expansion factor in deposits of about 3.5 to 1.

Accordingly, if customers of large city banks wanted to shift $1 billion of demand deposits into CDs, banks would, other things being equal, be able to carry about $3.5 billion in new CDs with the same volume of reserves. Total deposits could therefore be increased by $2.5 billion and banks would be able to lend or invest that additional amount. The banking system as a whole would increase both sides of its collective balance sheet simultaneously by $2.5 billion in the process, that is, it would add $2.5 billion overall to loans and investments outstanding while raising deposits by $2.5 billion.

In other words, if the banking system could get corporations to shift $1 billion out of demand deposits into CDs, the banks could also, with present reserves, get corporations to place about $2.5 billion more in CDs instead of lending in the money market themselves (so banks would become the lenders instead of the corporations).*

But is this the end? Can CD growth only come by pulling demand deposits down? I don't think so, but the burden of proof is on me since many, if not most, monetary theorists would go along with the orthodox analysis.

Before presenting my own analysis, let me suggest that the difficulty with the view we have just been discussing is that it is based on a static, moment-in-time approach. The volume of reserves is assumed to be fixed, so the arithmetic must be right.

As against the static analysis, let me introduce what I call the "dynamic" approach which brings in a different assumption, namely, that over a period of time, the Federal Reserve usually acts like a true navigator and considers in its monetary actions all the winds and currents in the financial position of the entire economy. It is normally quite willing, leaving out exceptional periods,† to provide additional reserves to permit bank customers to shift from short-term instruments to CDs if they wish, even if demand deposits do not decline. As noted earlier, the Federal Reserve does not restrict its considerations to the amount of credit extended by banks but considers also such factors as the growth pattern of the money supply, the volume of free reserves, interest rate developments, the degree of unemployment. the intensity of inflationary pressures, and, although to a lesser extent than formerly, the tone of the money market. It will also cast a look at the total volume of credit (debt) being extended, thus including loans made and securities purchased by financial intermediaries (such as savings banks, savings and loan associations, and insurance companies), by nonfinancial intermediaries (such as business corporations), and by individuals.

---

* This of course assumes that all other forces affecting the money supply are unchanged.

† Obviously, 1966, 1968, and 1969 were years in which the Federal Reserve was opposing the use of CDs by limiting interest rates payable on them, so the statement would not apply in those periods of tight money.

Sometimes it helps to look at extreme examples. Suppose that overnight all corporations as a group decided to sell the $19 billion of commercial paper they hold to the banks and to hold CDs instead. We are talking about a shift of, say, $19 billion of paper representing assets to the holders and debts to the borrowers. If it was concentrated in new CDs at the larger banks, it would require new reserves of about $1.0 billion. Banks as a group would have to borrow a large amount suddenly. The rate on Federal funds would skyrocket. Borrowings at the discount window would zoom and net borrowed reserves would soar.

It will help to remember here that I suggested that the Fed is like the navigator on a ship, looking at various dials and trying to compensate for excessive strength or weakness in the various "currents" deemed significant. The Fed would immediately see that the money market tone was under very heavy pressures. It would probably start to buy securities which would begin to offset the new money market pressures by creating reserves for the banks. The Fed would do this until the various indicators were back to the desired levels and thus it would validate the action, just as a navigator would compensate for the effects of a major shift of wind and current.

Most of the literature on CDs has stopped with the static approach described earlier, but when CDs first appeared, the Kansas City Federal Reserve Bank *Monthly Review* ran an interesting article which stated that the analysis commonly employed

> . . has the deficiency of assuming implicitly that the supply of bank reserves is fixed. Since the volume of bank reserves is controlled by the actions of the central bank, this assumption implies that the growth or lack of growth of commercial bank time deposits does not affect any of the variables which are significant in the formulation of central bank policy. Such a view is not acceptable, because the central bank scarcely would be indifferent to the marked variations in credit market conditions—changes in interest rates and credit availability—that might accompany

shifts by the public between time deposits and other forms of assets, given a constant volume of bank reserves. . . .

". . . A more logical analysis can be developed by beginning with the assumption that the economy is operating at full employment with stable prices. The central bank then shapes its policies so that the existing level of interest rates is maintained, in order that the stability of employment and prices will not be disrupted. Under such circumstances, the central bank is concerned with the changes in the composition of financial assets held by the public only when these changes affect market rates of interest." [1]

In writing this chapter I have had the benefit of a running debate with a friend of mine who held the traditional static point of view. After several discussions, I sent him the following letter:

Dear ———:

Your resistances on Chapter 16 are only making me more confident that I am right. All of your marginal comments on the matter of CDs essentially argue that, like predestination, nothing can change the volume of deposits—because they are controlled by reserves created by the Federal Reserve System. Like the song in Gigi, have you not been standing up too close or back too far?

What you do not appreciate is that I am talking about shifts of credit extension from corporations as a group to banks as a group. It is something like the monetization of the public debt in the late 1940s. What part of the total public debt was to be held by banks and what part by non-banks? As the debt moved to banks in larger degree it was monetized. It is similar here except we are talking about financial intermediation through CDs instead of monetization through demand deposits. If corporations as a group reduce their own lending and investing and "intermediate" it, so to speak, the steps will inevitably involve the banks holding more earning assets and corporations substituting CDs for direct credit extension. The size of total credit will not be changed so the Federal Reserve will be willing to provide the necessary reserves to banks.

He replied that I had convinced him but suggested that I had not carried the analysis through systematically to show the ef-

fects on both sides of the balance sheet of banks and corporations. So, with this in my mind, I would like to follow through
with some specifics of the synchronization by various investor
groups, if corporations acquire $5 billion of CDs over a period of
several months in substitution for various open market paper
and how the banking mechanism would respond to accommodate this. All the borrowers who had received credit from the
corporations would have to get credit elsewhere and these actions would precipitate other shifts. To round the circle we shall
examine six assumed interrelated actions occurring *pro rata*
over a period of time. All six steps should be followed through to
appreciate the entire interrelated sequence. The numbers cited
are in billions of dollars.

1. Corporations substitute $5 billion of CDs for Treasury
   bills, commercial paper, and dealer RPs they now hold.
   These actions of investing corporations can be summarized as follows on the asset side of their balance
   sheets:

   Investing Corporations

CDs	+5
Treasury bills	−3
Commercial paper	−1
Dealer RPs	−1

2. As deposits rise through the new CDs, banks will be increasing assets *pari passu*. Borrowing corporations will
   have to replace borrowings formerly done through the
   commercial paper market, so we will assume they borrow from banks instead. This shows up on the liability
   side of the corporations' balance sheets:

   Borrowing Corporations

Bank loans	+1
Commercial paper borrowings	−1

The reduction in commercial paper matches the action in Step 1.

3. As corporations reduce their advances of credit through RPs, dealers will also turn to the banks for funds. The liability side of the dealers' balance sheets is affected as follows:

Dealers

Bank loans	+1
RPs with Corporations	−1

The reduction in RPs matches the action in Step 1.

4. The increase of $300 million in bank required reserves as a result of the increase in CDs (rounded for convenience from $250 million, or 5% of $5 billion) might be borrowed initially at the discount window, but under our dynamic analysis we assume that the Federal Reserve will gradually add to its portfolio of Government securities. We assume that $300 million in bills will be purchased by the Fed in the market, presumably from corporations as they lighten their position. Both sides of the Fed's balance sheet are affected:

Federal Reserve

Treasury bills	+0.3	Member bank reserves	+0.3

5. In Step 1 we began with the assumption that corporations would reduce their holdings of Treasury bills by $3 billion, but we noted above that the Federal Reserve would pick up $300 million of bills, so the Treasury will lose buyers for $2.7 billion of bills. Now let us assume that the Treasury will offer notes to attract funds from commercial banks:

U.S. Treasury

Treasury notes	+2.7
Treasury bills	−2.7

241

6. Now let us bring all the factors affecting commercial banks together. Both sides of the balance sheet rise together:

Commercial Banks

Loans	+2.0	CDs outstanding	+5
Treasury notes	+2.7		
Reserves at F.R.	+0.3		
	+5.0		

Note that no reference was made to any change in demand deposits. Remember that the orthodox analysis called for a decline in demand deposits to release the reserves required for an increase in CDs. Instead, I have assumed a small increase in total reserves which was provided automatically, rather than grudgingly, by the Federal Reserve as needed because the increase in CDs did not involve an expansion in total credit and did not create inflationary pressures.

Bear in mind that the process we are describing usually takes place over a period of time. Note also that the dynamic approach here calls for a synchronized expansion of reserves, deposits, and bank assets. The Federal Reserve, of course, would not be taking sudden action in providing the extra reserves to permit the increase in deposits. Rather, it would provide reserves *pari passu* with the growth in deposits and bank assets. The Fed does not need to lead in providing the necessary reserves. It can follow closely behind the bank actions from hour to hour and day to day. Also, remember that the $300 million of bill purchases discussed here is isolated from all other Federal actions in order to relate it to the sequence of events involved in the increase of CDs by $5 billion. In real life it would be indistinguishably merged with a myriad of other transactions. No change in monetary policy is implied.

Most important, the Federal Reserve is constantly taking sights to judge the winds and currents influencing its course and making adjustments as necessary to keep on course. An increase in CDs occurring as described above would tend to tighten the market because of the need for additional reserves, so the Fed would accommodate by providing reserves. While the Fed's decisions are based on some necessarily imperfect facts and figures, it is as if a computer were printing out reports to Fed officials that it is all right to provide more bank reserves. Total credit is not growing rapidly, nor is the money supply; the commercial banks are simply taking a larger part of new credit, while the nonbank share is declining. It is as if the right hand (banks) provides more while the left hand (corporations) provides correspondingly less. The banks are acting as intermediaries, receiving the deposits from corporations in the form of CDs and lending the funds.

The implications of this kind of dynamic analysis, as against the usual static moment-in-time analysis, go far beyond the present example. I once wrote an analysis which argued that the customers of banks as a group have a good deal more power than they realize in determining the volume of commercial bank deposits as against the amount of funds placed in other financial institutions and money market instruments. The point was that if all individuals and businesses want to shift deposits from commercial banks to some nonbank form they can do so, given enough time and assuming that the Federal Reserve validates the change, in this case absorbing bank reserves rather than expanding them.

To illustrate the point again, let us consider a rather extreme situation. Suppose that the savings and loan industry had never been born in the United States. There are about $170 billion in accounts in these institutions. Now, on the assumption that these organizations had never been created, suppose that this $170 billion had simply gone into savings accounts in commercial banks over the years. The assumption may be extreme because some of the funds might have gone into savings banks or into life insurance companies or elsewhere but it will be useful to make it here to simplify the argument. Reserve requirements against savings accounts in commercial banks are now 3%. If this entire $170 billion had gone into member banks, $5.1 billion of reserves would be required in addition to present requirements. Shall we assume then that the Federal Reserve System would not have provided these reserves over the years and that accordingly there would be an extra $5.1 billion deficit in the reserve position of banks? Of course not. A much better assumption would be that the net surplus or shortage of reserves would still be about the same as it is today and that the Federal Reserve System, step by step, would have accommodated the larger volume of required reserves. At the margin, the degree of tightness or ease would have been kept about the same as it was at any particular time.

One way to visualize this is to combine the figures for member banks and savings and loan associations as shown below:

	Member banks	Savings and loan assns.	Combined
	October 1971		
		(In billions of dollars)	
Demand deposits	$146		$146
Time and savings deposits	203	$170	373
Total	$349	$170	$519
Reserves required	$ 30.6		$ 35.7

The first column shows that reserve requirements for member banks were $30.6 billion against total deposits of $349 billion in October 1971. If all savings in savings and loan associations were added to savings accounts of commercial banks, deposits would be $519 billion and required reserves would jump to about $35.7 billion, an increase of $5.1 billion. The net deficiency in free reserves averaged $165 million in October 1971, with the newly needed $5.1 billion there would have been a deficit in free reserves of about $5.3 billion *unless the Federal Reserve had taken action to create more reserves.* My contention is that the Fed would have taken care of this on a day-by-day basis over the years.

But would it not have required a heroic effort to provide another $5.1 billion of reserves? Not at all. Look at the table below showing the sources and uses of reserves which left $30 billion in reserve accounts of member banks in October 1971. The table has been set up like a balance sheet to show how reserves are provided.

(In Billion $)			
Assets (Factors Supplying Reserves)		**Liabilities (Factors Reducing Reserves)**	
Gold	$10.1	Currency in circulation	$59.2
Treasury currency	7.5	Treasury cash	.5
FR security holdings	67.7	Other FR accounts	5.3
FR discount window	.4	Total Factors Reducing	
FR float	3.1	Reserves	$65.0
Other FR assets	1.6	Net: Member Bank	
Cash in vault of banks	5.4	Reserves	30.8*
	$95.8		$95.8

* Of this amount required reserves are $30.6 billion, leaving a small amount ($195 million) of excess reserves. Free reserves are $−165 million (excess reserves of $195 million less $360 million of borrowings at the discount window).

As the numbers change from day to day and hour to hour, the Federal Reserve is watching, appraising, feeling the impact on markets, debating how to act, and ultimately buying or selling or holding Government securities as the great residual item in this whole array of numbers. Now it is my feeling that this is an *active,* not a passive role. If one of the ingredients changes, there is the Federal Reserve waiting to do something about it. Is gold down? The Federal Reserve must extend more credit to keep an even keel in the various market indicators. Is currency in circulation up? Again the Fed must act to offset the loss in reserves. Now if savings and loan associations had not been in existence, savings deposits at commercial banks would have expanded over a long period of time and the Fed would have responded and provided the necessary required reserves. The $5.1 billion of additional reserves needed to absorb accounts in savings and loan associations is not substantial when consideration is given to the fact that almost as large or even bigger amounts have been provided by the Fed in the past to offset various monetary factors. For example, currency in circulation has recently been expanding each year by $2.3 to $4.1 billion, and the nation's monetary gold stock declined about $5 billion from the end of 1964 to October 1971.

Clearly, the Federal Reserve watches the entire economic scene, using instinct and feel as well as good solid quantitative analysis. In this process, the Federal Reserve does, it seems to me, make it quite possible for individuals and businessmen as a group to shift their funds as they wish between deposits in commercial banks and other financial institutions or instruments in the money market. I challenge the notion that the Federal Reserve is so mechanical in practice that holders of financial assets cannot make these choices meaningfully.

In addition to the transfers into and out of commercial bank deposits, from and to nonbank groups, there is an occasional shifting of funds from demand to time deposits and back again within the commercial banking system. Recently, the trend has been toward time deposits. As the proportion of time deposits to the total advanced, the average percent of deposits required as reserves tended downward. Another factor influencing this downtrend from the 1940s was the reduction in reserve requirements as imposed by the Federal Reserve. Finally, there was also somewhat greater growth in the deposits of smaller banks which have lower reserve requirements than the larger banks and the introduction of graduated reserve requirements which favors smaller banks. These factors have brought the average reserve requirements of member banks down to about 9%, about half the peak reached in 1942 when war conditions prompted the Federal Reserve to raise requirements to the maximum. Before the Great Depression the figure averaged about 7¼% but

246

jumped sharply in the mid-thirties when reserve requirements were doubled to counteract the effects of the large inflow of gold. Since 1952, the figure has dropped steadily—from almost 16% to about 9%. The Federal Reserve, in adjusting its open market operations to meet these changing reserve requirements, must be considered, I believe, to have adopted the dynamic approach I am trying to explain.

In 1966, early 1968 and 1969, of course, the Fed took the opposite tack of deliberately squeezing CDs out of the banks by keeping interest rate ceilings too low in relation to market rates. I believe these episodes should be considered as *ad hoc* responses to special problems and that the Fed will permit the CD to expand over the years. This appears to be confirmed by the fact that when Regulation Q became no longer restrictive in 1970, the upward trend in time deposits was resumed and CDs rose to a new record volume.

Do CDs Bring in Hot Money?

An important controversy has developed over whether CDs bring in hot money—money which is so sensitive to interest rate changes that the chances of renewal at maturity are very uncertain. One school of thought argues that deposits from CDs are volatile and require unusual provision for liquidity in order to avoid difficulties, such as the inability to "roll over" maturing CDs. It is sometimes contended that the decline in the volume of CDs outstanding on three occasions in the late 1960s is evidence of the hot money attribute.

Admittedly, the future of the CD was clouded in those years because the Federal Reserve maintained interest rate ceilings on large CDs below open market rates on other short-term securities. More than one corporate treasurer let a CD mature on its scheduled date and placed the proceeds in Treasury bills or other securities in order to obtain a higher yield. It is clear, however, that it was the Federal Reserve interest rate ceilings that caused the switch rather than any basic lack of popularity or confidence in the CD.

I feel emphatically that although the individual CD is volatile the *pool* of CDs is not *hot money* unless the Federal Reserve causes it to be. We should remember, in this connection, that *total* corporate liquid assets in recent years have been tending upward with only occasional small interruptions. Substantial changes have taken place, however, in the composition of the total. The part invested in CDs has varied violently in response to the Fed's administration of Regulation Q. As already noted, from the moment when the negotiable CD came on the scene in 1961, the volume shot up very quickly. When large declines occurred in certain years the *total* of corporate liquid assets was not materially affected; there was simply a shift to other types of money market paper which had become more attractive as interest rates rose on Treasury bills, bankers' acceptances, and commercial paper.

Now this question of whether the CD is hot money or not is a vital one, because it inevitably must have a very serious bearing on how banks use CD funds and this affects the asset side of the balance sheet. If CDs represent hot money, banks are going to have to set up larger liquidity provisions for them than if they are more stable. It may be granted that some sort of temporary drain should be expected in certain periods (if the Federal Reserve uses Regulation Q interest rate ceilings to squeeze down the volume of CDs) but one hopes this will not be chronic. Accordingly, it would seem much more reasonable to assume that the CD does not pose exceptional requirements for liquidity.

Are CDs Profitable to Banks?

It is interesting to examine the CD from the point of view of cost, adjusted for hidden factors. To start with, reserve requirements have to be maintained and this, of course, adds a real cost. If commercial banks must maintain a reserve requirement of say 5% against CDs, only 95% may be put to work in an earning capacity. There is also the cost of the FDIC assessment, which currently is $\frac{1}{30}$%. In addition, CD interest rates are calculated on a 360-day year which slightly raises the effective interest cost. After allowing for these factors, what rate of earnings would be necessary to break even? As an example, assume that a bank is paying 6¼% on a CD of $1,000,000. The computations to obtain adjusted cost are shown below.

Practical Calculations to Determine True CD Interest Cost

1. Adjust Interest Rate to 365-day basis (R)

$$\frac{\text{Interest Rate}}{\text{Days}} = \frac{6.25\%}{360} = \frac{R}{365}$$

R = 6.3368%

2. Calculate Interest Cost

Interest Rate × Amount of CD
6.3368% × $1,000,000 = $63,368

3. Calculate FDIC Cost

1/30th of 1% of Amount of CD
.000333 × $1,000,000 = $333

4. Calculate Total Cost

Interest + FDIC Cost
$63,368 + $333 = $63,701

5. Calculate Funds Available for Investment

Amount of CD less 5% Reserve Requirement
$1,000,000 − $50,000 = $950,000

6. Derive Break-even Earnings Requirement Rate (R)

$$\frac{\text{Total Cost}}{\text{Funds Available for Investment}} = \frac{\$63,701}{\$950,000} = R$$

R = 6.71%

Thus the adjusted cost would be 6.71%, meaning that it would be necessary to earn 6.71% to break even. This is a convenient way to state the problem, because a bank will lose money on the CD unless it is able to invest funds at such a rate. If conditions require more liquidity against every dollar of CDs, the cost may go still higher; very short-term securities held in bank liquidity portfolios often earn less than the earnings rate on loan portfolios or the rates earned on longer-term investment assets.

A Glimpse
into the Future

PART V

The Inevitability of
Change: Some Near and
Long-Term Prospects

CHAPTER 17 Throughout this book I have pointed out how resourceful the money market is in developing instruments to meet new needs of borrowers and lenders. The money market is creative because it is free. And because it is competitive, it is indeed a true market in the classical sense. In spite of its enormous size, the market functions like the old-time farmers' market in bringing buyers and sellers together.

What about the future? Looking back at the cast of participants in the money market and at the pieces of paper they use in their daily business, let us speculate about some possible developments that may affect them in the years ahead.

1. More Interest Rate Ceilings on Deposits May Be Suspended (and Placed on a Stand-by Basis)

A constructive step, in my opinion, occurred in mid-1970 when the Federal Reserve "temporarily suspended" ceilings applicable to certificates of deposit over $100,000 with maturities up to eighty-nine days. It is not clear whether the Fed has authority to make such suspensions permanent.

It is sometimes suggested that legislation should be adopted clarifying the authority of the Federal Reserve and other banking agencies to suspend ceilings indefinitely, placing them on a stand-by basis until further notice. The question is a crucial one because the manner in which it is resolved may initiate significant changes in financial flows. On the several occasions during the Vietnam War when interest rates rose to levels not witnessed in more than a hundred years, thrift institutions and commercial banks lost a substantial volume of deposits as funds were diverted to new corporate, U.S. Government, and Federal agency issues offering substantially higher rates of return than on deposits subject to ceilings. Conversely, when interest rates declined in 1970–71, there was a record reintermediation of funds to savings institutions and commercial banks. Obviously, many depositors are very sensitive to interest rate changes. My feeling is that further suspensions of ceilings are highly desirable, since they would permit the money market to operate freely in a more competitive way; and all elements in the market would soon learn to live with the greater flexibility and the competition that would result.

2. CDs May Grow in Volume Faster Than Other Money Market Instruments

Although the CD was knocked about severely in the late 1960s, I expect it to continue to grow in importance. It is possible that CDs will some day approach the volume of demand deposits held by corporations or even the volume of Treasury bills in the hands of private holders.

Of course there will always be some questions about whether the Federal Reserve will restrict the growth of CDs through the administration of interest rate ceilings under Regulation Q or inhibit their profitability through imposition of severe reserve requirements. I am hopeful, however, that they will not do so. The Fed is vitally concerned with fostering a balanced growth of the commercial banking system in the interest of aiding sound economic expansion. Therefore, to supplement demand deposit growth, we should expect the monetary authorities over the long run to help the commercial banks expand CDs as well as other time and savings deposits.

Commercial banks may wish to extend maturities of CDs to beyond one year as Canadian banks do. It would, of course, take some promotional effort to persuade American corporations to buy CDs with maturities of up to two or three years, particularly since some boards of directors now limit investments to one-year maturities. But some finance companies have been successful in selling their paper with four- to five-year maturities. It may also be possible for banks to develop still longer CDs, perhaps with maturities of from three years to ten years or so. In contrast to capital notes of banks, these would not be subordinated to other deposits. Such longer term CDs would be particularly appropriate if the banks increase their emphasis on term loans, which I expect them to do.

Savings and loan associations will probably be in the market for substantial amounts of CDs. Associations that belong to the Home Loan Bank System have to maintain a liquidity reserve, the amount of which is established by the Federal Home Loan Bank Board. In late 1971 it was 7%. For a time CDs were not eligible for these reserves but the Housing Act of 1968 states that they are now included as a means of meeting requirements.

3. *Bank Capital Notes May Become a New Money Market Security*

Bank capital notes were first issued * only in long-term maturities, generally sold through underwriters to institutional investors such as municipal pension funds. When interest rates rose to peak levels in 1969, new offerings largely disappeared. The money market took special notice when shorter maturities began to be issued in recent years.

* Excluding earlier sales to the Reconstruction Finance Corporation by banks in the Depression.

Some banks sold short-term capital notes through their own offices rather than through underwriters. These issues were designed to attract funds from individuals at rates above those available on deposits under Regulation Q. For example, late in 1969, First Virginia Bankshares Corporation offered ten-year subordinated capital notes in denominations as low as $500. Notes in principal amounts of $20,000 or more bore interest at 8%, smaller amounts were issued at a rate of 7½%. Early in 1970, The First Pennsylvania Banking and Trust Company offered a two-and-a-half-year subordinated capital note at 7¼% in denominations as low as $100. These new money market instruments sold well. They tapped a new market and the rates were below what long-term capital note issues designed for institutional investors would have required. One aftermath was that the Federal Reserve adopted regulations limiting offerings of bank notes or debentures to a minimum denomination of $500 and a minimum maturity of seven years. In 1971, the Bank of America offered $100 million of 6¼% notes due 1978 to its customers; the offering was stopped when $70 million had been sold because increases in market rates had made it less attractive.

Several banks also sold maturities of about seven and a half years in the traditional way through underwriters. These were popular both with the issuing banks and the buyers. The banks found the rates well under what the traditional twenty- to twenty-five-year maturity would demand. For example, in March 1971 two New York City banks issued securities which provide a good comparison: Bankers Trust sold a twenty-five-year issue at a rate of 7.65% and about a week later Morgan Guaranty sold a seven-year note at 6.375%.

Buyers liked the yields on these short issues because they were in excess of rates available on deposits; also buyers felt less vulnerable to market price swings than in the long-term bond issues. It remains to be seen how viable these new shorter-term issues are. While negotiable, there are no active secondary markets as yet.

256

I believe that more and more banks will issue capital notes to raise capital funds necessitated by their growth. The range of maturities may vary widely at times, with some banks using fairly short maturities to appeal to individuals while others use long issues to appeal to institutional investors. The choice will depend on many factors including marketing possibilities and differences in interest rates. The short issues will probably develop a secondary market and thus in time could become money market securities.

4. Growth in the Commercial Paper Market May Be Strong but Erratic

As we have already noted, the commercial paper market has grown tremendously in recent years but growth stopped in 1970, when credit problems arose, and in 1971, when corporations were reducing short-term liabilities with the proceeds of bond issues. Probably the most important factor in the growth of corporate commercial paper was the double-barreled effect of tight monetary policies which diverted both corporate short-term investments and corporate borrowing away from banks. With Regulation Q ceilings below open market rates, corporations shifted investment funds to commercial paper. Simultaneously, many corporations borrowed through the commercial paper market for the first time. I find it interesting that corporations have carved out a sort of banking system of their own through commercial paper. Corporations borrow and corporations lend—to each other—and they bypass the regular banking system. The causes seem primarily to be various restrictive actions of the Federal Reserve, plus at times a sticky prime rate, reflecting such factors as high interest costs to banks on funds raised in the money market at home and abroad.

The prospects for this market in the future will undoubtedly continue to depend on monetary policy to a large extent. If banks cannot pay competitive rates on CDs, corporations will be more active in using the commercial paper market and other instruments for the investment of short-term funds. Borrowers will then find a supply of available funds, possibly below bank lending rates, allowing for compensating balances, if high borrowing costs to banks are present. However, the commercial paper market may also have periods of decline in activity, particularly if doubts arise in the market place concerning credit quality, as occurred in the Penn Central case in 1970.

One factor pointing toward expansion of commercial paper activity is that consumer credit should see further rapid growth, thus encouraging finance companies to borrow more in this market. In a little over one generation, we have seen the emergence of consumer credit from a somewhat controversial device to a system almost universally used and one that has contributed substantially to the standard of living of Americans. Tomorrow, many families which have not had sufficient economic stature to use consumer credit will be moving up the economic ladder and will use such credit much more actively. Also, the millions of new families resulting from the postwar population bulge are already familiar with the use of credit and will use it much more plentifully than even their parents do today. The result of all this should be an enormous increase in the amount of credit demanded of banks and the short-term market through institutions such as GMAC and other finance companies. The money market will need to generate considerably larger amounts of funds for this purpose.

The activity of banks as borrowers in the commercial paper market is uncertain and the extent to which banks draw on this market in the future will depend on many factors. Among these are the ceilings imposed under Regulation Q which, in relation to open market interest rates, will determine whether funds may be obtained through the issuance of CDs; the demand for loans; the relative attractiveness of alternate sources of funds, such as Euro-dollars; and the degree to which the Fed deters the issuance of commercial paper by bank holding and bank-related companies through continuance of reserve requirements or other

258

regulations. If conditions are favorable for issuance, banks will undoubtedly consider commercial paper as an important alternative source of new funds. Of course banks will be at a competitive disadvantage as long as a reserve requirement is imposed on their paper and not on the paper of nonfinancial corporations.

One further thought occurs to me, namely, that some banks and bank holding companies might become active as brokers or dealers in commercial paper. They learned about selling commercial paper themselves during the tight money period. Might they not therefore become agents for others in marketing such paper and thus help to broaden the market further?

5. *Growth in Bankers' Acceptances Could Be Much Stronger*

After almost dying out in the Great Depression, the active use of bankers' acceptances suddenly revived in the late 1960s. The combined effects of tight money and heavy loan demand encouraged banks to substitute acceptances for loans. Moreover, the squeeze on CDs under Regulation Q ceilings brought on the issuance of more "ineligible" acceptances. These instruments are defined as acceptances that are ineligible at the discount window or for purchase by the Federal Reserve because of the type of transaction being financed or the length of maturity. Such acceptances had occasionally been created previously but banks made every attempt to avoid doing so. Now that they are used as a money market instrument which may be traded even though ineligible, growth could be very large if banks push them in periods of tight money. One important factor is whether the Fed clarifies their use. It is not clear whether they must be included in a provision limiting the total amount of acceptance credit extended by a member bank to 50% of its capital stock, surplus and undivided profits, except with the special permission of the Board of Governors, which may allow a maximum of 100% of capital funds. Domestic acceptances, however, are limited to 50%. The Fed has been asked to act on this matter so as to free up ineligible acceptances for possible major use by banks.

259

It has been suggested that acceptances could be further encouraged by making bank charges more flexible. At present, banks charge a fee of 1½% or more to customers using bankers' acceptances. That is to say, the fee is charged as a bank stamps "Accepted" on the bank drafts and thereby puts its credit behind the credit of the original issuer. One possibility would be to establish a more flexible fee schedule, but any changes in fees would have to be considered in the light of bank costs and return on capital assigned to such an obligation. However, it is possible that profits might be increased, even with certain lower fees, if loan funds were preserved and used most effectively.

6. Arrangements for Financing of Government Securities Dealers May Be Improved

In spite of all of the skills developed by dealers in managing their needs for money to carry inventories, there may always be lingering doubts about whether everything will always work out right. It has been shown earlier that the money market banks, aside from servicing the dealers for whom they act as clearing agents, reserve the right to post changes in rates on dealer loans at any time in order to encourage or discourage them, in accordance with their own money needs. The dealers understand the routine well and have developed a flexible system of gathering funds from all across the country, both to round out their needs and sometimes to obtain lower rates than are available at the money market banks. The dealers also know that the Federal Reserve is constantly watching their condition, fitting it into the whole maze of signals which the Fed antennae are receiving, and that the Fed may at any time instigate special transactions with the dealers. But there are days when a dealer may struggle and not be too sure where the last needed dollar is coming from; he is always aware that at the last minute he may have to do something relatively unattractive, like dropping prices suddenly to unload some securities or paying higher interest rates to carry his position, with profits being hurt either way.

It seems likely that a key question regarding future trends in the money market must be whether some new "line of last resort" could be set up, even at a penalty rate, either directly with the Federal Reserve Banks or through the commercial banks accompanied by a special understanding that the Federal Reserve Banks in turn would take care of the commercial banks to cover the amounts so advanced to dealers. I understand that the subject has been under consideration by the Federal Reserve and the Treasury for some time.

7. *The Money Market Will Continue To Be Disrupted by "Symbolic" Restraints on Public Debt Management*

I think of the 4¼% ceiling on Treasury bonds and the public debt limit as symbolic of resistance by Congress to fiscal policy and to cumbersome budget machinery. The money market would breathe a big sigh of relief if these restraints could be eliminated or modified in some fashion to give the Treasury the flexibility it needs.

This is not to say that Congress is wrong in maintaining fiscal restraints. But the instincts of Congress seem to be that the budget is beyond understanding by any one person and that it is impossible to control. Under a kind of natural law of frustration, therefore, since it cannot be hit directly, it must be attacked indirectly by retaining the 4¼% interest ceiling on bonds (fortunately partially loosened by the $10 billion exemption recently adopted) and maintaining the debt limit as close as possible to the actual debt. Many members of Congress realize that these devices do not effectively attack the budget problem but they also feel that they force Government officials to be somewhat more conservative than they might otherwise be. From my vantage point in New York and from an earlier period of service in the United States Treasury Department, I feel that I understand both sides of the issue. Unfortunately, as more and more activities are taken on by Government, the budget gets more complex and the helplessness of the individual in understanding it becomes

261

more intense. It is difficult to conceive of a solution that might get things on a more understandable basis and thus help to get rid of some of these seemingly pointless restraints which muddy up Treasury operations in the money market.

8. *Operations of the Federal Reserve Discount Window Will Be Revitalized*

Over the years since the 1920s the Federal Reserve has leaned more and more heavily on open market operations to provide reserves while the discount window—except for recent periods of tight monetary policy—has shrunk in activity to almost nothing. It is my feeling that this has gone too far and that we will see the discount function made much more active through various steps in the years ahead.

It is interesting to compare the present situation with that of the 1920s, another period posing questions somewhat similar in the banking field to those which are discussed today. In the twenties the Federal Reserve leaned almost entirely on the discount window for its policy programs. Open market operations were so new that they were really not understood. The result was that the amount of discounts outstanding in 1929 averaged $952 million while Federal Reserve holdings of securities were only $208 million. Thus, the volume of Federal Reserve credit extended through the discount window was almost five times as great as the amount supplied through open market operations.

Today the picture is quite different. The volume of Federal Reserve credit being extended through security holdings during the first six months of 1968 was about $50 billion, or almost one hundred times the $560 million provided through the discount window. Even during the following year, when monetary policy was much more restrictive, the Fed's portfolio of securities averaged $53 billion, or almost forty times the $1.4 billion of member bank borrowings. Clearly the importance of the discount window has declined drastically since the twenties. A major reason for the decline has been that the Federal Reserve itself seems to have preferred open market operations. We have seen that another reason is that bankers have felt administration of the discount window by the Federal Reserve has been discouraging. There has been considerable confusion and doubt about certain aspects of the window. For example, granting that such borrowing has been a privilege and not a right, how far can the privilege be used before running into serious resistance? We have also noted that some bankers have contended that handling of requests at the twelve Federal Reserve banks has not been uniform.

In any event, the possibility of improving the use of the discount window has an important bearing on the question of how the Federal Reserve will provide bank reserves to support the economic growth of the country over the years ahead.

In mid-1971, Federal Reserve credit * outstanding averaged about $67 billion, or about 6½% of GNP. This was a higher percentage than for any year in the previous decade and about ¾% higher than the early years of the sixties. If the 6½% ratio is to be maintained as GNP grows to $1½ trillion in the mid-seventies, Federal Reserve credit outstanding would have to rise to almost $100 billion, meaning that close to $35 billion of additional credit would have to be provided. Assuming the bulk of the expansion were provided through open market operations, it could mean that an increasing proportion of the Federal debt would be held by the Federal Reserve Banks. Furthermore, if Federal Reserve purchases were concentrated in bills and other short-term issues, the short-term Government security market could be increasingly dominated by the Federal Reserve. Such domination could impair debt management and other monetary policies and objectives.

What about prospects for stepping up the use of the discount window? In Chapter 6 I mentioned briefly the proposals of a

---

* Federal Reserve credit comprises the total volume of funds injected into the banking system as a result of open market operations, *i.e.,* purchases of U.S. Government and agency issues and acceptances, advances to member banks at the discount window, and credits to member banks for checks in process of collection (F.R. float).

Steering Committee of the Federal Reserve System which would make the discount window much more viable. One very important part of these proposals would be to introduce a basic borrowing privilege for the first time. Substitute the word "right" for "privilege," and this comes into focus. Banks would be able under this proposal to borrow a certain amount with no questions asked by the Federal Reserve—which is an entirely new concept. Up to now questions have been asked and the threat of their being asked has deterred borrowing. This basic borrowing privilege would be fairly small but it would, however, be supplemented by the right to borrow under a supplemental adjustment credit which is really just a new name for the old system of borrowing with questions asked. A special proposal to provide seasonal credit for banks would also be introduced. Finally, a very important part of the plan would be to change the discount rate much more frequently and endeavor to keep it in fairly close touch with various other relevant rates.

How important would the new basic borrowing privilege be? The answer is that it would be just large enough to be significant and yet not so large that it would disrupt the whole scheme of Federal Reserve operations. Perhaps most important of all is the fact that it would represent a shifting of gears from the past. The discount window would assume a new role and the discount rate would become more viable. With such a program, I visualize that still further improvements could be made as time passes. In other words, the new program has to be tried out and, like any new model, adjustments may have to be made to put it on a smoothly working basis. Once that is accomplished, further improvements will be possible. Viewed in this way it is possible to be quite relaxed about the details of the new program. Even though the proposal has its critics it would be a start toward a better system which could be improved in the years ahead.

The Federal Reserve has also proposed to Congress that the types of collateral eligible for borrowings at the discount window be liberalized. The present system is outmoded. The volume of

Government securities in the hands of banks is not adequate to take care of borrowings at the discount window and probably will become even less adequate as the banking system grows. The use of business loans for collateral is rather awkward because the question of eligibility (to meet standards necessary to avoid penalty rates) has to be decided in each individual case, based on rules that were set up by the Federal Reserve a long time ago under a law which visualized bank credit as always being short-term. A large volume of today's bank loans is simply not eligible at the Federal Reserve discount window. The Federal Reserve is proposing that the statutes be modernized so that any sound business loan could be used for collateral. Sooner or later, this will be adopted, but it has been snarled in Congressional procedures.

9. Reserve Requirements May Be Overhauled but Bankers and the Federal Reserve Do Not Agree on the Prescription

An important alternative to continued expansion in Federal Reserve credit outstanding (and thus in bank reserves on deposit at the Federal Reserve), as discussed above, would be to gradually reduce the percentage of reserves required against various types of deposits. By scheduling a reduction in reserve requirements over a period of years, the present reserve base could support a larger volume of deposits and bank credit without the injection of any new reserves by the Federal Reserve System. The money market would be very interested because of the implications that banks might acquire more securities as Federal Reserve Banks purchased less.

The system of reserve requirements employed by the Federal Reserve System raises many questions, and I believe that most bankers think that it could be improved considerably. As noted earlier, requirements today are 13% for demand deposits of country banks and 17½% for demand deposits of reserve city banks, except that on the first $5 million of deposits requirements are ½% lower. Requirements on savings deposits (and on time deposits under $5 million) were reduced to 3% in March 1967, and a 5% requirement is in effect, as this is written, for time deposits over $5 million, including CDs. The particular figures do not seem to have any validity in themselves and study of the history of reserve requirements shows that in fact they are largely accidents of events at certain times.

Bankers would like to see the level of reserve requirements gradually reduced. A few years ago a committee of the American Bankers Association suggested that reserve requirements should be reduced to a standard 10% for demand deposits—with no requirements on time and savings deposits in order to equate such deposits with those of savings banks and savings and loan association. The committee suggested that there be no sudden change due to the proposed plan but that it should come into play as would be appropriate over a period of time so that there would be no disruptions in the money market.

More recently, the Federal Reserve System proposed that a graduated basis be adopted for reserve requirements on demand deposits based on the size of the bank. The plan would be for two or more brackets of reserve requirements to operate somewhat like the income tax does: each bank would first have the lowest bracket applied to it and then the second bracket and finally, if there are more than two brackets, the highest rate brackets. The objective of the Federal Reserve is to make reserve requirements lower for small banks so that they will be more willing to stay in or join the System. In effect, a start in this direction was made in 1966, when a higher requirement was imposed on time deposits over $5 million and in 1968 a ½% higher reserve was established on demand deposits over $5 million.

The Federal Reserve proposal also included the suggestion that insured nonmember banks be forced to carry the same reserve requirements as member banks, so that the "carrot" to be provided through fairly low reserve requirements for small banks would be matched by the "stick" of applying equal requirements to nonmember banks. No changes were proposed by the Federal Reserve with regard to time and savings deposits, nor was there any suggestion that the entire level of reserve requirements might be too high.

The evidence suggests that bankers do not favor the Federal Reserve proposal. Larger banks wonder why they should be penalized. They feel that there may be a proccupation with solving the problems of small banks and not enough attention to reducing the overall level of reserve requirements which, of course, would help all banks.

There is also resistance to the idea that nonmember banks should be forced to carry reserve requirements. As this is written, the Federal Reserve proposal appears to have little chance of being adopted by Congress soon. It seems unfortunate that the Fed has a plan that is unpopular with commercial banks while the commercial banks' plan apparently is not being taken seriously by the Federal Reserve.

Some people contend that bankers do not really understand the impact of reserve requirements; they argue that these requirements are costless to the banks because the Federal Reserve banks create credit which in turn becomes the reserves that the banks hold in meeting the requirements. Thus, as the Federal Reserve banks purchase Government securities or make loans to member banks, these actions create deposits on the Federal Reserve's books that are held by member banks in meeting their reserve requirements. But there is more to it than that. If the Federal Reserve creates credit and obtains earning assets, such as U.S. Government securities, it would seem that commercial banks would create that much less, assuming, of course, that the level of total credit is the same either way. In mid-1971, Federal Reserve credit was almost 13% of the combined total of commercial bank and Federal Reserve bank credit outstanding. In the twenties, it averaged 4%; in the thirties, it rose to as high as 6%, as reserve requirements were increased to offset the effect on reserves of a large inflow of gold. In 1948, the percentage was more than 16%, when reserve requirements were increased temporarily to help cope with inflationary pressures. So it is probable that the more credit the Federal Reserve Banks hold, in relative terms, the less the commercial banks will hold. I would suggest that a 10% figure might be an appropriate target today. We have already come down from 16% to 13%; the next objective might be 10% which would still be well above the 4% of the twenties and the 6% of the thirties.

10. *Federal Reserve Operations Will Be Sharpened by New Studies on Linkages Between the Money Market and Other Markets*

The tight money experiences of recent years showed in very dramatic fashion the importance of linkages between the money market, the bond market, and the stock market. The close connection between these markets and the well-being of thrift institutions, as well as housing starts, was vividly brought out for the public and members of Congress to see. The money market responded quite well to the challenges, but at times fears were aroused beyond anything that pure statistics on supply and demand alone could have suggested.

The whole question of linkages is elusive. The Federal Reserve has been conducting a number of research projects on the linkages between Federal Reserve actions and the various financial markets. For example, the Reserve Board's 1968 Annual Report listed four studies completed or under way during that year: reappraisal of the Federal Reserve discount mechanism, U.S. Government securities market study, foreign operations of member banks, economic model construction. The Board has also published from time to time economic studies on similar subjects made by staff members of the system. I am enthusiastic about the potential value of such studies. With better understanding of market linkages it is probable that Federal Reserve policies could be tailored more precisely in the future.

11. *The "Less Checks" Society Will Have Important Money Market Repercussions*

The transition to what has been called a "checkless" or "less-checks" society will be a major challenge and vital opportunity to commercial banks. What is visualized is the further rapid extension of credit cards and the transfer of funds between buyers and sellers on the computers of banks through tie-ins by wire. This will provide, among other things, instant credit which may importantly affect the activities of banks in the money market. Demands for credit could be larger under such a system than at present, because it would be so much easier to use credit. A corollary would seem to be that banks might need additional access to liquidity to meet sudden swings in demand for credit as computers contact each other. Moreover, the banks will not gain in reserves from the float * now generated as checks are sent physically from one location to another. Under the present system of check clearance, banks sometimes get credit for checks they have given the Federal Reserve to collect before they have in fact been collected from the banks on which they were drawn. This is because the Federal Reserve assumes it takes a stated number of days to collect a check from a certain distance but it may take longer. The assumptions used are based on a schedule of distances involved.

A nationwide computerized direct funds transfer system, which might be the end result of current trends in the direction of a less-checks society, would greatly increase the velocity of money. Money transfers from payer to payee would be instantaneous in most cases. A better synchronization of money receipts and expenditures under a direct funds transfer system would sharply reduce the length of time money must be held for transactions purposes. Such a system was vividly described in one of the closing paragraphs of a recent study by George Garvy and Martin R. Blyn:

> Such a large-scale and ultimately nationwide computerized system would revolutionize the entire payments mechanism by re-

---

* Credit for uncollected items is provided by the Federal Reserve and is shown as "Float" on the Federal Reserve statement. These credits would be eliminated for the entire banking system if transfers were made quickly by computers. Obviously, they would have to be replaced by another type of Federal Reserve credit if the volume of such credit outstanding is to be maintained.

placing the handling of checks with transmission signals that would activate electronic book-entry systems. A checkless, or rather less check-based, system would presumably involve some automatic extension of credit in the form of limited overdraft facilities. Under such conditions, the need to have enough cash in the bank, on which current management of cash flows and cash budgeting is based, would lose much of its meaning. The amount of money underlying that part of the payments flows which would be cleared by the new system presumably would be considerably smaller than that required to make the same amount of payments by check or currency, and the velocity of money will increase greatly. It is also conceivable that the wider use of overdrafts, only recently introduced for the household sector in the form of "ready cash" and similar plans, could spread to business accounts even before the advent of the less-cash society.[1]

Federal Reserve Governor Mitchell has gone even further in looking at possible developments.

A few people are interested in the implications of tomorrow's money for tomorrow's money managers. How will they deal with a monetary cyclotron built from a network of computers programmed to achieve the maximum efficiency for everyone's money? Could the system be programmed so that for a given day's work no one had more or less in his account, taking into account inflows, than needed to cover outflows? If so, velocity would approach infinity and money supply zero.[2]

12. Federal Funds May Play an Even Larger Role Than They Do Today

It has been proposed that all clearings between banks be settled in Federal funds rather than in Clearing House funds. The possibility exists that, as the computer is used more and more, it will be desirable and feasible to make almost instantaneous adjustments anywhere in the whole monetary system. Under such a sophisticated system, settlements in Clearing House funds, i.e., one day late, might well become an anachronism. As indicated previously, banking committees have been studying the feasibility of new procedures to effect prompt payment. The task is a difficult one and the solution will probably involve the introduction of settlement in Federal funds gradually to new segments of financial payments.

13. The Supply-Demand Situation in Some Securities Should Be Improved by Easing Pledging Requirements of Commercial Banks

Commercial banks have to hold substantial amounts of Government and municipal securities in order to pledge them against public deposits and borrowings from the Federal Reserve System and for trust accounts. In effect, securities are locked up for this purpose and therefore are not available for sale. Accordingly, the volume of securities held by banks usually considered to be available for liquidity purposes overstates the net free securities that banks could in fact liquidate. Recently, the needs for pledged securities have been growing so large that it has become a problem for some banks. The money market could be affected if a growing proportion of securities were locked up in this fashion and if the liquidity position of banks were further impaired.

Various proposals have been made which would eliminate pledging, in whole or in part, by having the FDIC insure public deposits, either fully or up to some percentage maximum in any bank. It is hard to say whether one of these proposals involving FDIC will be adopted, or whether some other approach will be found. One arrangement used in certain states has been to set up an insurance arrangement of their own to reduce the need for pledging. I believe that ways should be found to ease the pledging problem and that one result will be to free securities for more active use by the money market.

14. Private Debt Will Grow Faster Than Federal Debt, Causing Some Important Changes in Institutional Arrangements

As the money market grows in the 1970s and particularly with the decline in spending for Vietnam, it is likely that private debt instruments will grow faster in volume than Treasury securities.

271

A Glimpse into the Future

What I visualize is that private economic activity will be rising rapidly in the years ahead and this will require substantial increases in private debt, including short-term debt. It will also involve substantial increases in the demand for short-term money market instruments for liquidity purposes. These can just as well be private as Government, so far as the money market is concerned.

The foregoing may appear surprising in view of the large prospective increases in Government expenditures for aid to urban areas. But even assuming that such aid grows sharply, perhaps even to the level formerly spent on the Vietnam War, I believe that my prediction will still be right. The point is that the Federal revenue structure is very progressive and tax collections grow faster than Gross National Product. Therefore, growth in the Federal debt is likely to be more restrained than growth in private debt, which has increased more rapidly than Federal debt each year since 1946—even in exceptional periods like the Korean and the Vietnam wars, except for the year 1946.

One result will be that private debt instruments will be used more frequently for money market purposes. A corollary is that the Federal Reserve will consider broadening its operations. For example, it may purchase more acceptances and it may ease eligibility requirements at the discount window.

SOURCE NOTES

CHAPTER I

1   *Oxford English Dictionary* (London: Oxford University Press, 1961).
2   *Ibid.*
3   Walter Bagehot, *Lombard Street* (London: John Murray, 1917), pp. 3–4.
4   *Ibid.*, p. 16.

CHAPTER 4

1   "Bankers' Acceptances Used More Widely," *Business Conditions,* Federal Reserve Bank of Chicago, May 1965, pp. 9–16.

CHAPTER 5

1   *New York Times,* August 1, 1971, Section 3, p. 3.

CHAPTER 6

1   Robert V. Roosa, *Federal Reserve Operations in the Money and Government Securities Markets,* Federal Reserve Bank of New York, 1956, p. 13.
2   *Ibid.*, p. 14.
3   Federal Reserve Bank of New York, *Annual Report for 1967,* p. 26.
4   Federal Reserve Bank of New York, *Annual Report for 1968,* p. 23.
5   *Ibid.*, p. 26.
6   Andrew F. Brimmer, "Monetary Policy and the U.S. Balance of Payments," Speech at Wharton School of Finance & Commerce, University of Pennsylvania, Philadelphia, Pennsylvania, October 5, 1966.
7   Board of Governors of the Federal Reserve System, *Annual Report for 1966,* p. 101.

8   J. L. Robertson, "On Cutting Corners," Remarks at Annual Convention of West Virginia Bankers Association, White Sulphur Springs, West Virginia, July 25, 1969.

CHAPTER 9

1   *Wall Street Journal*, October 6, 1966.

CHAPTER 12

1   A book of this nature is Peter L. Bernstein's and Robert L. Heilbroner's, *A Primer on Government Spending* (New York: Random House, 1963).
2   Board of Governors of the Federal Reserve System, *Annual Report for 1967*, p. 204.

CHAPTER 15

1   Thomas O. Waage, "Some Problems of Monetary Policy," Speech before the New York Society of Security Analysts, New York, July 8, 1971.
2   Milton Friedman, *A Program for Monetary Stability* (New York: Fordham University Press, 1960).
3   Milton Friedman and Anna J. Schwartz, *A Monetary History of the United States, 1867–1960* (New York: National Bureau of Economic Research, 1963), p. 4.
4   George Garvy and Martin R. Blyn, *The Velocity of Money* (New York: Federal Reserve Bank of New York, 1969), pp. 49–53.
5   Dewey Daane, "Inflation and Financial Stability," Speech before the 15th Annual Bankers' Forum at Georgetown University, October 5, 1968.
6   Board of Governors of the Federal Reserve System, *Annual Report for 1965*, p. 148.
7   Board of Governors of the Federal Reserve System, *Annual Report for 1966*, p. 179.
8   Board of Governors of the Federal Reserve System, *Annual Report for 1970*, p. 110.
9   *American Banker*, January 25, 1971.

CHAPTER 16

1   "Profits on Commercial Bank Time Deposits," *Monthly Review*, Federal Reserve Bank of Kansas City, September 1961, p. 4.

CHAPTER 17

1   Garvy and Blyn, *The Velocity of Money*, p. 93.
2   George W. Mitchell, "Tomorrow's Money As Seen Today," Remarks at annual stockholders' meeting of Federal Reserve Bank of Boston, Boston, Mass., October 6, 1966.

GLOSSARY

Amortization—Used in connection with bonds, amortization refers to the writing down of a premium paid by a buyer. This premium is spread over the remaining years of the life of the bond, or, if callable, to the first call date. For example, if a bond is purchased at 102 and has ten years to go to maturity, the two points would be spread out over the ten years in equal amounts, or 0.20 per year. They would be offset against coupon interest payments to determine true net income. The calculations are made to the first call date on the assumption that the issuer might decide to refund at the first opportunity (first call date) when the bond is selling at a premium and therefore has a market yield below its coupon rate. If a premium is not amortized and not deducted from coupon income each year, a capital loss will be sustained when the issue is paid off; or, to put it differently, the investor who considers all of the coupon as income is actually consuming capital in part. To avoid this, it is advisable to spread the write-off of the premium over the life of the issue or to first call date as noted. Similarly, accretion refers to the writing up of a discount on bonds over the remaining years from date of purchase to maturity.

Arbitrage—Security arbitrage is usually undertaken when differences develop in prices of the same issue in different markets or in comparable issues within one market. In the case of U.S. Government securities, arbitrage-type dealings usually occur when spreads develop between the yields on securities with roughly comparable maturities and other features. Such transactions tend to correct any tendency for individual issues to sell far out of line in the market.

Balance of Payments— The term is applied to the difference between (a) all payments made by a nation outside its borders, and (b) payments received from foreign sources. It covers all international transactions, such as the export and import of merchandise and

277

services, and the movement of capital by individuals, business, and Government.

Bank Dealers—This refers to a group of commercial banks who act as dealers in government securities. This means that they carry inventories of U.S. Government and municipal securities and make a market in them. When a new security is offered, dealers begin trading it in the market on a when-issued basis. As dealers, when they buy or sell to someone else, they are acting as a principal for their own account.

Bankers' Acceptances—Assume that U.S. Corporation A has bought something from foreign corporation B in international trade and that A wants to pay for the merchandise in ninety days. However, B wishes the money immediately. He therefore requests A to arrange for the acceptance of B's ninety-day draft by A's bank. For a fee, A's bank will stamp B's draft "Accepted," thereby putting the bank's credit behind A's obligation. A's bank then sells the accepted draft and remits the money to B, directly or through B's bank. Such a bankers' acceptance is thus similar to a security and is traded readily in the money market.

Basis Point—In considering a yield expressed as 4.32%, the digits to the right of the decimal point are known in financial circles as basis points. Accordingly, one hundred basis points equals 1%.

Bond Market—This term is applied to the channels through which bonds and notes may be bought or sold. Some corporate and government issues, both domestic and foreign, are listed and traded in the bond trading departments of the New York and American Stock Exchanges. However, by far the greater volume is traded in the over-the-counter market, the market for securities not listed on any organized stock exchange. This market is not a centralized or organized trading center but is represented by hundreds of securities firms throughout the country which are linked by telephone and other means of communication and which stand ready to trade and make markets in unlisted securities.

Brokers and Dealers—A broker acts as an agent for his customer in completing buy and sell orders for securities, usually with other brokers. A dealer acts as a principal so that usually a sale is made from his own inventory and a purchase is added to his inventory.

278

Central Banks—The functions of a central bank are to issue currency, act as the bank for the Government, and administer monetary policy.

Certificates of Deposit—These are time deposits at commercial banks against which the bank has issued a receipt called a certificate. The certificate specifies the rate of interest and the final maturity of the deposit. Such certificates may be issued on a nonnegotiable or a negotiable basis. Beginning in 1961, negotiable CDs of large size issued to corporations developed into a very important money market instrument. Regulation Q ceilings on interest rates sharply limited the volume outstanding at times in the late sixties.

Clearing House Funds—See *Good Funds.*

Commercial Paper—Unsecured promissory notes of relatively short maturity issued by well-known corporations with good credit rating to finance short-term borrowing needs.

Compensating Balances—It is customary for customers to maintain balances with their banks to compensate for the volume of checking account and other services rendered and in consideration of outstanding loans, lines of credit, or loan commitments. For example, it is not unusual to require compensating balances of 10% against loan commitments and 20% when the commitment is converted into a loan.

Correspondent Bank—Commercial banks do business with one another. For example, a country bank may maintain a deposit account with a large city bank to facilitate check clearing operations or to obtain special investment services. The activity between such banks is usually described as a correspondent bank relationship.

Coupon Issues—In the Government bond market, coupon issues refer to certificates, notes, and bonds which bear a specified rate of interest as indicated by the coupon. They may be offered to the public for cash or in exchange for outstanding or maturing issues, generally ten or more days in advance of the issue date. In contrast, Treasury bills do not have coupons but are sold at a discount representing interest.

Creation of Bank Reserves—Member bank reserves at the Federal Reserve consist of deposits which can only be created, in the aggregate, by an increase in Federal Reserve credit of some kind (or gold). Both sides of the Federal Reserve balance sheet must go up or down at the same time. To make deposits rise, representing member bank reserves, the Fed must allow its assets to rise. The particular form may consist of Government securities, if the Federal Reserve takes the action through open market operations or through RPs with dealers, or it may consist of notes receivable from banks if they have borrowed at the discount window. (In this discussion we ignore decreases in other Federal Reserve assets which, of course, would affect reserves in the same way as increase in Federal Reserve liabilities, and vice versa. They are usually relatively unimportant.)

Occasional confusion about this is similar to that which arises when someone is trying to explain that the commercial banking system creates credit. When he points to the individual bank to explain it, he is bound to be wrong because the individual bank cannot make a loan until it has first received funds in the form of deposits or capital or possibly as borrowings. Funds for credit expansion for the commercial banking system *as a whole* can come only from additions to bank reserves provided by the Federal Reserve. These then provide for a multiple expansion of credit—roughly eleven times for the entire banking system based on average reserve requirements of 9%. Thus, an increase of, say, $1 billion in reserves will support an expansion of $11 billion in deposits of commercial banks. Since the balance sheet again must go up equally on both sides, there will be an increase of $11 billion in commercial bank assets. This will be almost entirely loans or securities held, except for the $1 billion of reserves held in the Federal Reserve System.

Sometimes the individual bank resists the idea that the Federal Reserve creates the reserves the bank must put up for deposit growth. The individual bank may feel that it must pay over deposit funds to the Federal Reserve bank in order to provide for required reserves, so it is hard to see that the Federal Reserve System had a hand in creating such reserves. The point is that the individual bank is not the entire banking system. Obviously, if one bank has an increase in its deposits of, say, $10 million, it will have to put up perhaps one million dollars in the form of deposits at the Federal Reserve to

280

meet its legal reserve requirements. It will rightfully feel that some portion of the new deposits has been diverted away from earning assets. Looking at the entire commercial banking system, however, the picture will be quite different. A deposit rise in one bank will merely mean a deposit decrease in some other bank—unless the Federal Reserve is taking some action of its own. The real key to understanding the creation of credit by the commercial banks or the creation of reserves by the Federal Reserve System is to think in terms of the total system, not the individual bank.

Dealers—See *Brokers and Dealers*.

Discount Window—This refers to the function of the twelve Federal Reserve Banks in making loans to member banks. In a technical sense, the original idea was that commercial banks would discount paper, *i.e.*, sell commercial loans to the Federal Reserve Bank at a discount representing the interest charge. The Federal Reserve Bank sets a rate on such loans—the discount rate. The function is administered by a discount officer in the Federal Reserve Bank. Most transactions in recent years have not technically been discounts, however, but rather have represented advances or loans made on the basis of collateral consisting of U.S. Government securities or customer loans of high quality and short maturity.

Disintermediation—A new term developed in 1966 to describe the process by which depositors of financial institutions withdrew savings and purchased securities in the markets. The earlier term, intermediation, developed from the idea that financial institutions gathered funds from depositors and invested for them collectively by making loans or purchasing securities.

Edge Act Corporation—A foreign banking corporation organized under Section 25(a) of the Federal Reserve Act to aid in financing and stimulating foreign trade. It may be chartered by the Board of Governors of the Federal Reserve System for twenty years with a minimum capital of $2 million.

Euro-dollars—These are dollar demand deposits in the United States which various holders have acquired and redeposited in banks outside the United States.

281

For an illustration of one way Euro-dollars are created, assume an American manufacturer imports $100,000 of merchandise and the contract calls for a German exporter to receive payment in United States dollars by means of a check drawn on a New York bank. The German exporter takes the check to his bank in Germany. He can ask for conversion to marks or may open a time deposit which specifies he will receive another check in American dollars at a certain date. He thus has a claim on dollars in the future and earns interest in the interim. It is obviously a loan of the dollars to the German bank, which will quickly lend them to someone else who needs dollars.

The mechanics would be that, on the books of the New York bank, ownership of the demand deposits would be shifted from the American manufacturer to someone else abroad. On the books of the German bank the Euro-dollar deposit liability to the German exporter is offset by a Euro-dollar loan to someone else.

The increasing volume of dollars received by foreigners through the U.S. balance of payments deficits and the continuing demand for dollars has created the Euro-dollar market where United States dollars may be borrowed from European banks or loaned to them via deposits. The market is particularly active in London. The German bank, therefore, might loan its dollars either overnight or for varying periods of time through the London market. Banks in London and elsewhere actively seek Euro-dollars to meet the needs of customers or to make a profit between rates paid on deposits and rates received on Euro-dollars sold (*i.e.*, loaned).

Federal Funds—When a bank has deposits in its Federal Reserve Bank in excess of its reserve requirements, that is, excess reserves, it can sell them to a bank which has a shortage or deficiency in its required reserves. Such transactions are known as purchases and sales of Federal funds. Such funds are also known as "Good Funds" because they may be used immediately in settlement of a transaction, such as the purchase of Treasury bills.

Finance Paper—This is similar to commercial paper except that it is issued by a finance company. One large borrower would be General Motors Acceptance Corporation.

Financial Intermediary—In general a financial intermediary is a savings institution which accepts savings from individuals and puts them to work in loans or purchases of securities. Such intermediaries consist of savings banks, savings and loan associations, insurance companies, and commercial banks—although commercial banks are hybrid institutions in that they are credit-creating institutions as well as financial intermediaries.

Fiscal Drag—The country's progressive income tax system is a form of fiscal drag because it tends to bring in tax receipts at a faster rate than the growth in the Gross National Product. Thus if Gross National Product grows at a rate of 5%, tax obligations accruing at the same time may increase at a rate one-and-a-half or two times this amount. In 1964, there was concern in Government circles that the existing tax structure, together with Government spending policies, were exerting such a strong fiscal drag on the economy that it might remain at less than full employment for an extended period of time. This argument was used to justify the 1964 reduction in tax rates.

Fiscal Policy—The simplest concept is to consider fiscal policy as the budget policy of the Federal Government. Most people think of fiscal policy as the size of the deficit, or more rarely the surplus, in the budget of the Federal Government. A better approach would be to think of the economic effects arising from all of the receipt items and from all of the expenditure items in the budget. Obviously, the deficit has great significance but the source of taxes and the types of spending which produce the deficit are also very important. Generally, fiscal policy is used in an economic context. For example, "We need a tighter fiscal policy to cope with inflationary pressures," or, "We need a more expansive fiscal policy to help generate more production and cope with unemployment."

Full Employment Budget Surplus or Deficit—This refers to calculations of the Federal Budget based on the assumption that the economy would be operating at a level of unemployment of only 4% instead of the actual level. The idea is to test the appropriateness of the budget at full employment so that a deficit at a high level of unemployment will be understood to have been caused by the extra

283

unemployment. Presumably, then, the budget should be balanced on a full employment basis.

Good Funds vs. Clearing House Funds—Clearing House funds represent checks drawn on another clearing house bank which are deposited in a commercial bank on a given day. They will be collected or "cleared" on the following day, at which time they will be good funds, because the acquiring bank will then have them to increase its deposit at the Federal Reserve Bank or to sell as Federal funds. Good funds represent cash in hand, deposits at the Federal Reserve, or Federal funds sold.

Incomes Policy—Any programs designed to hold down price increases by using moral suasion on business to restrict price increases and on labor to limit wage demands.

Interest Rate Ceilings—These refer to the maximum rates which may be paid by banks and other financial institutions on time and savings deposits. They are established by the Federal Reserve Board under Regulation Q for banks which are members of the Federal Reserve System, by the FDIC for mutual savings banks and commercial insured nonmember banks, and by the Federal Home Loan Bank Board for savings and loan associations. See *Regulation Q*.

Liquidity—In the money market sense, liquidity refers to the ability to turn an asset into cash quickly with a minimum risk of loss.

Member Bank Reserves—These are balances maintained at the Federal Reserve banks by commercial banks which are members of the Federal Reserve System to meet the legal reserves required against their deposits. Vault cash is also eligible for meeting reserve requirements.

Monetarists—Refers to the ideas propounded by followers of Professor Milton Friedman of the University of Chicago, who argues that the growth of money should be on a steady predetermined basis rather than on a flexible basis resulting from Federal Reserve discretionary management.

Monetary Policy—Monetary policy usually refers to the composite actions of the Federal Reserve System affecting the growth of the money supply. A given monetary policy can be expansive, restrictive, or neutral. It is useful, also, to think of the impact of monetary policy on the entire banking system. Even this idea is not broad enough, for monetary policy has effects beyond the banking system and throughout the entire financial and economic structure.

Money Market—The money market encompasses activity in short-term, high-grade credit. Being short term and high grade, the element of risk is minimized and such credit instruments may be readily turned into money. Accordingly, the money market is very important in providing instruments for liquidity investments of banks, corporations, and other investors. Borrowers tap the money market through loans or by issuing short-term securities. The largest borrower in this market is the United States Government. Other borrowers include Federal agencies, corporations, and municipalities. Banks are important in the money market both as investors and borrowers (*e.g.*, CDs, bankers' acceptances, and Federal funds).

Municipals—This word is applied to all securities issued by States and political subdivisions in the United States which have a tax-exempt status.

"Near Money"—Top grade credit instruments representing claims on others. They may be notes and securities which may soon be turned into money by redeeming at maturity or by selling in the money market. They also include loans to brokers which may be called.

Nonbank Dealers—This refers to a group of firms who perform the same function of trading in government securities as the bank dealers. There are eleven firms. They act as principals in the Government and municipal securities markets and in many cases in other markets, accumulating inventories and buying or selling from their own account when dealing with customers.

PCs—These are participation certificates which were issued by Federal agencies, such as the Federal National Mortgage Association and the Export-Import Bank. They represent participation in a pool of assets held by these agencies. These instruments carry a definite coupon and maturity date and are considered as securities in the money market. They are of very high quality since they are backed not only by the assets themselves but also by a statement of the

285

Attorney General of the United States, dated September 30, 1966, that "FNMA's guaranty of a participation certificate brings into being a general obligation of the United States backed by its full faith and credit," and that "the holders of a participation guaranteed by FNMA hold valid general obligations of the United States and are in a position to reach beyond the assets of FNMA to the United States for payment, if necessary." In September 1968, when FNMA became a private organization, these obligations were assumed by the Government National Mortgage Association.

Prime Rate—This is the rate charged by commercial banks on short-term loans to substantial depositors with the highest credit rating.

Public Debt—The table shows the public debt of the United States Government broken down into two broad classifications: marketable and other issues.

	(Billions of Dollars) Marketable Debt						**Other Debt***	**Total Debt**
	Under 1 Year							
	Treasury Bills	Other	1–5 Years	5–10 Years	Over 10 Years	Total		
June 30, 1913	—	—	.1	.1	.8	1.0	—	1.0
" 30, 1919	—	3.6	3.5	4.1	13.1	24.3	1.0	25.2
" 30, 1930	.2	1.9	1.6	6.3	5.2	15.2	.8	15.9
" 30, 1941	1.6	1.1	13.1	9.9	12.0	37.7	10.7	48.4
" 30, 1946	17.0	45.0	18.9	45.0	63.7	189.6	78.5	268.1
" 30, 1965	53.7	33.9	56.2	39.2	25.7	208.7	104.4	313.1
June 30, 1971	86.7	26.1	89.1	24.5	19.1	245.5	150.8	396.3

* Nonmarketable and special issues held by U.S. Government agencies, trust accounts, etc.

Marketable debt is issued to the public in various forms: bills, certificates of indebtedness, notes, and bonds. Anything classified as marketable is negotiable—it may be sold and ownership transferred to another investor. Nonmarketable debt consists primarily of United States savings bonds issued in the name of an individual or two individuals as co-owners. Such bonds may be cashed on the basis of a stated redemption schedule but ownership may not be shifted to another person. Special issues are those sold only to United States Government agencies and trust accounts. They are especially tailored in accordance with the legal provisions governing the agency's operations so that each special issue tends to be different from another issue designed for some other agency or trust fund. These thus have a strong fiduciary flavor, like a parent setting up special arrangements for a child. If funds are needed, these issues can be redeemed under stated conditions at the Treasury.

Registered Bonds vs. Bearer Bonds—A registered bond has the owner's name recorded in the office of the registrar appointed by the issuer of the bond, whereas a bearer bond has no such recording and ownership simply goes along with possession. If a registered bond is sold in the secondary market the name of the owner is changed on the books of the registrar. Interest on registered bonds is paid by check but, in case of bearer bonds, the owner must clip the coupons attached to the bond as they come due and have them sent to the issuing company (or its bank) for collection.

Regulation Q—This is a Federal Reserve regulation governing the maximum rate which banks may pay on various types of time and savings deposits. The table "Maximum Interest Rates Payable on Time and Savings Deposits" shows rates in effect since its inception.

Reserve Requirements—Every bank is required by law to maintain reserves against its deposits. A bank which is not a member of the Federal Reserve System maintains reserves in its vault or on deposit with correspondent banks. A member bank must maintain its reserves on deposit at the Federal Reserve Bank of its district, except for its vault cash. The percentage of reserves required for member banks is established by the Board of Governors of the Federal Reserve System. The record of changes in reserve requirements is shown in the table "Reserve Requirements of Member Banks."

RPs—A repurchase agreement is represented by a contract to sell certain assets with understanding to repurchase. It may be considered as an advance secured by 100% of the collateral offered. Eligible collateral includes Treasury securities, bankers' acceptances, and commercial paper.

287

Maximum Interest Rates Payable on Time and Savings Deposits
(Percent per annum)

Rates Nov. 1, 1933–July 19, 1966

Type of Deposit	11/1 1933	2/1 1935	1/1 1936	1/1 1957	1/1 1962	7/17 1963	11/24 1964	12/6 1965
	Effective Date							
Savings and postal savings deposits	3	2½	2½	3	3½–4[1]	3½–4[1]	4	4
Other time deposits:[2]								
30–89 days			1	1	1	1	4	
90 days to 6 months	3	2½	2	2½	2½	4	4½	5½
6 months to 12 months			2½	3	3½–4[1]			

Rates beginning July 20, 1966

Type of Deposit	7/20 1966	9/26 1966	4/19 1968	1/21 1970
	Effective Date			
Savings deposits	4	4	4	4½
Other time dep.:[2]				
Multiple maturity:[3]				
30–89 days	4	4	4	4½
90 days to 1 year				5
1 year to 2 years	5	5	5	5½
2 years and over				5¾
Single maturity:				
Less than $100,000				
30 days to 1 year				5
1 year to 2 years	5½	5	5	5½
2 years and over				5¾
$100,000 or more				
30–59 days			5½	5¼[4]
60–89 days			5¾	6½[4]
90–179 days	5½	5½	6	6¾
180 days to 1 year			6¼	7
1 year and over				7½

[1] Higher rate applied to twelve months or more.
[2] Beginning October 15, 1962, deposits of foreign governments, monetary and financial authorities of foreign governments, and international institutions of which the United States is a member were exempted from these limitations.
[3] Multiple-maturity time deposits include deposits that are automatically renewable at maturity without action by the depositor and deposits that are payable after written notice of withdrawal.
[4] Effective June 24, 1970, maximum interest rates on these maturities were suspended until further notice.
SOURCE: Board of Governors of Federal Reserve System

Reserve Requirements of Member Banks

| Effective Date | | On Net Demand Deposits [a] | | | On Time |
		Country banks	Reserve city banks	Central reserve city banks	Deposits [b]
1917 – June	21	7	10	13	3
1936 – Aug.	16	10½	15	19½	4½
1937 – Mar.	1	12¼	17½	22¾	5¼
May	1	14	20	26	6
1938 – Apr.	16	12	17½	22¾	5
1941 – Nov.	1	14	20	26	6
1942 – Aug.	20			24	
Sept.	14			22	
Oct.	3			20	
1948 – Feb.	27			22	
June	11			24	
Sept.	16, 24	16	22	26	7½
1949 – May	1, 5	15	21	24	7
June	30, July 1	14	20		6
Aug.	1	13			
Aug.	11, 16	12	19½	23½	5
18			19	23	
25			18½	22½	
Sept.	1		18	22	
1951 – Jan.	11, 16	13	19	23	6
Jan.	25, Feb. 1	14	20	24	
1953 – July	9, 1	13	19	22	
1954 – June	24, 16			21	5
July	29, Aug. 1	12	18	20	
1958 – Feb.	27, Mar. 1	11½	17½	19½	
Mar.	20, Apr. 1	11	17	19	
Apr.	17			18½	
Apr.	24		16½	18	
1960 – Sept.	1			17½	
Nov.	24	12			
Dec.	1			16½	
1962 – July	28			[c]	
Oct.	25, Nov. 1				4

[a] Net demand deposits are gross demand deposits minus cash items in process of collection and demand balances due from domestic banks.
[b] Applicable to all classes of banks.
[c] Classification of central reserve city banks was abolished on July 28, 1962.

289

Glossary

| | On Net Demand Deposits | | | Other Time Deposits | |
	Country banks	Reserve city banks	Savings deposits	$5 million	Over $5 million
1966 – July	14, 21	12	16½	4	4	5
Sept.	8, 15					6
1967 – Mar.	2			3½	3½	
Mar.	16			3	3	
1968 – Jan.	11, 18	12–12½ [d]	16½–17 [d]			
1969 – Apr.	17	12½–13 [d]	17–17½ [d]			
1970 – Oct.	1					5
Present legal range:		7–14	10–22	3–10	3–10	3–10

[d] Lower figure applies to deposits under $5 million.
Note: See text for discussion of new reserve requirements imposed on Euro-dollar and other borrowings in 1969 and 1970.

Risk Assets—In commercial banking the usual definition of risk assets is all assets on a bank's balance sheet except cash and U.S. Government securities. Cash is riskless and Government securities are considered riskless from the point of view of credit even though there is, of course, market risk resulting from changes in the level of interest rates.

Secondary Market—After new marketable securities are sold to subscribers on original issuance they may be traded in the market. This market is known as the secondary market, in counterdistinction to new issues of securities which are called original or primary offerings.

Stock Market—The stock market handles trading in outstanding stock issues.

Strip Bills—This refers to an auction by the Treasury Department in which several bill issues are offered as a group. This might consist of a basket comprising additions to, say, each of ten weekly issues of Treasury bills, or to each of three or more different monthly issues of Treasury bills. The important point is that it refers to a multiple group of issues of Treasury bills rather than to a single issue.

Swap Agreements—The Special Manager of the Open Market Account for foreign currency operations was authorized in 1962 by the Federal Open Market Committee to negotiate a series of reciprocal credit or swap facilities with foreign central banks and the Bank for International Settlements. Details of the swap arrangements vary some-

290

what in the different agreements but in effect a swap constitutes a reciprocal credit facility under which a central bank agrees to exchange on request its own currency for the currency of the other party up to a maximum amount over a limited period of time. Starting with seven central banks and the BIS in 1962, the swap agreements were expanded to fourteen central banks and the BIS by 1971.

Syndicate—A group of investment banking houses, or broker-dealer firms, which organize to underwrite a new issue offered by a corporate or government entity. Banks participate in syndicates that underwrite state and municipal obligations.

Tax and Loan Account—This is the United States Treasury Department's demand deposit account in a commercial bank. Funds are placed in this account by the individual commercial banks from two sources, namely, proceeds from sales of new issues of U.S. Government securities to the bank or its customers and payments by taxpayers to meet their tax obligations. The Tax and Loan Account is thus a collection account for the Treasury which draws the funds as it wishes, not by check but by shifting them to the Treasury's account in the Federal Reserve System. Hence a Treasury call on a commercial bank's Tax and Loan Account will authorize the Federal Reserve Bank to charge the commercial bank's reserve account and credit the Treasury's account in the Federal Reserve.

Tax-exempts—These refer to state and municipal government securities which are exempt from Federal income taxation.

Treasury Bills—An obligation of the U.S. Government sold weekly or monthly on an auction basis, *i.e.*, to the highest bidders. The maximum maturity is one year. There is no interest coupon; rather the interest return is the difference between the amount bid at the time of the auction and par, or 100, received at the time of maturity. Bills constitute the largest volume of security trading in the money market. The difference between cash paid (at the auction or in the market on purchase) and cash received (at maturity or in the market on resale) is interest for tax purposes.

Underwriters—A person or company which individually or as a member of a syndicate purchases new securities from the issuing corporation or a government entity at a stated price and guarantees its sale and distribution to investors.

When Issued Basis—This refers to a price or interest rate quotation on a security which has been sold but not yet issued and paid for. It is thus purchased by a buyer on the basis of expectation that it will be issued.

Yield—The annual rate of return on an investment computed as though held to maturity, or first call date, if purchased at a premium. It is determined by relating the interest, or coupon rate, to the price paid and to the remaining life, or the maturity of the investment.

Yield Curve—This refers to the plotting of yields versus maturities of Treasury securities (or any homogenous group of issues) on a chart showing maturity dates on the horizontal axis and yields on the vertical axis. In other words, to plot an issue with a ten-year maturity and a yield of 4.53%, the chartist would move out sideways on the chart to ten years, and then upward, according to the scale on the left-hand side, to the level corresponding to a yield of 4.53% and indicate with a dot or X the intersection of the two readings. When a number of issues are plotted in this way, it is apparent that yields tend to line up according to a pattern and a kind of curve may be derived. This curve may slope in various directions at different times or may even be flat. It is a useful tool in analyzing market issues of bonds and in searching for issues which may be out of line with the market.

BIBLIOGRAPHY

BOOKS

Aschheim, Joseph. *Techniques of Monetary Control.* Baltimore: Johns Hopkins Press, 1961.

Ahearn, Daniel S. *Federal Reserve Policy Reappraised 1951–1959.* New York: Columbia University Press, 1963.

Bagehot, Walter. *Lombard Street.* London: John Murray, 1917.

Bernstein, Peter L. *Primer on Money, Banking and Gold.* New York: Random House, 1965.

———, and Heilbroner, Robert L. *A Primer on Government Spending.* New York: Random House, 1963.

Burgess, W. R. *The Reserve Banks and the Money Market.* New York: Harper & Brothers, 1936.

Chandler, Lester V. *Economics of Money and Banking.* New York: Harper & Row, 1964.

Commission on Money and Credit. *Fiscal and Debt Management Policies.* New York: Prentice-Hall, Inc., 1963.

Conrad, Joseph W. *The Behavior of Interest Rates.* New York: National Bureau of Economic Research, 1966.

Crosse, Howard D. *Management Policies for Commercial Banks.* New York: Prentice-Hall, Inc., 1962.

Friedman, Milton. *A Program for Monetary Stability.* New York: Fordham University Press, 1960.

———, and Schwartz, Anna J. *A Monetary History of the United States, 1867–1960.* National Bureau of Economic Research. Princeton, New Jersey: Princeton University Press, 1963.

Garvy, George, and Blyn, Martin R. *The Velocity of Money.* New York: Federal Reserve Bank of New York, 1969.

Goldenweiser, E. A. *American Monetary Policy.* New York: McGraw-Hill Book Company, Inc., 1951.

Gurley, John G., and Shaw, Edward S. *Money in a Theory of Finance.* Washington, D.C.: Brookings Institution, 1960.

Harris, S. E. *Twenty Years of Federal Reserve Policy.* 2 vols. Cambridge: Harvard University Press, 1933.

Homer, Sidney. *The Bond Buyer's Primer.* New York: Salomon Brothers & Hutzler, 1968.

Bibliography

————, *A History of Interest Rates*. New Brunswick: Rutgers University Press, 1963.

Jacobs, Neil. *United States Monetary Policy*. New York: F. A. Praeger, Inc., 1964.

Keynes, John Maynard. *The General Theory of Employment, Interest and Money*. New York: Harcourt, Brace & World, Inc., 1936.

Meigs, A. James. *Free Reserves and the Money Supply*. Chicago: University of Chicago Press, 1962.

Oxford English Dictionary. London: Oxford University Press, 1961.

Prochnow, Herbert V., and Faulke, Roy A. *Practical Bank Credit*. New York: Harper & Row, 1963.

Riefler, Winfield. *Money Rates and Money Markets in the United States*. New York: Harper & Brothers, 1930.

Ritter, Lawrence. *Money and Economic Activity*. Boston: Houghton Mifflin Co., 1967.

Robinson, Roland L. *The Management of Bank Funds*. 2nd edition. New York: McGraw-Hill Book Company, Inc., 1962.

Roosa, Robert V. *Federal Reserve Operations in the Money and Government Securities Market*. Federal Reserve Bank of New York, 1956.

Stein, Herbert. *The Fiscal Revolution in America*. Chicago: University of Chicago Press, 1969.

Whittlesey, Charles R. *Money and Banking*. New York: Macmillan Company, 1963.

ARTICLES

Anderson, Leonall C., and Jordan, Jerry L. "Monetary and Fiscal Actions: A Test of Their Relative Importance—Reply." *Monthly Review*, Federal Reserve Bank of St. Louis, 51 (April 1969): 10–17.

Bernstein, Edward M. "The Euro-dollar Market and National Credit Policy." *Quarterly Review* (second quarter). New York: Model Roland & Co., 1969.

Davis, Richard G. "The Role of the Money Supply in Business Cycles." *Monthly Review*, Federal Reserve Bank of New York, 50. (April 1968): 63–73.

Federal Reserve Bank of Chicago. "Bankers' Acceptances Used More Widely." *Business Conditions*. May 1965.

Klopstock, Fred H. "Euro-Dollars in the Liquidity and Reserve Man-

agement of United States Banks." *Monthly Review,* Federal
Reserve Bank of New York, 50 (July 1968): 129–34.

———, and Holmes, Alan R. "The Market for Dollar Deposits in
Europe." *Monthly Review,* Federal Reserve Bank of New York,
42 (November 1960): 3–8.

Polakoff, Murray E. "Federal Reserve Discount Policy and Its Critics."
Banking and Monetary Studies, edited by Deane Carson.
Homewood, Illinois: Richard D. Irwin, Inc., 1963.

Roosa, Robert V. "Credit Policy at the Discount Window: Comment."
Quarterly Journal of Economics, 73 (May 1959): 333–8.

Smith, Warren L. "The Discount Rate As a Credit Control Weapon."
Journal of Political Economy, 66 (April 1958): 171–7.

Whittlesey, Charles R. "Credit Policy at the Discount Window."
Quarterly Journal of Economics, 73 (May 1959): 207–16.

OTHER

Bank for International Settlements. *Annual Reports* (1958–71).

Banking and Financial Research Committee. *The Discount Function.*
New York: American Bankers Association, 1968.

Baughn, William W., and Walker, Charles E., eds. *Bankers' Handbook.* Illinois: Dow-Jones Irwin, Inc., 1966.

Board of Governors of the Federal Reserve System. *Annual Reports*
(1958–70).

———. *Federal Reserve Bulletins* (1958–70).

———. *Report of a System Committee: Reappraisal of the Federal
Reserve Discount Mechanism.* July 1968.

——— and the United States Treasury. *The Federal Reserve and
the Treasury: Answers to Questions from the Commission on
Money and Credit.* Englewood Cliffs, New Jersey: Prentice-
Hall, Inc., 1963.

Brimmer, Andrew F. "Monetary Policy and the U.S. Balance of Payments." Speech at Wharton School of Finance & Commerce,
University of Pennsylvania, Philadelphia, Pennsylvania. October 5, 1966.

Burns, Arthur F. Various speeches and testimony before Congressional Committees usually reprinted in Federal Reserve
Bulletin.

Crosse, Howard D. "Bank Liquidity and Time Deposits." Speech before American Bankers Association National Credit Conference, Chicago, Illinois, January 23, 1960.

295

Bibliography

Daane, Dewey. "Inflation and Financial Stability." Speech before the 15th Annual Bankers' Forum at Georgetown University, October 5, 1968.

Federal Reserve Bank of New York. *Annual Reports* (1958–70).

———. *Monthly Review* (1958–70).

Heebner, Gilbert A. "Negotiable Certificates of Deposit: The Development of a Money Market Instrument." *The Bulletin*. New York University, nos. 53–4, February 1969.

Joint Economic Committee of the United States Congress. Hearings on Balance of Payments Statistics before Subcommittee on Economic Statistics, May 11 to June 9, 1965.

Kansas City Federal Reserve Bank. "Profits on Commercial Bank Time Deposits." *Monthly Review*. September 1961.

Leach, Ralph F. Remarks at Panel Session on "Alternative Market Sources of Funds" at the International Monetary Conference in Munich, Germany, May 26, 1971.

Lindow, Wesley. "The Federal Funds Market." *Bankers Monthly*. September 15, 1960.

Mitchell, George W. "Tomorrow's Money As Seen Today." Remarks at annual stockholders' meeting of Federal Reserve Bank of Boston, Mass., October 6, 1966.

Nichols, Dorothy M. *Trading in Federal Funds*. Washington, D.C.: Board of Governors of the Federal Reserve System, 1965.

Robertson, J. L. "On Cutting Corners." Remarks at Annual Convention of West Virginia Bankers Association, White Sulphur Springs, W. Va., July 25, 1969.

Waage, Thomas O. "Some Problems of Monetary Policy." Speech before the New York Society of Security Analysts, New York, New York, July 8, 1971.

Willis, Parker B. *The Federal Funds Market*. Boston: Federal Reserve Bank of Boston, 1964.

———. *A Study of the Market for Federal Funds*. Prepared in connection with the Federal Reserve System's Reappraisal of the Discount Mechanism, March 28, 1967.

INDEX

Index

About the Author

WESLEY LINDOW is a leading member of New York's financial community, widely known for his expert knowledge of money and security markets in the United States and throughout the world.

He is Vice Chairman of Charter New York Corporation, the bank holding company that owns Irving Trust Company and nine upstate banks in New York State. Mr. Lindow also holds the post of Executive President of Irving Trust. He was Senior Investment Officer of Irving for many years and supervised the Personal Trust Division. Earlier he was head of the Economics Department.

Before joining the bank he was Head Economic Analyst of the U.S. Treasury Department with a major role in public debt management. Later he served as Consultant to the Secretary of the Treasury.

Mr. Lindow has been active in banking groups. He is a member of the Reserve City Bankers Association, the Administrative Committee of the Economic Advisory Committee of the American Bankers Association, the Research Committee of the Association of Registered Bank Holding Companies and the Pledged Assets Committee of the New York State Bankers Association. Until recently he was Chairman of the Banking and Financial Research Committee of the American Bankers Association. For many years he served on the A.B.A. Executive Council, the Bank Management Committee and the Resolutions Committee. He has also been active in the International Monetary Conference, including service as speaker and as Program Chairman and has testified many times before Congressional Committees.

DISCHARGED

APR 14 1971

DISCHARGED